Modern JavaScript Applications

An example-driven guide that explores the world of modern web development with JavaScript

Narayan Prusty

[PACKT] open source*
PUBLISHING   community experience distilled

BIRMINGHAM - MUMBAI

Modern JavaScript Applications

First published: July 2016

Production reference: 1140716

Published by Packt Publishing Ltd.
Livery Place
35 Livery Street
Birmingham B3 2PB, UK.

ISBN 978-1-78588-144-2

www.packtpub.com

Credits

Author
Narayan Prusty

Reviewer
Olivier Pons

Commissioning Editor
Wilson D'souza

Acquisition Editor
Dharmesh Parmar

Content Development Editor
Arshiya Ayaz Umer

Technical Editor
Mohit Hassija

Copy Editor
Madhusudan Uchil

Project Coordinator
Kinjal Bari

Proofreader
Safis Editing

Indexer
Pratik Shirodkar

Graphics
Kirk D'Penha

Production Coordinator
Shantanu N. Zagade

Cover Work
Shantanu N. Zagade

About the Author

Narayan Prusty is a full-stack developer. He works as a consultant for various startups around the world. He has worked on various technologies and programming languages but is very passionate about JavaScript, WordPress, Ethereum, Solr, React, Cordova, MongoDB, and AWS.

Apart from consulting for various startups, he also runs a blog titled QNimate (`http://qnimate.com`) and a video-tutorial site titled QScutter (`http://qscutter.com`), where he shares information about a lot of the technologies he works on. Previously, he wrote a book titled *Learning ECMAScript 6*, which was published by Packt Publishing.

You can reach Narayan on LinkedIn (`https://in.linkedin.com/in/narayanprusty`).

About the Reviewer

Olivier Pons is a senior developer who's been building websites for many years. He's a teacher at the University of Sciences (IUT) of Aix-en-Provence, France, ISEN (Institut Supérieur de l'Électronique et du Numérique), G4 Marseille, and École d'Ingénieurs des Mines de Gardanne, where he teaches state-of-the-art web techniques: Node.js, big data/NoSQL, MVC fundamentals, Django/Python, Symfony basics, Wordpress, PHP, HTML, CSS, jQuery/jQuery mobile, AngularJS, Apache, Linux basics, and advanced VIM techniques. He has already done some technical reviews, including the Packt books *Learning ExtJS*, *ExtJS 4 First Look*, *jQuery hotshots*, *jQuery Mobile Web Development Essentials*, *Wordpress 4 Complete*, and *jQuery 2.0 for Designers Beginner's Guide*. In 2011, he left a full-time job as a Delphi developer and PHP expert to concentrate on his own company, HQF Development (`http://hqf.fr`). He currently runs a number of websites, including `http://krystallopolis.fr`, `http://artsgaleries.com`, `http://www.battlesoop.fr`, `http://www.cogofly.com`, `http://www.papdevis.fr`, and `http://olivierpons.fr`, his own web development blog. He's currently polishing `http://cogofly.com` and making a keyboard for geek here `http://ergofip.com`. He works as a consultant, teacher, and project manager and sometimes helps big companies as a senior/highly skilled developer.

www.PacktPub.com

eBooks, discount offers, and more

Did you know that Packt offers eBook versions of every book published, with PDF and ePub files available? You can upgrade to the eBook version at www.PacktPub. com and as a print book customer, you are entitled to a discount on the eBook copy. Get in touch with us at customercare@packtpub.com for more details.

At www.PacktPub.com, you can also read a collection of free technical articles, sign up for a range of free newsletters and receive exclusive discounts and offers on Packt books and eBooks.

https://www2.packtpub.com/books/subscription/packtlib

Do you need instant solutions to your IT questions? PacktLib is Packt's online digital book library. Here, you can search, access, and read Packt's entire library of books.

Why subscribe?

- Fully searchable across every book published by Packt
- Copy and paste, print, and bookmark content
- On demand and accessible via a web browser

Table of Contents

Preface

"JavaScript is the only language that I'm aware of that people feel they don't need to learn before they start using it."

– Douglas Crockford

The book begins by covering an enterprise-level application with the microservices architecture, using Node.js to build web services. As we move forward, the book shows you how to build a browser-browser application using WebRTC. We then focus on building a real-time web application with WebSockets.

When you've gained a solid grip on the different architectures, you'll see how to write better reactive code using functional reactive programming (FRP). Then, we'll move onto what's new in Bootstrap 4 and how it makes it easier then ever to build responsive sites. As we near the end of this book, you'll see how to build a modern single-page application that builds on the innovative component-based architecture using React and Angular 2.

After reading this book, you will have a solid knowledge of the latest JavaScript techniques, tools, and architecture required to build modern web apps.

What this book covers

Chapter 1, Breaking into Microservices Architecture, teaches what the microservices architecture is and why enterprise-level applications are built using it. We will then explore Seneca.js, which is a microservices toolkit for Node.js.

Chapter 2, Building a Coupon Site, shows you how to build a basic coupon site to demonstrate Seneca.js and the microservices architecture.

Chapter 3, Communication between Browsers in Real Time, teaches you what WebRTC is and how to use it to implement features such as audio/video chat or some other features in websites that need real-time browser-to-browser data transfer or to retrieve audio/video streams from microphones, webcams, or any other device. We will learn to write WebRTC-based applications using PeerJS, which simplifies WebRTC-based application development.

Chapter 4, Building a Chatroulette, shows you how to build a chatroulette to demonstrate WebRTC and PeerJS.

Chapter 5, Bidirectional Communication in Real Time, teaches what WebSockets are and how to achieve bidirectional communication in real-time using WebSockets. We will then explore Socket.IO, which utilizes WebSockets to enable bidirectional communication in real time.

Chapter 6, Building a Live Score Site, shows you how to build a simple live-score site using Socket.IO.

Chapter 7, Functional Reactive Programming, teaches you reactive code and how to write better reactive code using functional reactive programming. We will then explore Bacon.js, which is a functional reactive programming library for JavaScript.

Chapter 8, Building an Advanced Profile Search Widget, helps you build an advanced profile-search widget using Bacon.js.

Chapter 9, New Features of Bootstrap 4, teaches you what's new in Bootstrap 4 and how it makes it easier then ever to create responsive sites.

Chapter 10, Building User Interfaces Using React, teaches you what React.js is and how it makes writing of code for reactive UI easier and takes care of rendering performance and reusability.

Chapter 11, Building an RSS Reader Using React and Flux, shows you how to build a simple RSS reader using React and the Flux architecture.

Chapter 12, New Features of Angular 2, teaches you how to use Angular 2 to build the client side of websites. We will also learn about web components in this chapter.

Chapter 13, Building a Search Engine Template Using AngularJS 2, shows you how to build a search engine template using Angular 2. We will also learn how to build an SPA using Angular 2.

Chapter 14, Securing and Scaling Node.js Applications, teaches you how to make Node.js applications more secure and what the common technologies used for scaling Node.js applications are.

What you need for this book

You can use any operating system that supports Node.js and MongoDB. You will need a browser, but I would recommended you to use the latest version of Chrome as it's way ahead with supporting the new technologies that are covered in this book. You will also need a webcam and microphone. And finally, you will need a working Internet connection.

Who this book is for

This book is for existing JavaScript developers who want to explore some modern JavaScript features, techniques, and architectures in order to develop cutting-edge web applications.

Conventions

In this book, you will find a number of text styles that distinguish between different kinds of information. Here are some examples of these styles and an explanation of their meaning.

Code words in text, database table names, folder names, filenames, file extensions, pathnames, dummy URLs, user input, and Twitter handles are shown as follows: "Here we are first calling the `make` method of the `senena` object. It's used to get reference of an entity's store. For example, in case of MySQL, the `make` method gets reference to a table."

A block of code is set as follows:

```
var script_start_time = Bacon.constant(Date.now()).map(function(value)
{
  var date = new Date(value);
  return (date).getHours() + ":" + (date).getMinutes() + ":" + (date).
getSeconds();
});
```

New terms and **important words** are shown in bold. Words that you see on the screen, for example, in menus or dialog boxes, appear in the text like this: "Now click on the **Admin** button to visit the admin panel and accept the coupon. Here is how the admin panel will look."

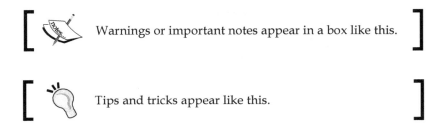

Warnings or important notes appear in a box like this.

Tips and tricks appear like this.

Reader feedback

Feedback from our readers is always welcome. Let us know what you think about this book—what you liked or disliked. Reader feedback is important for us as it helps us develop titles that you will really get the most out of.

To send us general feedback, simply e-mail feedback@packtpub.com, and mention the book's title in the subject of your message.

If there is a topic that you have expertise in and you are interested in either writing or contributing to a book, see our author guide at www.packtpub.com/authors.

Customer support

Now that you are the proud owner of a Packt book, we have a number of things to help you to get the most from your purchase.

Downloading the example code

You can download the example code files for this book from your account at http://www.packtpub.com. If you purchased this book elsewhere, you can visit http://www.packtpub.com/support and register to have the files e-mailed directly to you.

You can download the code files by following these steps:

1. Log in or register to our website using your e-mail address and password.
2. Hover the mouse pointer on the **SUPPORT** tab at the top.
3. Click on **Code Downloads & Errata**.
4. Enter the name of the book in the **Search** box.
5. Select the book for which you're looking to download the code files.

6. Choose from the drop-down menu where you purchased this book from.

7. Click on **Code Download**.

You can also download the code files by clicking on the **Code Files** button on the book's webpage at the Packt Publishing website. This page can be accessed by entering the book's name in the **Search** box. Please note that you need to be logged in to your Packt account.

Once the file is downloaded, please make sure that you unzip or extract the folder using the latest version of:

* WinRAR / 7-Zip for Windows

* Zipeg / iZip / UnRarX for Mac

* 7-Zip / PeaZip for Linux

The code bundle for the book is also hosted on GitHub at `https://github.com/PacktPublishing/Modern-JavaScript-Applications`. We also have other code bundles from our rich catalog of books and videos available at `https://github.com/PacktPublishing/`. Check them out!

Downloading the color images of this book

We also provide you with a PDF file that has color images of the screenshots/diagrams used in this book. The color images will help you better understand the changes in the output. You can download this file from `https://www.packtpub.com/sites/default/files/downloads/ModernJavaScriptApplications_ColorImages.pdf`.

Errata

Although we have taken every care to ensure the accuracy of our content, mistakes do happen. If you find a mistake in one of our books—maybe a mistake in the text or the code—we would be grateful if you could report this to us. By doing so, you can save other readers from frustration and help us improve subsequent versions of this book. If you find any errata, please report them by visiting `http://www.packtpub.com/submit-errata`, selecting your book, clicking on the **Errata Submission Form** link, and entering the details of your errata. Once your errata are verified, your submission will be accepted and the errata will be uploaded to our website or added to any list of existing errata under the Errata section of that title.

To view the previously submitted errata, go to `https://www.packtpub.com/books/content/support` and enter the name of the book in the search field. The required information will appear under the **Errata** section.

Piracy

Piracy of copyrighted material on the Internet is an ongoing problem across all media. At Packt, we take the protection of our copyright and licenses very seriously. If you come across any illegal copies of our works in any form on the Internet, please provide us with the location address or website name immediately so that we can pursue a remedy.

Please contact us at copyright@packtpub.com with a link to the suspected pirated material.

We appreciate your help in protecting our authors and our ability to bring you valuable content.

Questions

If you have a problem with any aspect of this book, you can contact us at questions@packtpub.com, and we will do our best to address the problem.

1
Breaking into Microservices Architecture

The architecture of server-side application development for complex and large applications (applications with huge number of users and large volume of data) shouldn't just involve faster response and providing web services for wide variety of platforms. It should be easy to scale, upgrade, update, test, and deploy. It should also be highly available, allowing the developers write components of the server-side application in different programming languages and use different databases. Therefore, this leads the developers who build large and complex applications to switch from the common monolithic architecture to microservices architecture that allows us to do all this easily. As microservices architecture is being widely used in enterprises that build large and complex applications, it's really important to learn how to design and create server-side applications using this architecture. In this chapter, we will discuss how to create applications based on microservices architecture with Node.js using the Seneca toolkit.

In this chapter, we'll cover the following topics:

- Understanding monolithic architecture
- Scaling, upgrading, deploying, and writing applications based on monolithic architecture
- Discussing microservices architecture in depth
- Scaling, upgrading, deploying, and writing applications based on microservices architecture
- Getting started with Seneca
- Creating and calling services using Seneca

What is monolithic architecture?

To understand microservices architecture, it's important to first understand monolithic architecture, which is its opposite.

In monolithic architecture, different functional components of the server-side application, such as payment processing, account management, push notifications, and other components, all blend together in a single unit.

For example, applications are usually divided into three parts. The parts are HTML pages or native UI that run on the user's machine, server-side application that runs on the server, and database that also runs on the server. The server-side application is responsible for handling HTTP requests, retrieving and storing data in a database, executing algorithms, and so on. If the server-side application is a single executable (that is, running is a single process) that does all these tasks, then we say that the server-side application is monolithic.

This is a common way of building server-side applications. Almost every major CMS, web servers, server-side frameworks, and so on are built using monolithic architecture.

This architecture may seem successful, but problems are likely to arise when your application is large and complex.

Demerits of monolithic architecture

The following are some of the issues caused by server-side applications built using the monolithic architecture.

Scaling monolithic architecture

As traffic to your server-side application increases, you will need to scale your server-side application to handle the traffic.

In case of monolithic architecture, you can scale the server-side application by running the same executable on multiple servers and place the servers behind a load balancer or you can use round robin DNS to distribute the traffic among the servers:

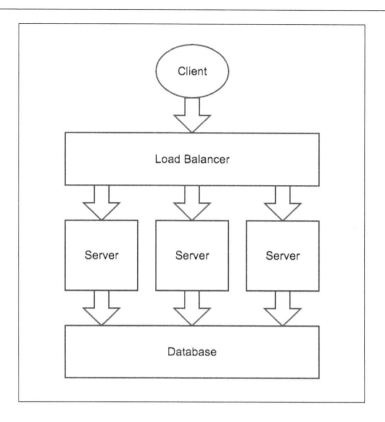

In the preceding diagram, all the servers will be running the same server-side application.

Although scaling is easy, scaling monolithic server-side application ends up with scaling all the components rather than the components that require greater resource. Thus, causing unbalanced utilization of resources sometimes, depending on the quantity and types of resources the components need.

Let's consider some examples to understand the issues caused while scaling monolithic server-side applications:

- Suppose there is a component of server-side application that requires a more powerful or special kind of hardware, we cannot simply scale this particular component as all the components are packed together, therefore everything needs to be scaled together. So, to make sure that the component gets enough resources, you need to run the server-side application on some more servers with powerful or special hardware, leading to consumption of more resources than actually required.

- Suppose we have a component that requires to be executed on a specific server operating system that is not free of charge, we cannot simply run this particular component in a non-free operating system as all the components are packed together and therefore, just to execute this specific component, we need to install the non-free operating system on all servers, increasing the cost greatly.

These are just some examples. There are many more issues that you are likely to come across while scaling a monolithic server-side application.

So, when we scale monolithic server-side applications, the components that don't need more powerful or special kind of resource starts receiving them, therefore deceasing resources for the component that needs them. We can say that scaling monolithic server-side application involves scaling all components that are forcing to duplicate everything in the new servers.

Writing monolithic server-side applications

Monolithic server-side applications are written in a particular programming language using a particular framework. Enterprises usually have developers who are experts in different programming languages and frameworks to build server-side applications; therefore, if they are asked to build a monolithic server-side application, then it will be difficult for them to work together.

The components of a monolithic server-side application can be reused only in the same framework using, which it's built. So, you cannot reuse them for some other kind of project that's built using different technologies.

Other issues of monolithic architecture

Here are some other issues that developers might face, depending on the technology that is used to build the monolithic server-side application:

- It may need to be completely rebuild and redeployed for every small change made to it. This is a time-consuming task and makes your application inaccessible for a long time.

- It may completely fail if any one of the components fails. It's difficult to build a monolithic application to handle failure of specific components and degrade application features accordingly.

- It may be difficult to find how much resources are each components consuming.

- It may be difficult to test and debug individual components separately.

Microservices architecture to the rescue

We saw the problems caused by monolithic architecture. These problems lead developers to switch from monolithic architecture to microservices architecture.

In microservices architecture, the server-side application is divided into services. A service (or microservice) is a small and independent process that constitutes a particular functionality of the complete server-side application. For example, you can have a service for payment processing, another service for account management, and so on; the services need to communicate with each other via a network.

What do you mean by "small" service?

You must be wondering how small a service needs to be and how to tell whether a service is small or not. Well, it actually depends on many factors such as the type of application, team management, availability of resources, size of application, and how small you think is small. However, a small service doesn't have to be the one that is written is fewer lines of code or provides a very basic functionality. A small service can be the one on which a team of developers can work independently, which can be scaled independently to other services, scaling it doesn't cause unbalanced utilization of recourses, and overall they are highly decoupled (independent and unaware) of other services.

You don't have to run each service in a different server, that is, you can run multiple services in a single computer. The ratio of server to services depends on different factors. A common factor is the amount and type of resources and technologies required. For example, if a service needs a lot of RAM and CPU time, then it would be better to run it individually on a server. If there are some services that don't need much resources, then you can run them all in a single server together.

The following diagram shows an example of the microservices architecture:

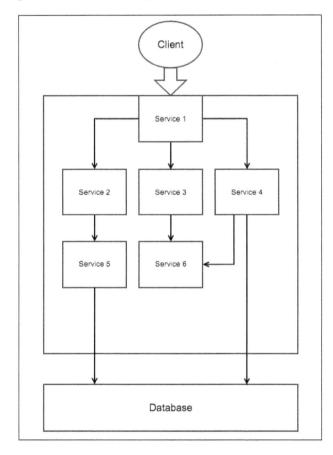

Here, you can think of **Service 1** as the web server with which a browser communicates and other services providing APIs for various functionalities. The web services communicate with other services to get data.

Merits of microservices architecture

Due to the fact that services are small and independent and communicate via network, microservices architecture solves many problems that monolithic architecture had. Here are some of the benefits of microservices architecture:

- As the services communicate via a network, they can be written in different programming languages using different frameworks
- Making a change to a service only requires that particular service to be redeployed instead of all the services, which is a faster procedure
- It becomes easier to measure how much resources are consumed by each service as each service runs in a different process
- It becomes easier to test and debug, as you can analyze each service separately
- Services can be reused by other applications as they interact via network calls

Scaling services

Apart from the preceding benefits, one of the major benefits of microservices architecture is that you can scale individual services that require scaling instead of all the services, therefore preventing duplication of resources and unbalanced utilization of resources.

Suppose we want to scale **Service 1** in the preceding diagram. Here is a diagram that shows how it can be scaled:

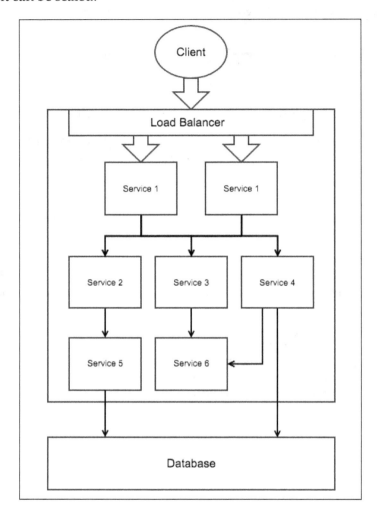

Here, we are running two instances of **Service 1** on two different servers kept behind a load balancer, which distributes the traffic between them. All other services run the same way, as scaling them wasn't required. If you wanted to scale **Service 3**, then you can run multiple instances of **Service 3** on multiple servers and place them behind a load balancer.

Demerits of microservices architecture

Although there are a lot of merits of using microservices architecture compared to monolithic architecture, there are some demerits of microservices architecture as well:

- As the server-side application is divided into services, deploying, and optionally, configuring each service separately is a cumbersome and time-consuming task.

 Note that developers often use some sort automation technology (such as AWS, Docker, and so on) to make deployment somewhat easier; however, to use it, you still need a good level of experience and expertise with that technology.

- Communication between services is likely to lag as it's done via a network.
- This sort of server-side applications more prone to network security vulnerabilities as services communicate via a network.
- Writing code for communicating with other services can be harder, that is, you need to make network calls and then parse the data to read it. This also requires more processing. Note that although there are frameworks to build server-side applications using microservices that make fetching and parsing data easier, it still doesn't deduct the processing and network wait time.
- You will surely need some sort of monitoring tool to monitor services as they may go down due to network, hardware, or software failure. Although you may use the monitoring tool only when your application suddenly stops, to build the monitoring software or use some sort of service, monitoring software needs some level of extra experience and expertise.
- Microservices-based server-side applications are slower than monolithic-based server-side applications as communication via networks is slower compared to memory.

When to use microservices architecture

It may seem like its difficult to choose between monolithic and microservices architecture, but it's actually not so hard to decide between them.

If you are building a server-side application using monolithic architecture and you feel that you are unlikely to face any monolithic issues that we discussed earlier, then you can stick to monolithic architecture. In future, if you are facing issues that can be solved using microservices architecture, then you should switch to microservices architecture.

If you are switching from a monolithic architecture to microservices architecture, then you don't have to rewrite the complete application, instead you can only convert the components that are causing issues to services by doing some code refactoring. This sort of server-side applications where the main application logic is monolithic but some specific functionality is exposed via services is called microservices architecture with monolithic core. As issues increase further, you can start converting more components of the monolithic core to services.

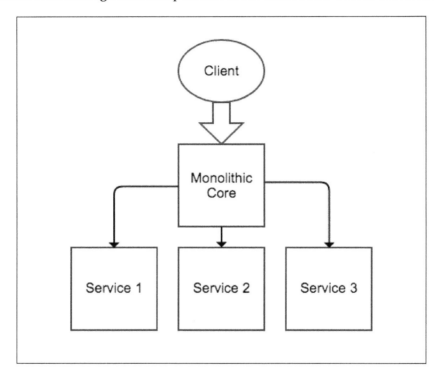

If you are building a server-side application using monolithic architecture and you feel that you are likely to face any of the monolithic issues that we discussed earlier, then you should immediately switch to microservices architecture or microservices architecture with monolithic core, depending on what suits you the best.

Data management

In microservices architecture, each service can have its own database to store data and can also use a centralized database.

Some developers don't use a centralized database at all, instead all services have their own database to store the data. To synchronize the data between the services, the services omit events when their data is changed and other services subscribe to the event and update the data. The problem with this mechanism is that if a service is down, then it may miss some events. There is also going to be a lot of duplicate data, and finally, it is difficult to code this kind of system.

Therefore, it's a good idea to have a centralized database and also let each service to maintain their own database if they want to store something that they don't want to share with others. Services should not connect to the centralized database directly, instead there should be another service called **database service** that provides APIs to work with the centralized database. This extra layer has many advantages, such as the underlying schema can be changed without updating and redeploying all the services that are dependent on the schema, we can add a caching layer without making changes to the services, you can change the type of database without making any changes to the services and there are many other benefits. We can also have multiple database services if there are multiple schemas, or if there are different types of database, or due to some other reason that benefits the overall architecture and decouples the services.

Implementing microservices using Seneca

Seneca is a Node.js framework for creating server-side applications using microservices architecture with monolithic core.

Earlier, we discussed that in microservices architecture, we create a separate service for every component, so you must be wondering what's the point of using a framework for creating services that can be done by simply writing some code to listen to a port and reply to requests. Well, writing code to make requests, send responses, and parse data requires a lot of time and work, but a framework like Seneca makes all this easy. Also, converting the components of a monolithic core to services is also a cumbersome task as it requires a lot of code refactoring, but Seneca makes it easy by introducing the concepts of actions and plugins. Finally, services written in any other programming language or framework will be able to communicate with Seneca services.

In Seneca, an action represents a particular operation. An action is a function that's identified by an object literal or JSON string called the action pattern.

In Seneca, these operations of a component of monolithic core are written using actions, which we may later want to move from monolithic core to a service and expose it to other services and monolithic cores via a network.

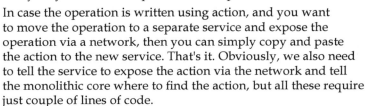

Why actions?

You might be wondering what is the benefit of using actions instead of functions to write operations and how actions make it easy to convert components of monolithic core to services? Suppose you want to move an operation of monolithic core that is written using a function to a separate service and expose the function via a network, then you cannot simply copy and paste the function to the new service, instead you need to define a route (if you are using Express). To call the function inside the monolithic core, you will need to write code to make an HTTP request to the service. To call this operation inside the service, you can simply call a function so that there are two different code snippets depending from where you are executing the operation. Therefore, moving operations requires a lot of code refactoring. However, if you would have written the preceding operation using the Seneca action, then it would have been really easy to move the operation to a separate service.

In case the operation is written using action, and you want to move the operation to a separate service and expose the operation via a network, then you can simply copy and paste the action to the new service. That's it. Obviously, we also need to tell the service to expose the action via the network and tell the monolithic core where to find the action, but all these require just couple of lines of code.

A Seneca service exposes actions to other services and monolithic cores. While making requests to a service, we need to provide a pattern matching an action's pattern to be called in the service.

Why patterns?

Patterns make it easy to map a URL to an action. Patterns can overwrite other patterns for specific conditions, therefore it prevents editing the existing code, as editing the existing code in a production site is not safe and has many other disadvantages.

Seneca also has a concept of plugins. A `seneca` plugin is actually a set of actions that can be easily distributed and plugged in to a service or monolithic core.

As our monolithic core becomes larger and complex, we can convert components to services. That is, move actions of certain components to services.

Creating your first Seneca application

Let's create a basic application using Seneca to demonstrate how to use it. We will create an application that allows users to log in and register. This will be a demo application just to demonstrate how actions, plugins, and services can be created, and not how login and registration functionality works.

Before you proceed further, create a directory named seneca-example and place a file named package.json in it. Inside the seneca-example directory, we will place our services and monolithic core. Inside the package.json file, place the following code so that npm will be able to download the dependencies for our application:

```
{
  "name": "seneca-example",
  "dependencies": {
    "seneca": "0.6.5",
    "express" : "latest"
  }
}
```

Here we are using Seneca version 0.6.5. Make sure that you are also using the same version to avoid code incompatibility.

Now run the npm install command inside the seneca-example directory to install Seneca and other packages locally.

Now create a file named main.js that will be the monolithic core of our server side application.

The monolithic core and services are all seneca instances programmatically. Place this code in the main.js file to create a seneca instance:

```
var seneca = require("seneca")();
```

Now using this seneca object, we are going to add actions, call actions, add plugins, and everything.

Creating actions

Let's create actions for login and registration functionality and place them in the main.js file. To create actions, we need to use the `add` method of the `seneca` object. The first argument of the `add` method takes a JSON string or object that is the action identifier (called **pattern** to identify the action). The second argument is a callback that will be executed when the action is invoked.

Place this code in the main.js file that creates two actions for login and registration, as follows:

```
seneca.add({role: "accountManagement", cmd: "login"}, function(args,
respond){
});

seneca.add({role: "accountManagement", cmd: "register"},
function(args, respond){
});
```

We will see the code for the body of the actions later in this chapter.

There is nothing special about `role` and `cmd` properties. You can use any property names you wish too.

The second argument is a callback, which will be invoked when the action is called.

If there are multiple actions with the same pattern, then the later overrides the others.

We need to use the `act` method of the `seneca` object to invoke an action that's local to the instance or resides on some other service. The first argument of the `act` method is a pattern to match an action, and the second argument is a callback that will be executed once the action has been invoked.

Here is an example code that shows how to call the preceding two actions:

```
seneca.act({role: "accountManagement", cmd: "register", username:
"narayan", password: "mypassword"}, function(error, response){
});

seneca.act({role: "accountManagement", cmd: "login", username:
"narayan", password: "mypassword"}, function(error, response){
});
```

The callback passed to the `act` method is executed asynchronously once the result of the action arrives.

Here, the object we passed to the act method has two extra properties than the action's pattern it is supposed to match. However, the action is still matched and invoked because in case the pattern passed to the act method has more properties than the action's pattern it is supposed to match, Seneca finds all the action's patterns whose properties are in the pattern passed to the act method and invokes the one that has the highest number of matching properties.

If Seneca finds multiple action patterns with equal number of matching properties, then they are matched in ascending alphabetical order.

 You can learn more about Seneca pattern matching at `http://senecajs.org/getting-started.html#patterns-unique-override`.

Creating plugins

A Seneca plugin is just a set of related actions packed together. Programmatically, a seneca plugin can be created using a function or module.

A plugin makes it easy to distribute a set of actions among applications. You will also find seneca plugins in online public package registry maintained by npm. For example, there is a seneca plugin that provides actions to work with the MongoDB database. This plugin can be inserted into monolithic cores or services with just a single line of code.

By default, Seneca installs four built-in plugins when we create a seneca instance. These plugins are **basic**, **transport**, **web**, and **mem-store**.

Let's first create a plugin using a function. The function name is the plugin name, and a plugin can also have an initialization action, which will be invoked as soon as the plugin is attached to the seneca instance.

So, let's create a plugin named account and place the login and register actions in that, as later on, we will be creating a service and moving the actions there. Remove the actions we defined earlier in the main.js file and place the following code instead:

```
function account(options)
{
  this.add({init: "account"}, function(pluginInfo, respond){
    console.log(options.message);
    respond();
  })
```

```
    this.add({role: "accountManagement", cmd: "login"}, function(args,
respond){
  });

    this.add({role: "accountManagement", cmd: "register"},
function(args, respond){
  });
}

seneca.use(account, {message: "Plugin Added"});
```

Here we defined a function named `account` and attached it using the `use` method of the `seneca` object. To attach multiple plugins, we can call the `use` method multiple times.

The `init:account` action is the initialization action invoked by Seneca once the plugin is added. This can be used to do things such as establishing database connection or other things that the actions of the plugin depend on.

The `this` keyword inside the plugin refers to the `seneca` instance.

Let's create the same plugin using a module so that it's easily distributable and can be put up in the `npm` registry. Create a file named `account.js` and place it in the `seneca-example` directory. `account.js` is the plugin module. Place this code inside the `account.js` file:

```
module.exports = function(options)
{
  this.add({init: "account"}, function(pluginInfo, respond){

    console.log(options.message);

    respond();
  })

    this.add({role: "accountManagement", cmd: "login"}, function(args,
respond){
  });

    this.add({role: "accountManagement", cmd: "register"},
function(args, respond){
  });

  return "account";
}
```

Here is the plugin name in the string returned by the anonymous function.

Remove the plugin code that we previously defined in the `main.js` file and place the following code instead:

```
seneca.use("./account.js", {message: "Plugin Added"});
```

Here, to attach the plugin, we are providing the module path.

 You can learn more about creating Seneca plugins at `http://senecajs.org/write-a-plugin.html`, and you can find all the Seneca plugins at `http://senecajs.org/plugins.html`.

Creating services

A service is a seneca instance that exposes some actions via network. Let's create a service that exposes the login and register actions.

Create an `account-service.js` file in the `seneca-example` directory that will act as the service. Then place the following code in it to create a service that exposes the login and register actions:

```
var seneca = require("seneca")();

seneca.use("./account.js", {message: "Plugin Added"});

seneca.listen({port: "9090", pin: {role: "accountManagement"}});
```

Here, we first created a `seneca` instance. Then we added actions via a plugin. You can also manually add actions using the `add` method of the `seneca` object. Finally, we exposed the actions via an HTTP protocol. Seneca also supports other protocols, but we will stick to HTTP, as it's the most commonly used one.

`seneca.listen` creates an HTTP server to listen to requests. We also provided the port number and pin, which are optional. The default port is `10101`, and by default, there is no pin if not provided.

You must be wondering what is a pin and what is it used for? Well, you may not always want to expose all the actions of the service via a network. In that case, you can provide a pattern to the `pin` property and the server will handle these requests that match the `pin` pattern.

Now, for other services or monolithic cores to be able to call the actions of this service, they need to register this service.

Remove the previous plugin attachment code from the `main.js` file and add the following code to register the service:

```
seneca.client({port: "9090", pin: {role: "accountManagement"}});
```

Here we are registering the service by providing the `port` number and `pin`. Both of them are optional. In case if we don't use any port number, then it defaults to `10101`. In case the service is on different server, then you should use the `host` property to provide the IP address.

The `pin` attached to the `client` method is used to tell the `seneca` instance about what actions are exposed by the service. It's completely optional. Seneca won't send requests to a service that doesn't match the `pin` pattern.

You can add as many services as you want by calling the client method multiple times.

When you call the `act` method to invoke an action, the `seneca` instance first looks for the action locally before requesting services. If it's not found locally, then it checks for the services that have a pin to see if it matches any. If a pin matches, then it sends request to this particular service. Finally, if any of the pin doesn't match, it sends the requests one by one to all other services that don't have a pin till it gets a valid response from one of them.

You can also manually call an action of a service by sending the GET request to these types of URL:

```
http://localhost:9090/act?role=accountManagement&cmd=login&usernam
e=narayan&password=mypassword
```

You can also call a service by using the POST request. Here is how to do it using CURL:

```
curl -d
'{"role":"accountManagement","cmd":"login","username":"narayan","passw
ord":"mypassword"}' -v http://localhost:9090/act
```

Storing data

Seneca provides a built-in mechanism to store data. Seneca provides some built-in actions that allow us to store data. The built-in actions use `mem-store` to store data by default. **mem-store** is an asynchronous in-memory storage system.

You can create your application using the default storing mechanism. In case you want to change the underlying store system, you just need to install plugin for this particular storage system that will overwrite the built-in storage actions, therefore you will not have to refactor any code.

The built-in actions to do the CRUD operations are as follows:

- `role:entity,cmd:load,name:<entity-name>`: This is used to retrieve an entity using its ID. An entity can be thought of as a row in MySQL. Every entity gets a unique ID.

- `role:entity,cmd:save,name:<entity-name>`: This is used to update (if you provide entity ID) or add an entity if it does not exist. Entities are stored and retrieved in form of objects.

- `role:entity,cmd:list,name:<entity-name>`: This is used to list all the entities that are matching a query.

- `role:entity,cmd:remove,name:<entity-name>`: This is used to remove an entity using its ID.

Seneca also provides some wrapper functions that extract these actions and make it easy to call these actions. These functions are `load$`, `save$`, `list$`, and `remove$`.

Let's implement the login and register actions to allow us to log in and also register new accounts.

Here is the implementation of the account action. Update this code in the `account.js` file:

```
this.add({role: "accountManagement", cmd: "login"}, function(args,
respond){
  var accounts = this.make("accounts");

  accounts.list$({username: args.username, password: args.password},
function(error, entity){
    if(error) return respond(error);

    if(entity.length == 0)
    {
      respond(null, {value: false});
    }
    else
    {
      respond(null, {value: true});
    }
  });
});
```

The first argument of the callback passed to the `add` method holds reference to the object that matched against the pattern of the action.

Here we are first calling the `make` method of the `seneca` object. It's used to get reference of an entity's store. For example, in case of MySQL, the `make` method gets reference to a table.

Then, we will find whether there are any entities with the username and password passed by the `act` method. As entities are added as objects, to query for entities, we need to pass an object. Now `list$` looks for all entities with the same username and password.

We are passing a callback to the `$list` method that will be invoked asynchronously once the data is retrieved. This callback takes two parameters, that is, the first parameter is an `error` object if there is an error, otherwise `null`. Similarly, the second parameter is an array of entities found matching the given object.

For the action to respond back, it needs to call the second parameter of the action callback by passing it an object as the second argument. In case an error has occurred, we need to pass the error in the first argument.

Similarly, now let's write the code for the register action, as follows:

```
this.add({role: "accountManagement", cmd: "register"}, function(args,
respond){
  var accounts = this.make("accounts");

  accounts.list$({username: args.username}, function(error, entity){
    if(error) return respond(error);

    if(entity.length == 0)
    {
      var data = accounts.data$({username: args.username, password:
args.password})

      data.save$(function(error, entity){
        if(error) return respond(error);

        respond(null, {value: true});
      });
    }
    else
    {
      respond(null, {value: false});
    }
  });
});
```

Here, most of the code is understandable as it works the same way as the previous action. To store data, we are creating a new entity store reference using the data$ method by passing the entity we want to store. Then we are calling the save$ method to save the entity.

 To learn more about storing data in Seneca, visit http://senecajs. org/data-entities.html.

Integrating Express and Seneca

We have completed creating our login and register actions. Now, as our backend will be used by an app or it may represent as a website, we need to provide URLs to the clients who will use them to talk to the server.

Monolithic core is the part of our server-side application that the client interacts with for most of the functionality. Clients can also interact with services directly for some specific functionality if required.

So, we need to use some sort of website development framework in the monolithic core and services of our server-side application. We will be using Express, as it's the most popular one.

Seneca also provides a built-in way to map the URLs to actions, that is, requests made to an HTTP server can be automatically mapped to a particular action to invoke them. This is done using a definition object whose properties define a route mapping from URLs to action patterns. This built-in method defines route mapping independent of the framework being used. Once we have defined the definition objects, we need a plugin specific to the web server framework that will capture and resolve the URLs to action patterns using the definition objects. Definition object allows you to attach callbacks that will get the response of the action via a parameter, and then the callbacks can return the data to the user in whatever format they want. This can be useful in case you are creating a plugin for distribution that exposes a few actions that need to be called for specific URL requests, then you will have to use the built-in method, as it defines route mapping independent of the framework being used.

 You can learn more about how to use the built-in way to integrate Seneca and Express at https://github.com/rjrodger/seneca-web.

Add the following code to the `main.js` file to start the Express server in it:

```
var app = require("express")();
app.use(seneca.export("web"))
app.listen(3000);
```

On the second line, we are exporting a middleware function provided by the `seneca-web` plugin. `seneca-web` is the plugin to integrate Seneca and Express directly, that is, to translate URLs into action patterns using the definition object for Express framework. This is only required if we use the definition object to define route mapping. We won't be using definition objects, but we should still use `seneca-web`, as some third-party plugins may use definition objects if we are using these plugins. For example, if you are using the `seneca-auth` plugin, then you will have to include second line.

We want the user to be able to log in using the `/account/login` path and register using the `/account/register` path. The user will provide a username and password via query string. Here is the code to define routes to handle HTTP requests for login and registration:

```
app.get('/account/register', function(httpRequest, httpResponse, next)
{
  httpRequest.seneca.act({role: "accountManagement", cmd: "register",
username: httpRequest.query.username, password: httpRequest.query.
password}, function(error, response){
    if(error) return httpResponse.send(error);

    if(response.value == true)
    {
      httpResponse.send("Account has been created");
    }
    else
    {
      httpResponse.send("Seems like an account with same username
already exists");
    }
  });
});

app.get('/account/login', function(httpRequest, httpResponse, next){
  httpRequest.seneca.act({role: "accountManagement", cmd: "login",
username: httpRequest.query.username, password: httpRequest.query.
password}, function(error, response){
    if(error) return httpResponse.send(error);
```

```
    if(response.value == true)
    {
      httpResponse.send("Logged in!!!");
    }
    else
    {
      httpResponse.send("Please check username and password");
    }
  });
});
```

Here we are calling the appropriate actions depending on the path of the URL request.

Here, instead of using `seneca.act`, we are using `httpRequest.seneca.act` as the middleware function that we exported earlier adds a new `seneca` property to request the object of every HTTP requests. This property inherits the actual `seneca` instance. Actions in the third-party plugins add information in form of properties to the `seneca` property in order to share information related to a particular HTTP request with other route handers. The preceding code will behave in the same way even if we use `seneca.act`, but it's a good practice to use `httpRequest.seneca.act` as we may use such types of plugins. Your own route handlers can also use `httpRequest.seneca.act` to pass information related to `seneca` to each other.

Now, to run the application, first run the `account-service.js` file and then the `main.js` file. You can then log in and register using the following URLs:

* `http://localhost:8080/account/login?username=narayan&password=mypassword`
* `http://localhost:8080/account/register?username=x&password=mypassword`

Here, we saw how to create a web interface, which can be used by an app or to serve HTML pages in case it's a website.

We can also move the routes of Express to a service if we want a different service to handle certain requests.

Summary

In this chapter, we saw the difference between monolithic and microservices architecture. Then we discussed what microservices architecture with monolithic core means and its benefits. Finally, we jumped into the Seneca framework for implementing microservices architecture with monolithic core and discussed how to create a basic login and registration functionality to demonstrate various features of the Seneca framework and how to use it.

In the next chapter, we will create a fully functional e-commerce website using Seneca and Express frameworks.

2
Building a Coupon Site

The best way to understand Seneca and microservices architecture is by building a server-side application that would benefit from the microservices architecture. In previous chapter, we saw how large and complex server-side application benefits from the microservices architecture and why enterprises use microservices architecture. In this chapter, we will build a coupon website to practically demonstrate the benefits of using microservices architecture and Seneca to create a server-side application. While building this coupon site, you will also learn how to design a server-side application using the microservices architecture from scratch, how to split the functionality of the application into services, how a client can directly communicate with the services, and many other things.

Some of the things that we will cover in this chapter, apart from things related to Seneca and microservices architecture, are as follows:

- Using the `seneca-mongo-store` plugin to store data in MongoDB
- Creating a basic image storage server
- Discussing HTTP basic authentication using the basic-auth npm package
- Using the connect-multiparty npm package to parse HTTP POST requests with the `multipart/form-data` content type
- Moving, deleting, and renaming files in Node.js using the `fs` npm package
- Implementing pagination with MongoDB and Express

Getting started

The coupon site that we will build will allow users to submit coupons. For the coupon to be publicly visible, the administrator of the site should accept the coupon. Every coupon will have an image attached to it that will be stored and served by an image storage server.

We will be using MongoDB to store the coupons. Before you continue further, make sure that you have MongoDB installed and running. I am assuming that you have basic knowledge of MongoDB.

The exercise files contain two directories: `Initial` and `Final`. Inside the `Final` directory, you will find the complete coupon site source code. In the `Initial` directory, you will find the HTML code and directories for the monolithic core, services, image storage server, and so on. You will put code related to them in their respective directories. The `Initial` directory will help you quickly get started with building the coupon site.

We won't get into designing the frontend of our coupon site. We will only be concentrating on building the architecture and functionalities of the site. Therefore, the HTML code is already included in the `Initial` directory.

Architecture of our site

Our server-side application will be composed of a monolithic core, three services, MongoDB server, and image storage server.

The monolithic core will serve pages to the site visitors and administrators.

The three services are database service, URL configuration service, and upload service. The following is what each of these services do:

- **Database service**: Adding, retrieving, updating, and deleting coupons in MongoDB is done through database service. The monolithic core retrieves coupons from MongoDB through database service, and upload service stores coupons through database service.

- **Upload service**: When a user submits a coupon, the HTML form is submitted to the upload service. The upload service then sends the image to the image storage server and adds metadata about the coupon to the database using the database service. We moved these operations to a different service, because if we are resizing and converting the uploaded image, then it will consume more memory and CPU time and keep the port open for more time, which will flood the server and break the monolithic core in case there are a large number of submissions at a time, so moving these operations to a different service makes sure that if there is a rise in submissions, it doesn't affect the site visitors who are looking for the coupons. We won't be resizing and converting images, but if you want to add this functionality, you can add this by simply updating the upload service. While the upload service is being updated, the form submissions will not work, but everything else will work. Therefore, we can say that this functionality can be independently updated without affecting other functionalities.

- **URL config service**: The client communicates with the monolithic core, image storage server, and upload service. In a production site, these three servers will remain in three different physical computers with three different IP addresses. So, for the client to be able to communicate with them, these three need to be exposed via different domain names (that is the monolithic core can be pointed using the main domain and the other two using sub domains) or we can use a load balancer or reverse proxy that supports URL rerouting so that we can have a single domain name and route the requests to the respective server based on the path of the URL. The URL config service will serve the base URL to communicate with these three servers. To follow this chapter, you can simply run these servers in the same physical computer using different ports, and when you are ready to make the site live, you can change the base URLs in the URL config service, depending on what technique you used to make the client able to communicate with the servers. You don't have to modify the source code of the servers directly, which is a cumbersome and risky task.

We will be creating our own image storage server. However, in a production site, I would recommend that you use Amazon S3 or something similar to store images, as it makes it easy to serve images via CDN. You don't have to worry about scaling and reliability, and it's low cost. The image storage server that we will be creating will be a basic one to just demonstrate how to store images in a separate server and serve from there.

The following is the diagram that shows all the architecture's looks and how the servers in the architecture communicate with each other:

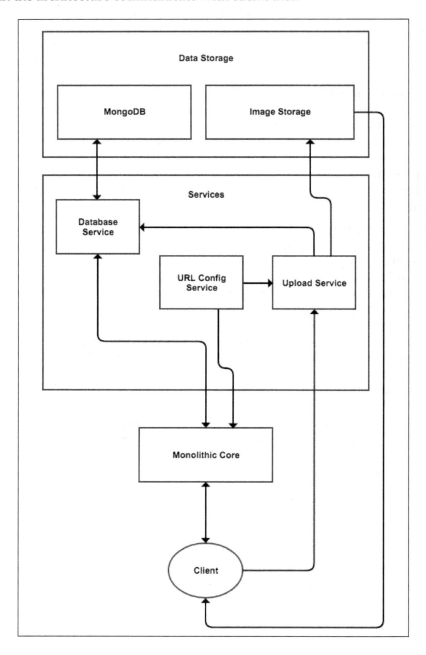

Creating the services

Let's first build the services before building the image storage server and monolithic core.

We will build the database service first, as it only depends on the MongoDB server, which is already running. The upload service and monolithic core depend on it, therefore it needs to be built before these.

Database service

The database service will provide actions to add coupons, list verified coupons, list unverified coupons, verify a coupon, and delete a coupon. These actions will be used by the upload service and monolithic core.

Open the `Initial/database-service` directory. Inside the directory, you will find a `package.json` file and an `app.js` file. The `app.js` file is where you will write the code, and `package.json` lists the dependencies for the database service. The database service is dependent on the `seneca` and `seneca-mongo-store` plugins. Run the `npm install` command inside `Initial/database-service` to install the dependencies locally.

Here is the code to import the `seneca` module, create the `seneca` instance, attach the `seneca-mongo-store` plugin, and initialize the plugin to connect to MongoDB:

```
var seneca = require("seneca")();

seneca.use("mongo-store", {
  name: "gocoupons",
  host: "127.0.0.1",
  port: 27017
});
```

Here we are using `gocoupons` as the database name. I am assuming that the MongoDB server is running locally on the default port `27017`.

The following is the code to create an action that allows you to add a coupon:

```
seneca.add({role: "coupons-store", cmd: "add"}, function(args,
respond) {
  var coupons = seneca.make$("coupons");
  var data = coupons.data$({title: args.title, desc: args.desc, email:
args.email, url: args.url, price: args.price, discount: args.discount,
thumbnail_id: args.thumbnail_id, verified: false});
  data.save$(function(err, entity) {
```

```
        if(err) return respond(err);

        respond(null, {value: true});
    });
});
```

We will store the coupons in a collection named coupons. Here we are setting the verified property of the document to false, that is, whenever a new coupon is submitted by a user, we will make it unverified so that the administrator can retrieve this newly submitted coupon and verify it manually.

The thumbnail_id property doesn't hold the complete URL of the coupon thumbnail, instead it's just the filename.

Here is the code to create an action to retrieve the verified coupons:

```
seneca.add({role: "coupons-store", cmd: "list"}, function(args,
respond){
  var coupons = seneca.make$("coupons");
  coupons.list$({verified: true, limit$:21, skip$: args.skip},
function (err, entity){
    if(err) return respond(err);

    respond(null, entity);
  })
});
```

This action retrieves maximum 21 coupons and it takes a skip argument that is used to skip some documents, making it possible to implement pagination using this action.

The following is the code to create an action to retrieve the unverified coupons:

```
seneca.add({role: "coupons-store", cmd: "admin_list"}, function(args,
respond){
  var coupons = seneca.make$("coupons");
  coupons.list$({verified: false}, function (err, entity){
    if(err) return respond(err);

    respond(null, entity);
  })
});
```

This action will be used to retrieve coupons to display on the admin panel for the administrator to accept or reject a coupon.

Here is the code to create an action to verify a coupon, that is, change the `verified` property from `false` to `true`:

```
seneca.add({role: "coupons-store", cmd: "verified"}, function(args,
respond){
  var coupons = seneca.make$("coupons");
  var data = coupons.data$({id: args.id, verified: true});
  data.save$(function(err, entity){
  if(err) return respond(error);

    respond(null, {value: true});
  });
});
```

This action will be invoked when the admin accepts a coupon to be displayed publicly.

Here is the code to create an action to delete a coupon:

```
seneca.add({role: "coupons-store", cmd: "delete"}, function(args,
respond){
  var coupons = seneca.make$("coupons");
  coupons.remove$({id: args.id});
  respond(null, {value: true});
});
```

This action will be invoked when the admin rejects a coupon.

Now that we have created all the actions for our database service, let's expose these actions via the network so that the other servers can call them. Here is the code to do this:

```
seneca.listen({port: "5010", pin: {role: "coupons-store"}});
```

Now go ahead and run the database service using the `node app.js` command.

URL config service

The upload services use the URL config service to find the base URL of the monolithic core so that it can redirect the user there once the coupon is submitted successfully. Also, the monolithic core uses this service to find the base URL of the image storage server and upload service so that it can include them in the HTML code.

Open the `Initial/config-service` directory. Inside the directory, you will find a `package.json` file and an `app.js` file. The `app.js` file is where you will write the code and `package.json` lists the dependencies for the config service. URL config service is only dependent on seneca. Run the `npm install` command inside `Initial/config-service` to install the dependencies locally.

The following is the code to import the `seneca` module and create actions to return the base URLs of the upload service, monolithic core, and image storage server:

```
var seneca = require("seneca")();

seneca.add({role: "url-config", cmd: "upload-service"}, function(args,
respond) {
  respond(null, {value: "http://localhost:9090"});
});

seneca.add({role: "url-config", cmd: "monolithic-core"},
function(args, respond) {
  respond(null, {value: "http://localhost:8080"});
});

seneca.add({role: "url-config", cmd: "image-storage-service"},
function(args, respond) {
  respond(null, {value: "http://localhost:7070"});
});

seneca.listen({port: "5020", pin: {role: "url-config"}});
```

Now go ahead and run the URL config service using the `node app.js` command.

Upload service

The upload service handles the new coupon form submission. The form consists of a coupon title, URL, description, price, discount price, and a thumbnail. The content type of form submission is `multipart/form-data`, as it is uploading an image file.

Open the `Initial/upload-service` directory. Inside the directory, you will find a `package.json` file and an `app.js` file. The `app.js` file is where you will write the code and `package.json` lists the dependencies for the upload service. The upload service is dependent on `seneca`, `express`, `connect-multiparty`, `path`, `fs` and `request` packages. Run the `npm install` command inside `Initial/upload-service` to install the dependencies locally.

The following is the code to import the modules:

```
var seneca = require("seneca")();
var app = require("express")();
var multipart = require("connect-multiparty")();
var path = require("path");
var fs = require("fs");
var request = require("request");
```

There are chances that the users may upload images with the same name. We don't want images with the same name to overwrite each other. Therefore, we need rename every image with a unique name. The following is the code for defining a function to generate a unique number, which will be used as an image name:

```
function uniqueNumber() {
  var date = Date.now();

  if (date <= uniqueNumber.previous) {
    date = ++uniqueNumber.previous;
  } else {
    uniqueNumber.previous = date;
  }

  return date;
}

uniqueNumber.previous = 0;

function ID(){
  return uniqueNumber();
};
```

Now, for the upload service to be able to communicate with the database and URL config services, we need to add them to the upload service `seneca` instance. The following is the code to do this:

```
seneca.client({port: "5020", pin: {role: "url-config"}});
seneca.client({port: "5010", pin: {role: "coupons-store"}});
```

Now we need to define an express route to handle POST requests submitted to the /submit path. Inside the route handler, we will rename the image, upload the image to image storage server, add the metadata of the coupon to MongoDB using the database service, and redirect to the monolithic core with the status stating that the form was submitted successfully. Here is the code to define the route:

```
//declare route and add callbacks
app.post('/submit', multipart, function(httpRequest, httpResponse,
next){

  var tmp_path = httpRequest.files.thumbnail.path;
  var thumbnail_extension = path.extname(tmp_path);
  var thumbnail_directory = path.dirname(tmp_path);
  var thumbnail_id = ID();
  var renamed_path = thumbnail_directory + '/' + ID() + thumbnail_
extension;

  //rename file
  fs.rename(tmp_path, renamed_path, function(err) {
    if(err) return httpResponse.status(500).send("An error occured");

    //upload file to image storage server
    seneca.act({role: "url-config", cmd: "image-storage-service"},
function(err, storage_server_url){
      var req = request.post(storage_server_url.value + "/store",
function (err, resp, body){
        fs.unlink(renamed_path);

        if(err) return httpResponse.status(500).send("An error
occured");

        if(body == "Done")
        {
          //store the coupon
          seneca.act({role: "coupons-store", cmd: "add", title:
httpRequest.body.title, email: httpRequest.body.email, url:
httpRequest.body.url, desc: httpRequest.body.desc, price: httpRequest.
body.price, discount: httpRequest.body.price, thumbnail_id: thumbnail_
id + thumbnail_extension}, function(err, response){
            if(err)
            {
              //delete the stored image
              request.get(storage_server_url + "/delete/" + thumbnail_
id + thumbnail_extension);
              httpResponse.status(500).send("An error occured");
```

```
                return;
            }
            seneca.act({role: "url-config", cmd: "monolithic-core"},
function(err, response){
                if(err) return httpResponse.status(500).send("An error
occured");

                //redirect to monolithic core
                httpResponse.redirect(response.value +
"/?status=submitted");
            });
        });
    }
    });

    var form = req.form();
    form.append("thumbnail", fs.createReadStream(renamed_path));
    form.append("name", thumbnail_id + thumbnail_extension);
    });
  });
});
```

Here is how the preceding code works:

- First we added a callback provided by the connect-multiparty module, which parses the `multipart/form-data` body and moves the files to a temporary location.

- In the second callback, we performed our custom operations. In the second callback, we first renamed the file so that every image file gets a unique name. Renaming is done using the `rename` method of the filesystem module.

- Then we uploaded the image file to the image storage server using the `post` method of the request module.

- After this, we deleted the local version of the image file using the `unlink` method of the filesystem module.

- If uploading the image to the image storage server failed for some reason, then we will return an HTTP internal server error to the client.

- If the image got uploaded to the image storage server successfully, then we will add the coupon metadata to MongoDB via the database service.

- If, for some reason, the metadata did not get added, we will delete the previously stored image in the image storage server and then return an HTTP internal server error to the client.

- If the coupon metadata got added successfully, we will retrieve the base URL of monolithic core from the URL config service and redirect there with a /?status=submitted query string, which indicates that the form was submitted successfully. When the monolithic core sees this query string, it displays a message saying that the coupon was submitted successfully.

- In case the URL config service didn't respond for some reason, we will return an HTTP internal server error to the client.

So what you need to keep in mind while coding such services is that you need to handle all sorts of failures and also roll back changes if a failure occurs. Now, this also makes it easy to update and redeploy the database service, URL config service, and image storage server as the upload service handles the failure of these services and provides a feedback to the user.

Now we have defined our routes. Finally, we need to start the Express server. The following is the code to do so:

```
app.listen(9090);
```

Now go ahead and run the upload service using the node app.js command.

Creating the image upload server

We have finished building the services. Now let's build the image storage server. The image storage server defines the routes using which an image can be stored, deleted, or retrieved.

Open the Initial/image-storage directory. Inside the directory, you will find a package.json file and an app.js file. The app.js file is where you will write the code, and package.json lists the dependencies for the image storage server. The upload service is dependent on express, connect-multiparty, path, and fs. Run the npm install command inside Initial/image-storage to install the dependencies locally.

The following is the code to import the modules:

```
var express = require("express");
var app = express();
var fs = require("fs");
var multipart = require("connect-multiparty")();
```

Now let's define the route using which the upload service can store images in the image storage server. The upload service makes the POST request to the `/store` URL path to store the image. Here is the code to define the route:

```
app.post("/store", multipart, function(httpRequest, httpResponse,
next){
  var tmp_path = httpRequest.files.thumbnail.path;
  var target_path = "public/images/" + httpRequest.body.name;
  fs.rename(tmp_path, target_path, function(err) {
    if(err) return httpResponse.status(500).send("An error occured");

    httpResponse.send("Done");
  });
});
```

Here, at first, we are adding the callback provided by the connect-multiparty module, which parses the `multipart/form-data` content type body and also moves the files to a temporary location.

Then, we are moving the file from temporary directory to another directory. The directory we are moving the file to is `public/images/`. We are moving the file using the `rename` method of the filesystem module. Finally, we are sending a `Done` string as the body of HTTP response to tell the upload service that the file is stored successfully.

Now let's define the route using which the upload service can delete an image stored in the image storage server. The upload service makes the GET request to the `/delete/:id` URL path, where the `id` parameter indicates the image name. The following is the code to define the route:

```
app.get("/delete/:id", function(httpRequest, httpResponse, next){
  fs.unlink("public/images/" + httpRequest.params.id,
  function(err) {
    if(err) return httpResponse.status(500).send("An error
    occured");

    httpResponse.send("Done");
  });
});
```

Here we are deleting the image file using the `unlink` method of the `fs` module.

Finally, we need to serve images to the browser. Looking for static file in the `public/images/` directory can do this. The following is the code to do this:

```
app.use(express.static(__dirname + "/public/images"));
```

Here we are using the static middleware that looks for static files in the directory provided by arguments and serves directly to the browser.

Now we have defined our routes. Finally, we need to start the Express server. Here is the code to do so:

```
app.listen(9090);
```

Now go ahead and run the image storage server using the `node app.js` command.

Creating the monolithic core

We have finished creating the services and image storage server. The users interact with the monolithic core to view coupons and the admin interacts with the monolithic core to view unverified coupons, and then it either rejects or accepts a coupon. Other than new coupon submission by the user, everything else by the user and admin is done in the monolithic core.

Open the `Initial/monolithic` directory. Inside the directory, you will find a `package.json` file and an `app.js` file. The `app.js` file is where you will write the code, and `package.json` lists the dependencies for the monolithic core. The monolithic core is dependent on `express`, `seneca`, `request` and `basic-auth npm` packages. Run the `npm install` command inside `Initial/monolithic` to install the dependencies locally.

We will use the `ejs` template engine with Express. Inside the `views` directory, you will find `ejs` files for home, new coupon submit forms, and admin pages. The files already contain the templates and HTML code. The site is designed using Bootstrap.

The following is the code to import the modules:

```
var seneca = require("seneca")();
var express = require("express");
var app = express();
var basicAuth = require("basic-auth");
var request = require("request");
```

Now, for the monolithic core to be able to communicate with the database and `url-` `config` services, we need to add them to the monolithic core `seneca` instance. The following is the code to do this:

```
seneca.client({port: "5020", pin: {role: "url-config"}});
seneca.client({port: "5010", pin: {role: "coupons-store"}});
```

Now we need to set `ejs` as the `view` `engine`. Here is the code to set `ejs` as the view engine:

```
app.set("view engine", "ejs");
```

All the static files such as CSS, JS, and fonts are kept on the `public` directory. We need to serve them to the client. Here is the code to serve the static files:

```
app.use(express.static(__dirname + "/public"));
```

Here we are serving the static files in the same way as we served the static files (that is, images) in the image upload server.

Now we need to add a route to the server of the home page of our website that displays the first 20 coupons. It also displays the **Next** and **Previous** buttons to navigate between the next or previous 20 buttons.

The home page is accessed via the root URL. The following is the code to add a route to the server of the home page:

```
app.get("/", function(httpRequest, httpResponse, next){
  if(httpRequest.query.status == "submitted") {
    seneca.act({role: "coupons-store", cmd: "list", skip: 0},
    function(err, coupons){
      if(err) return httpResponse.status(500).send("An error
      occured");

      seneca.act({role: "url-config", cmd: "image-storage-
      service"}, function(err, image_url){
        if(err) return httpResponse.status(500).send("An error
        occured");

        if(coupons.length > 20)
        {
          var next = true;
        }
        else
        {
```

```
            var next = false;
        }

        var prev = false;

        httpResponse.render("index", {prev: prev, next: next,
        current: 0, coupons: coupons, image_url: image_url.value,
        submitted: true});
      })
    })

    return;
};

if(parseInt(httpRequest.query.current) !== undefined &&
httpRequest.query.next == "true")
{
    seneca.act({role: "coupons-store", cmd: "list", skip:
    parseInt(httpRequest.query.current) + 20}, function(err,
    coupons){
        if(err) return httpResponse.status(500).send("An error
        occured");

        seneca.act({role: "url-config", cmd: "image-storage-
        service"}, function(err, image_url){
            if(err) return httpResponse.status(500).send("An error
            occured");

            if(coupons.length > 20)
            {
                var next = true;
            }
            else
            {
                var next = false;
            }

            var prev = true;

            httpResponse.render("index", {prev: prev, next: next,
            current: parseInt(httpRequest.query.current) + 20,
            coupons: coupons, image_url: image_url.value});
        })
    })
}
```

```
else if(parseInt(httpRequest.query.current) != undefined &&
httpRequest.query.prev == "true")
{
  seneca.act({role: "coupons-store", cmd: "list", skip:
  parseInt(httpRequest.query.current) - 20}, function(err,
  coupons){
    if(err) return httpResponse.status(500).send("An error
    occured");

    seneca.act({role: "url-config", cmd: "image-storage-
    service"}, function(err, image_url){
      if(err) return httpResponse.status(500).send("An error
      occured");

      if(coupons.length > 20)
      {
        var next = true;
      }
      else
      {
        var next = false;
      }

      if(parseInt(httpRequest.query.current) <= 20)
      {
        var prev = false;
      }
      else
      {
        prev = true;
      }

      httpResponse.render("index", {prev: prev, next: next,
      current: parseInt(httpRequest.query.current) - 20,
      coupons: coupons, image_url: image_url.value});
    })
  })
}
else
{
  seneca.act({role: "coupons-store", cmd: "list", skip: 0},
  function(err, coupons){
    if(err) return httpResponse.status(500).send("An error
    occured");
```

```
seneca.act({role: "url-config", cmd: "image-storage-
service"}, function(err, image_url){
  if(err) return httpResponse.status(500).send("An error
  occured");

  if(coupons.length > 20)
  {
    var next = true;
  }
  else
  {
    var next = false;
  }

  var prev = false;

  httpResponse.render("index", {prev: prev, next: next,
  current: 0, coupons: coupons, image_url:
  image_url.value});
  })
  })
  }
});
```

The index.ejs file is the view of the home page of our site. The preceding code renders this view to generate the final HTML code for the home page.

The preceding code implements pagination by checking whether prev or next keys are present in the query string. If these keys are undefined, then it displays the first 20 coupons, otherwise it calculates the skip value argument by adding 20 to the value of the current key in the query string.

Then, the code checks whether the total number of coupons retrieved is 21 or less. If they are less than 21, then it doesn't display the **Next** button by assigning the next variable to false, otherwise it displays the **next** button by assigning the next variable to true. However, the total number of coupons it displays is 20. We retrieved an extra coupon to just check whether we should display the **next** button or not. To find out whether we should display the **previous** button or not is fairly easy, that is, if the next key is true in the query string, then we must display the **previous** button.

The preceding code also checks for the `status=submitted` query string that indicates the user was redirected back from the upload service. If it's present, then it assigns the `submitted` local variable for the view to `true`. This is the `ejs` template present in the view that checks whether the `submitted` local variable is `true` or `undefined` and displays a successful form submission message:

```
<% if(typeof submitted !== "undefined"){ %>
  <% if(submitted == true){ %>
    <div class="alert alert-success" role="alert">Coupon has been
    submitted. Our administrator will review and the coupon
    shortly.</div>
  <% } %>
<% } %>
```

Here is the `ejs` template present in the view that displays the coupons and the **next** and **previous** buttons:

```
<% if(coupons.length < 21){ %>
  <% var cut = 0; %>
<% } %>
<% if(coupons.length == 21){ %>
  <% var cut = 1; %>
<% } %>
<% for(var i = 0; i < coupons.length - cut; i++) {%>
  <div class="col-sm-3 col-lg-3 col-md-3">
    <div class="thumbnail">
      <img src="<%= image_url + '/' + coupons[i].thumbnail_id %>"
      alt="">
      <div class="caption">
        <h4 class="pull-right"><del><%= coupons[i].price %></del>
        <%= coupons[i].discount %></h4>
        <h4><a href="<%= coupons[i].url %>"><%= coupons[i].title
        %></a>
        </h4>
        <p><%= coupons[i].desc %></p>
      </div>
    </div>
  </div>
<% } %>
</div>
```

```
<ul class="pager">
<% if(prev == true){ %>
  <li class="previous"><a href="/?prev=true&current=<%= current
%>">Previous</a></li>
<% } %>
<% if(next == true){ %>
  <li class="next"><a href="/?next=true&current=<%= current %>">Next</
a></li>
<% } %>
</ul>
```

We are done creating our home page. Now we need to create a route with the /add URL path that will display a form to submit a new coupon. The view for this coupon submission page is add.ejs. Here is the code to create the route:

```
app.get("/add", function(httpRequest, httpResponse, next){
  seneca.act({role: "url-config", cmd: "upload-service"},
  function(err, response){
    if(err) return httpResponse.status(500).send("An error
    occured");

    httpResponse.render("add", {upload_service_url:
    response.value});
  })
});
```

Here we are retrieving the base URL of the upload service from the URL config service and assigning it to the upload_service_url local variable so that the form knows where to submit the POST request.

The following is the template in the add.ejs view that displays the coupon submission form:

```
<form role="form" method="post" action="<%= upload_service_url %>/
submit" enctype="multipart/form-data">
  <div class="form-group">
    <label for="email">Your Email address:</label>
    <input type="email" class="form-control" id="email"
    name="email">
  </div>
  <div class="form-group">
    <label for="title">Product Title:</label>
    <input type="text" class="form-control" id="title"
    name="title">
  </div>
  <div class="form-group">
    <label for="desc">Product Description:</label>
```

```
    <textarea class="form-control" id="desc"
    name="desc"></textarea>
  </div>
  <div class="form-group">
    <label for="url">Product URL: </label>
    <input type="text" class="form-control" id="url" name="url">
  </div>
  <div class="form-group">
    <label for="price">Original Price:</label>
    <input type="text" class="form-control" id="price"
    name="price">
  </div>
  <div class="form-group">
    <label for="discount">Discount Price:</label>
    <input type="text" class="form-control" id="discount"
    name="discount">
  </div>
  <div class="form-group">
    <label for="thumbnail">Product Image: <i>(320 x
    150)</i></label>
    <input type="file" class="form-control" id="thumbnail"
    name="thumbnail">
  </div>
  <button type="submit" class="btn btn-default">Submit</button>
</form>
```

Now we need to provide a path for the site admin to access the admin panel. The path to access admin panel is going to be /admin. The admin panel will be protected using HTTP basic authentication.

We will create two more routes that will be used by the admin to accept or reject a coupon. The routes are /admin/accept and /admin/reject.

The following is the code to protect the admin panel using the HTTP basic authentication:

```
var auth = function (req, res, next){
  var user = basicAuth(req);

  if (!user || !user.name || !user.pass)
  {
    res.set("WWW-Authenticate", "Basic realm=Authorization
    Required");
    res.sendStatus(401);
  }
```

```
  //check username and password
  if (user.name === "narayan" && user.pass === "mypassword")
  {
    next();
  }
  else
  {
    res.set("WWW-Authenticate", "Basic realm=Authorization
    Required");
    res.sendStatus(401);
  }
}

app.all("/admin/*", auth);
app.all("/admin", auth);
```

Here we are executing the `auth` callback for all the admin panel paths. The callback checks whether the user is logged in or not. If user is not logged in, we will ask the user to log in. If the user tries to log in, then we will check whether the username and password is correct. If the username and password are wrong, we will ask the user to log in again. We will parse the HTTP basic authentication based the headers using the `basic-auth` module, that is, we will pass the `req` object to the `basicAuth` function to parse it. Here we are hardcoding the username and password.

Now we need to define the routes to access the admin panel. The `admin.ejs` file is the view for the admin panel. The following is the code to add the routes:

```
app.get("/admin", function(httpRequest, httpResponse, next){
  seneca.act({role: "coupons-store", cmd: "admin_list", skip: 0},
  function(err, coupons){
    if(err) return httpResponse.status(500).send("An error
    occured");

    seneca.act({role: "url-config", cmd: "image-storage-service"},
    function(err, image_url){
      httpResponse.render("admin", {coupons: coupons, image_url:
      image_url.value});
    });
  });
});

app.get("/admin/accept", function(httpRequest, httpResponse,
next){
  seneca.act({role: "coupons-store", cmd: "verified", id:
  httpRequest.query.id}, function(err, verified){
```

```
    if(err) return httpResponse.status(500).send("An error
    occured");

    if(verified.value == true)
    {
      httpResponse.redirect("/admin");
    }
    else
    {
      httpResponse.status(500).send("An error occured");
    }
  });
});

app.get("/admin/reject", function(httpRequest, httpResponse,
next){
  seneca.act({role: "url-config", cmd: "image-storage-service"},
  function(err, storage_server_url){
    if(err) return httpResponse.status(500).send("An error
    occured");

    request.get(storage_server_url.value + "/delete/" +
    httpRequest.query.thumbnail_id, function(err, resp, body){
      if(err) return httpResponse.status(500).send("An error
      occured");

      seneca.act({role: "coupons-store", cmd: "delete", id:
      httpRequest.query.id}, function(err, deleted){
        if(err) return httpResponse.status(500).send("An error
        occured");

        if(deleted.value == true)
        {
          httpResponse.redirect("/admin");
        }
        else
        {
          httpResponse.status(500).send("An error occured");
        }
      });
    });
  })
});
```

When the admin visits /admin, unverified coupons are displayed along with buttons to accept or reject a coupon. When the admin clicks on the **Accept** button, then a request is made to the /admin/accept path to mark the coupon as verified, and when the admin clicks on the **Reject** button, a request is made to the /admin/reject path to delete the coupon. After accepting or deleting a coupon, the admin is redirected to the /admin path.

The following is the template that displays the **coupons** and **verification** buttons to the admin:

```
<% for(var i = 0; i < coupons.length; i++) {%>
  <tr>
    <td><%= coupons[i].title %></td>
    <td><%= coupons[i].desc %></td>
    <td><%= coupons[i].url %></td>
    <td><img style="width: 300px !important" src="<%= image_url +
    '/' + coupons[i].thumbnail_id %>" alt=""></td>
    <td><%= coupons[i].price %></td>
    <td><%= coupons[i].discount %></td>
    <td>
      <form role="form" method="get" action="/admin/accept">
        <div class="form-group">
          <input type="hidden" value="<%= coupons[i].id %>"
          name="id">
          <input type="hidden" value="<%= coupons[i].thumbnail_id
          %>" name="thumbnail_id">
          <input type="submit" value="Accept" class="btn btn-
          default">
        </div>
      </form>
    </td>
    <td>
      <form role="form" method="get" action="/admin/reject">
        <div class="form-group">
          <input type="hidden" value="<%= coupons[i].id %>"
          name="id">
          <input type="hidden" value="<%= coupons[i].thumbnail_id
          %>" name="thumbnail_id">
```

```
        <input type="submit" value="Reject" class="btn btn-
        default">
      </div>
    </form>
  </td>
</tr>
<% } %>
```

We have defined our routes. Finally, we need to start the Express server. Here is the code to do so:

```
app.listen(9090);
```

Now go ahead and run the monolithic core server using the `node app.js` command.

Website walkthrough

We have completed creating our website. Now, let's walkthrough our site to see how it works overall. Before that, make sure that everything is running.

You can visit the home page of the website using the `http://localhost:8080/` URL. The following is how the web page will look when you will visit it for the first time:

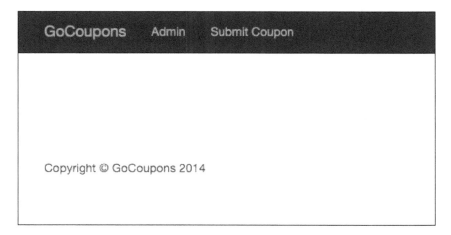

Now to add a coupon, click on the **Submit Coupon** button. Now you will see a form. Fill in the form. Here is how it looks:

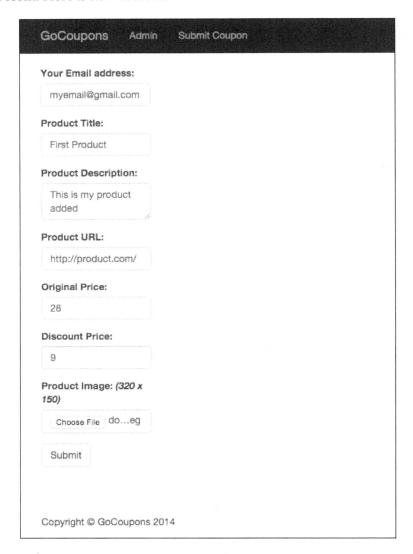

Now submit the form. After submitting the form, you will be redirected to the home page. The following is how the home page will look after redirect:

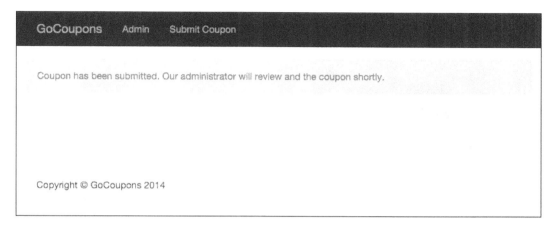

Now click on the **Admin** button to visit the admin panel and accept the coupon. Here is how the admin panel will look:

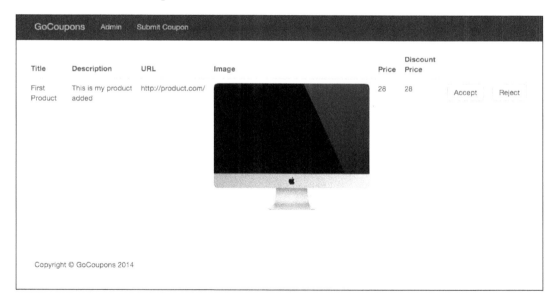

Click on the **Accept** button to accept it. Now go back to the home page. This is how the home page will look now:

In the preceding image, you can see that the product is listed.

Further improvements to the site

Here is a list of things we can do now to make the site architecture even better and add some extra features. You will also get some practice writing code involving the microservices architecture by performing the following actions:

- Create a separate service for the admin panel. The benefit of this is that you can update the admin panel without affecting the visitors, that is, while the admin panel is being updated, the users will still be able to visit and browse coupons. For this, you need to move the route of the admin panel to a new service.

- Fetch the username and password from the database. For this, you need to add some actions to the database service.

- Resize or crop images to thumbnail size, as that's the size of an image being displayed on the frontend. This will save the disk space. This needs to be done with the help of the upload service.

- You can create a mobile app for the website. For this, you need to create a service that provides APIs for the mobile app. New coupons can be submitted to the upload service by adding a query string, indicating that the request has arrived from the mobile app so that it won't redirect, instead send a response once coupon is submitted successfully.

These are just some ideas to make the site even better.

Summary

In this chapter, we saw how to build a website using Seneca and microservices architecture from scratch. The website we built was simple in terms of features, but involved a lot of important techniques that are used while building sites using the microservices architecture. Now you are ready to choose the architecture that suits your site best. I also mentioned the things you can do to make the site even better.

In the next chapter, we will discuss real-time communication among browsers using WebRTC.

3
Communication between Browsers in Real Time

To implement features such as audio/video chat or some other features in websites that require real-time peer-to-peer (browser-to-browser) data transfer, or need to retrieve audio/video stream from a microphone, webcam, or any other device, we had to use browser plugins such as Java and Flash. There are various issues with making websites depend on browser plugins, such as mobile browsers not supporting plugins and plugins requiring to be kept up to date. Therefore, WebRTC was introduced to solve these problems, that is, browsers that support WebRTC provide APIs to exchange data in real time directly between browsers and also retrieve stream from physical media sources without the use of plugins. In this chapter, we will discuss WebRTC and also the PeerJS library that wraps the WebRTC APIs to provide an easy to use API to work with WebRTC.

In this chapter, we'll cover the following topics:

- Discussing various APIs provided by WebRTC
- Retrieving stream from physical media input devices
- Displaying a media stream
- Discussing protocols used by WebRTC
- Exchanging media stream and arbitrary data between peers using PeerJS
- Discussing topics related to the fundamentals of WebRTC and PeerJS

Terminologies

Before we get into WebRTC and PeerJS, you need to know the meaning of some terms that we are going to use. These terms are discussed in the following sections.

Stream

A **stream** is a sequence of any kind of data that is made available over time. A stream object represents a stream. Usually, an event handler or callback is attached to the stream object, which is invoked whenever new data is available.

A **media stream** is a stream whose data is either audio or video. Similarly, a **media source** is a physical device, file, or something that provides data that is audio or video. A **media consumer** is also a physical device, API, or something that uses media stream.

WebRTC allows us to retrieve a media stream of physical media sources, such as microphones, webcams, screens, and so on. We will discuss more about it later in this chapter.

Peer-to-peer network model

Peer-to-peer model is the opposite of the client-server model. In the client-server model, the server provides resources to the clients, whereas in peer-to-peer model, every node in the network acts as a server and client, that is, every node provides and consumes resources. Peers in the peer-to-peer model communicate with each other directly.

To establish a peer-to-peer connection, we need a signaling server, which is used for signaling. **Signaling** refers to the exchange of data by peers that is required to establish a peer-to-peer connection. Data such as session control messages, network configuration, and so on is required to establish a peer-to-peer connection. A signaling server implements a signaling protocol such as SIP, Jingle, or some other protocol.

A model is selected depending on the requirements and resource availability for the application. Let's consider some examples:

- To build a video chat app, we should use the peer-to-peer model instead of the client-server model. As each node, in this case, is going to produce a lot data (or frames), and send the data to other node in real time, the server requires a lot of networks and other resources, increasing the server running cost. So, the peer-to-peer model is the best option for a video chat app. For example, Skype video chat is based on the peer-to-peer model.

- To build a text chat app that stores messages in a centralized database, we should use the client-server model as the amount of data that a client produces is not very high and you would also want to store the messages in a centralized database. For example, the Facebook messenger is based on the client-server model.

To establish a peer-to-peer connection using WebRTC, you will need a signaling server, STUN server, and optional TURN server. We will discuss more about it later in this chapter.

Real-time data

Real-time data is the data that needs to be processed and transferred without much delay. For example, video chatting, live analytics, live stock price, live streaming, text chat, live score, online multiplayer game data, and so on are all real-time data.

Real-time data transfer is a difficult task to achieve. The techniques and technologies used for real-time data transfer depend on the amount of data and whether the loss of data during data transfer is tolerable or not. If the real-time data is large, and the loss of data is intolerable, then it requires a lot of resources to achieve real-time data transfer, making it practically impossible to achieve real-time data transfer. For example, while video chatting, every user generates a lot of frames. If some frames are lost, then it is tolerable, therefore in this case, we can use the UDP protocol as a transport layer protocol that is unreliable and also has less overhead than TCP, making UDP very suitable for video chat application.

WebRTC allows us to transfer real-time media stream produced by it using the SRTP protocol. To transfer arbitrary data, it uses the SCTP protocol. We will discuss more about what these protocols are later in this chapter.

Introduction to WebRTC

Web Real-Time Communications (WebRTC) is a browser technology that enables retrieval of media stream of physical media sources and exchange media stream or any other data in real time. It comprises of three APIs: the `MediaStream` constructor, `RTCPeerConnection` constructor, and `RTCDataChannel` interface.

In short, `MediaStream` is used to retrieve the stream of physical media source, `RTCPeerConnection` is used to exchange `MediaStream` among peers in real time, and finally, `RTCDataChannel` is used to exchange arbitrary data among peers.

Let's see how these APIs work.

MediaStream API

Two main components of MediaStream API are the `MediaStream` constructor and `MediaStreamTrack` interface.

A track represents the stream of a media source. A track implements the `MediaStreamTrack` interface. A track can either be an audio track or be a video track. That is, a track attached to an audio source is an audio track, and a track attached to a video source is a video track. There can be multiple tracks attached to a particular media source. We can also attach constraints to a track. For example, a track attached to a webcam can have constraints such as the minimum video resolution and FPS. Each track has its own constraints.

You can change the constraints of a track after it's created using the `applyConstraints()` method of the `MediaStreamTrack` interface. You can retrieve the constraints applied to a track anytime using the `getSettings()` method of the `MediaStreamTrack` interface. To detach a track from a media source, that is, to stop the track permanently, we can use the `stop()` method of the `MediaStreamTrack` interface. To pause a track, that is, to stop the track temporarily, we can assign `false` to the `enabled` property of the `MediaStreamTrack` interface.

 Find out more about the `MediaStreamTrack` interface at `https://developer.mozilla.org/en-US/docs/Web/API/MediaStreamTrack`.

A track can either be a local or remote track. A local track represents the stream of a local media source; whereas, a remote track represents the stream of a remote media source. You cannot apply constraints to the remote track. To find whether a track is local or remote, we can use the `remote` property of the `MediaStreamTrack` interface.

We will come across the remote track while exchanging tracks between peers. When we send a local track to a peer, the other peer receives the remote version of the track.

A MediaStream holds multiple tracks together. Technically, it doesn't do anything. It just represents a group of tracks that should be played, stored, or transferred together in a synchronized manner.

 Find out more about the MediaStream constructor at https://developer.mozilla.org/en/docs/Web/API/MediaStream.

The getSources() method of the MediaStreamTrack object allows us to retrieve the ID of all the media devices, such as speakers, microphones, webcams, and so on. We can use the ID to create a track if the ID represents a media input device. The following is an example that demonstrates this:

```
MediaStreamTrack.getSources(function(sources){
  for(var count = 0; count < sources.length; count++)
  {
    console.log("Source " + (count + 1) + " info:");
    console.log("ID is: " + sources[count].id);

    if(sources[count].label == "")
    {
      console.log("Name of the source is: unknown");
    }
    else
    {
      console.log("Name of the source is: " +
      sources[count].label);
    }

    console.log("Kind of source: " + sources[count].kind);

    if(sources[count].facing == "")
    {
      console.log("Source facing: unknown");
    }
    else
    {
      console.log("Source facing: " + sources[count].facing);
    }
  }
})
```

The output will vary for everyone. Here is the output I got:

```
Source 1 info:
ID is:
0c1cb4e9e97088d405bd65ea5a44a20dab2e9da0d298438f82bab57ff9787675
Name of the source is: unknown
Kind of source: audio
Source facing: unknown
Source 2 info:
ID is:
68fb69033c86a4baa4a03f60cac9ad1c29a70f208e392d3d445f3c2d6731f478
Name of the source is: unknown
Kind of source: audio
Source facing: unknown
Source 3 info:
ID is:
c83fc025afe6c7841a1cbe9526a6a4cb61cdc7d211dd4c3f10405857af0776c5
Name of the source is: unknown
Kind of source: video
Source facing: unknown
```

navigator.getUserMedia

There are various APIs that return `MediaStream` with tracks in it. One such method is `navigator.getUserMedia()`. Using `navigator.getUserMedia()`, we can retrieve a stream from media input sources, such as microphones, webcams, and so on. The following is an example to demonstrate:

```
navigator.getUserMedia = navigator.getUserMedia || navigator.
webkitGetUserMedia || navigator.mozGetUserMedia;

var constraints = {
  audio: true,
  video: {
    mandatory: {
      minWidth: 640,
      minHeight: 360
    },
    optional: [{
      minWidth: 1280
    }, {
      minHeight: 720
    }]
```

```
    }
  }

  var av_stream = null;

  navigator.getUserMedia(constraints, function(mediastream){
    av_stream = mediastream; //this is the MediaStream
  }, function(err){
    console.log("Failed to get MediaStream", err);
  });
```

When you run the preceding code, the browser will display a popup seeking permission from the user. The user has to give the permission to the code to access the media input devices.

By default, the media input devices to which the tracks are attached while using `getUserMedia()` depends on the browser. Some browsers let the user choose the audio and video device that they want to use, while other browsers use the default audio and video devices listed in the operating system configuration.

We can also provide the `sourceId` property assigned to the ID of the media input device in the constraint object's `audio` or `video` property's `mandatory` property to make `getUserMedia()` attach tracks to these devices. So, if there are multiple webcams and microphones, then you can use `MediaStreamTrack.getSources()` to let the user choose a media input device and provide this media input device ID to `getUserMedia()` instead of relying on the browser, which doesn't guarantee whether it will let the user choose a media input device.

The first parameter that it takes is a constraint object with audio and video track constraints. Mandatory constraints are those constraints that must be applied. Optional indicates that they are not very important, so they can be omitted if it's not possible to apply them.

Some important constraints of an audio track are `volume`, `sampleRate`, `sampleSize`, and `echoCancellation`. Some important constraints of a video track are `aspectRatio`, `facingMode`, `frameRate`, `height`, and `width`. If a constraint is not provided, then its default value is used.

You can simply set the `audio` or `video` property to `false` if you don't want to create the audio or video tracks respectively.

We can retrieve the tracks of MediaStream using the getTracks() method of MediaStream. Similarly, we can add or remove a track using the addTrack() and removeTrack() methods, respectively. Whenever a track is added, the onaddtrack event is triggered. Similarly, whenever a track is removed, the onendtrack is triggered.

If we already have some tracks, then we can directly use the MediaStream constructor to create MediaStream with the tracks. The MediaStream constructor takes an array of tracks and returns MediaStream with the reference of the tracks added to it.

An API that reads data from tracks of MediaStream is called a MediaStream consumer. Some of the MediaStream consumers are the <audio> tag, <video> tag, RTCPeerConnection, Media Recorder API, Image Capture API, Web Audio API, and so on.

Here is an example that demonstrates how to display data of tracks of MediaStream in the video tag:

```html
<!doctype html>
<html>
  <body>

    <video id="myVideo"></video>
    <br>
    <input value="Pause" onclick="pause()" type="button" />

    <script type="text/javascript">

      navigator.getUserMedia = navigator.getUserMedia ||
      navigator.webkitGetUserMedia || navigator.mozGetUserMedia;

      var constraints = {
        audio: true,
        video: true
      }

      var av_stream = null;

      navigator.getUserMedia(constraints, function(mediastream){

        av_stream = mediastream;

        document.getElementById("myVideo").setAttribute("src",
        URL.createObjectURL(mediastream));
```

```
    document.getElementById("myVideo").play();
  }, function(err){
    console.log("Failed to get MediaStream", err);
  });

  function pause()
  {
    av_stream.getTracks()[0].enabled =
   !av_stream.getTracks()[0].enabled;
    av_stream.getTracks()[1].enabled =
   !av_stream.getTracks()[1].enabled;
  }

  </script>
  </body>
</html>
```

Here we have a `<video>` tag and a button to pause it. A video tag takes a URL and displays the resource.

 Before HTML5, HTML tags and CSS attributes could only read data from `http://` and `file://` URLs. However, in HTML5, they can read `blob://`, `data://`, `mediastream://`, and other such URLs.

To display the output of `MediaStream` in the `<video>` tag, we need to use the `URL.createObjectURL()` method, which takes a blob, file object, or `MediaStream` and provides a URL to read its data. `URL.createObjectURL()` takes extra memory and CPU time to provide access to the value passed on to it via a URL, therefore, it is wise to release the URL using `URL.revokeObjectURL()` when we don't need the URL anymore.

If there are multiple audio and video tracks in `MediaStream`, then `<video>` reads the first audio and video tracks.

RTCPeerConnection API

`RTCPeerConnection` allows two browsers to exchange `MediaStream` in real time. `RTCPeerConnection` is an instance of the `RTCPeerConnection` constructor.

Establishing peer-to-peer connection

For a peer-to-peer connection to be established, a signaling server is needed. Through the signaling server, the peers exchange data required to establish a peer-to-peer connection. Actual data transfer takes place directly between peer-to-peer. The signaling server is just used to exchange pre-requirements to establish a peer-to-peer connection. Both the peers can disconnect from the signaling server once the peer-to-peer connection has been established. The signaling server doesn't need to be a highly configured server as the actual data is not transferred through it. Data transfer for a single peer-to-peer connection will be in some KB, so a decent server can be used for signaling.

A signaling server usually uses a signaling protocol, but it is also okay if it's an HTTP server as long as it can pass messages between two peers. WebRTC doesn't force us to use any particular signaling protocol.

For example, say that there are two users, Alice and Bob, on two different browsers. If Alice wants to establish a peer-to-peer connection with Bob for chatting, then this is how a peer-to-peer connection would be established between them:

1. They both will connect to a signaling server.

2. Alice will then send a request to Bob via the signaling server, requesting to chat.

3. The signaling server can optionally check whether Alice is allowed to chat with Bob, and also if Alice and Bob are logged in. If yes, then the signaling server passes the message to Bob.

4. Bob receives the request and sends a message to Alice via the signaling server, confirming to establish a peer-to-peer connection.

5. Now both of them need to exchange messages related to session control, network configuration, and media capabilities. All these messages are exchanged between them by the RTCPeerConnection. So, they both need to create an RTCPeerConnection, initiate it, and attach an event handler to RTCPeerConnection that will be triggered by RTCPeerConnection when it wants to send a message via the signaling server. RTCPeerConnection passes the message to the event handler in the **Session Description Protocol (SDP)** format, and the messages for the RTCPeerConnection received from the signaling server must be fed to RTCPeerConnection in the SDP format, that is, RTCPeerConnection only understands the SDP format. You need to use your own programming logic to split custom messages and messages for RTCPeerConnection.

The preceding steps seem to have no problem; however, there are some major problems. The peers may be behind a NAT device or firewall, so finding their public IP address is a challenging task, sometimes it is practically impossible to find their IP address. So, how does RTCPeerConnection find an IP address of the peers when they may be behind a NAT device or firewall?

RTCPeerConnection uses a technique called **Interactive Connectivity Establishment (ICE)** to resolve all these issues.

ICE involves **Session Traversal Utilities for NAT (STUN)** and **Traversal Using Relays around NAT (TURN)** server to solve the problems. A STUN server is used to find the public IP address of a peer. In case the IP address of a peer cannot be found, or due to some other reason a peer-to-peer cannot be established, then a TURN server is used to redirect the traffic, that is, both the peers communicate via the TURN server.

We just need to provide the addresses of the STUN and TURN servers and RTCPeerConnection handles the rest. Google provides a public STUN server, which is used by everyone. Building a TURN server requires a lot of resources as the actual data flows throw it. Therefore, WebRTC makes it optional to use a TURN server. If RTCPeerConnection fails to establish a direct communication between two peers and a TURN server is not provided, there is no other way for the peers to communicate and a peer-to-peer connection establishment fails.

[WebRTC doesn't provide any way to make signaling secure. It's your job to make the signaling secure.]

Transferring MediaStream

We saw how RTCPeerConnection establishes a peer-to-peer connection. Now, to transfer MediaStream, we just need to pass the reference of MediaStream to RTCPeerConnection and it will transfer MediaStream to the connected peer.

[When we say that MediaStream is transferred, we mean the stream of individual tracks is transferred.]

The following are some of the things you need to know regarding the transfer of MediaStream:

- RTCPeerConnection uses SRTP as an application layer protocol and UDP as a transport layer protocol to transfer MediaStream. SRTP is designed for media stream transfer in real time.

- UDP doesn't guarantee the order of packets, but SRTP takes care of the order of the frames.

- The **Datagram Transport Layer Security (DTLS)** protocol is used to secure the `MediaStream` transfer. So, you don't have to worry about the security while transferring `MediaStream`.

- Constraints of the tracks that the remote peer receives may be different from the constraints of the local tracks, as `RTCPeerConnection` modifies the stream automatically, depending on the bandwidth and other network factors to speed up the transfer, achieving real-time data transfer. For example, `RTCPeerConnection` may decrease the resolution and frame rate of video stream while transferring.

- If you add or remove a track from `MediaStream` that is already being sent, then `RTCPeerConnection` updates `MediaStream` of the other peer by communicating to the other peer via the signaling server.

- If you pause a track that is being sent, then `RTCPeerConnection` pauses transfer of the track.

- If you stop a track that is being sent, `RTCPeerConnection` stops the transfer of the track.

You can send and receive multiple `MediaStream` instances via single `RTCPeerConnection`, that is, you don't have to create multiple `RTCPeerConnection` instances to send and receive multiple `MediaStream` instances to and from a peer. Whenever you add or remove a new `MediaStream` to or from `RTCPeerConnection`, the peers exchange information related to this via the signaling server.

RTCDataChannel API

`RTCDataChannel` is used to transfer data other than `MediaStream` between peers to transfer arbitrary data. The mechanism to establish a peer–to-peer connection to transfer arbitrary data is similar to the mechanism explained in the earlier section.

`RTCDataChannel` is an object that implements the `RTCDataChannel` interface.

The following are some of the things you need to know regarding `RTCDataChannel`:

- `RTCDataChannel` uses SCTP over UDP as a transport layer protocol to transfer data. It doesn't use unlayered SCTP protocol as the SCPT protocol is not supported by many operating systems.

- SCTP can be configured for reliability and delivery order, unlike UDP, which is unreliable and unordered.

- `RTCDataChannel` also uses DTLS to secure data transfer. So, you don't have to worry about the security at all while transferring data via `RTCDataChannel`.

 We can have multiple peer-to-peer connections open between browsers. For example, we can have three peer-to-peer connections, that is, first one for webcam stream transfer, second one for text message transfer, and third one for file transfer.

WebRTC applications using PeerJS

PeerJS is a client-side JavaScript library that provides an easy-to-use API to work with WebRTC. It only provides an API to exchange `MediaStream` and arbitrary data between peers. It doesn't provide an API to work with `MediaStream`.

PeerServer

PeerServer is an open source signaling server used by PeerJS to establish a peer-to-peer connection. PeerServer is written in Node.js. If you don't want to run your own PeerServer instance, then you can use PeerServer cloud, which hosts PeerServer for public use. PeerServer cloud allows you to establish a maximum of 50 concurrent connections for free.

A unique ID identifies every peer connected to PeerServer. PeerServer itself can generate the ID, or else the peers can provide their own ID. For a peer to establish a peer-to-peer connection with another peer, it just needs to know the other peer's ID.

You might want to run your own PeerServer instance when you want to add more functionality to PeerServer or you want to support more than 50 concurrent connections. For example, if you want to check whether the user is logged in to PeerServer, then you need to add this feature and host your own customized PeerServer.

In this chapter, we will use PeerServer cloud, but in the next chapter, we will create our own instance of PeerServer. Therefore, to continue further with this chapter, create an account on the PeerServer cloud and retrieve the API key. Every application gets an API key to access the PeerServer cloud. If you are hosting your own PeerServer, then you won't need an API key. The API key is used by PeerServer cloud to track the total connections established by an application. To create an account and retrieve an API key, visit `http://peerjs.com/peerserver`.

PeerJS API

Let's discuss the PeerJS API by creating a simple app that allows the users to exchange video and text messages with any user whose ID they have.

Create a `peerjs-demo` directory in your web server and place a file named `index.html` in it.

In the `index.html` file, we need to first enqueue the `PeerJS` library. Download `PeerJS` from `http://peerjs.com/`. At the time of writing, the latest version of PeerJS was 0.3.14. I would recommend that you stick to this version for the following examples. Place this starting code in the `index.html` file:

```
<!doctype html>
<html>
  <head>
    <title>PeerJS Demo</title>
  </head>
  <body>

    <!-- Place HTML code here -->

    <script src="peer.min.js"></script>
    <script>
      //place JavaScript code here
    </script>
  </body>
</html>
```

Here, I enqueued the minified version of PeerJS.

PeerJS API comprises of three main constructors, as follows:

- `Peer`: An instance of `Peer` represents a peer in the network. A peer is connected to the signaling server and STUN, and optionally, to a TURN.

- `DataConnection`: DataConnection (that is, the instance of `DataConnection`) represents a peer-to-peer connection, which is used to exchange the arbitrary data. Technically, it wraps `RTCDataChannel`.

- `MediaConnection`: MediaConnection (that is, the instance of `MediaConnection`) represents a peer-to-peer connection that is used to exchange `MediaStream`. Technically, it wraps `RTCPeerConnection`.

If a peer wants to establish `DataConnection` or `MediaConnection` with another peer, then it simply needs to know the other peer's ID. PeerJS doesn't give the other peer an option to accept or reject `DataConnection`. Also, in the case of `MediaConnection`, PeerJS doesn't give the other peer an option to accept or reject `MediaConnection`, but `MediaConnection` will be inactive until it is activated programmatically by the other peer so that `MediaStream` can be transferred, otherwise `MediaStream` will not be transferred. So, we can write our own logic to let the other user accept or reject `DataConnection` or `MediaConnecton`, that is, as soon as `DataConnection` or `MediaConnection` is established, we can cancel it by asking the user for their opinion.

 At present, one `MediaConnection` can transfer only one `MediaStream`. In future releases of PeerJS, a single `MediaConnection` will support the transfer of multiple MediaStreams.

Now, we need to create a `<video>` tag where the video will be displayed, a button to connect to a peer, and also a text box to send message. Here is the HTML code to display all these:

```
<video id="remoteVideo"></video>
<br>
<button onclick="connect()">Connect</button>
<br>
<input type="text" id="message">
<button onclick="send_message()">Send Message</button>
```

Now as soon as the page loads, we need to connect to `PeerServer` and ICE servers so that other peers can talk to us, and also when a user clicks on the connect button, we can establish `DataConnection` and `MediaConnection`. The following is the code for this:

```
var peer = null;

window.addEventListener("load", function(){
  var id = prompt("Please enter an unique name");

  peer = new Peer(id, {key: "io3esxy6y43zyqfr"});

  peer.on("open", function(id){
    alert("Connected to PeerServer successfully with ID: " + id);
  });

  peer.on("error", function(err){
    alert("An error occured. Error type: " + err.type);
```

```
    })

    peer.on("disconnected", function(){
      alert("Disconnected from signaling server. You ID is taken
      away. Peer-to-peer connections is still intact");
    })

    peer.on("close", function(){
      alert("Connection to signaling server and peer-to-peer
      connections have been killed. You ID is taken away. You have
      been destroyed");
    })

    peer.on("connection", function(dataConnection){
      setTimeout(function(){
        if(confirm(dataConnection.peer + " wants to send data to
        you. Do you want to accept?"))
        {
          acceptDataConnection(dataConnection);
        }
        else
        {
          dataConnection.close();
        }
      }, 100)
    })

    peer.on("call", function(mediaConnection){
      setTimeout(function(){
        if(confirm("Got a call from " + mediaConnection.peer + ". Do
        you want to pick the call?"))
        {
          acceptMediaConnection(mediaConnection);
        }
        else
        {
          mediaConnection.close();
        }
      }, 100);
    })
  });
```

Here is how the code works:

- First we displayed a prompt box to take the ID as an input so that every peer can decide their own ID.

- Then we created an instance of `Peer` with ID and PeerServer cloud key. Here we didn't provide signaling and ICE server's URLs, therefore, PeerJS will use PeerServer cloud as the signaling server and Google's public STUN server. It will not use any TURN server. As soon as a `Peer` instance is created, the instance connects to the signaling server and registers the given ID.

- Then we attached five event handlers to the `peer` object.

- The `open` event is triggered when the connection to `PeerServer` was successful.

- The `error` event is triggered for errors on the `peer` object.

- The `disconnected` event is triggered when the connection with the signaling server is disconnected. The connection with the signaling server may get disconnected due to network problem or if you manually call the `peer.disconnect()` method. Once you are disconnected, your ID can be taken by someone else. You can try to reconnect with the same ID using the `peer.reconnect()` method. You can check whether `peer` is connected to the signaling server using the `peer.disconnect` Boolean property.

- The `close` event is triggered when `peer` is destroyed, that is, it cannot be used anymore, all `MediaConnections` and `DataConnections` are killed, connection with the signaling server is killed, the ID is taken away, and so on. You may want to manually destroy `peer` when you don't need it anymore. You can destroy a peer using the `peer.destroy()` method.

- The `connection` event is triggered when some other peer establishes `DataConnection` with you. As I said earlier, `DataConnection` is established without further permission, but you can close it as soon as it's established if you want. Here we let the user decide if they want to continue or close `DataConnection` established by another peer. The event handler attached to the event receives an instance of `DataConnection` via the parameter that represents the currently established `DataConnection`.

- The `call` event is triggered when some other peer establishes `MediaConnection` with you. Here, we also let the user decide if they want to continue or close `MediaConnection` established by another peer. The event handler attached to the event receives an instance of `MediaConnection` via the parameter that represents the currently established `MediaConnection`.

- Here, in the `call` and `connection` event handlers, we asynchronously displayed the confirm popup boxes to prevent blocking the execution of the event handler that causes issues in some browsers, that is, blocking it fails to establish `DataConnection` and `MediaConnection`.

Now, let's implement the `acceptDataConnection()` and `acceptMediaConnection()` functions so that we can display the text messages and remote `MediaStream` when other peer establishes `DataConnection` or `MediaConnection` with us. Here's the code:

```
navigator.getUserMedia = navigator.getUserMedia ||
navigator.webkitGetUserMedia || navigator.mozGetUserMedia;

var myDataConnection = null;
var myMediaConnection = null;

function acceptDataConnection(dataConnection)
{
  myDataConnection = dataConnection;

  dataConnection.on("data", function(data){
    alert("Message from " + dataConnection.peer + ".\n" + data)
  })

  dataConnection.on("close", function(data){
    alert("DataConnecion closed");
  })

  dataConnection.on("error", function(err){
    alert("Error occured on DataConnection. Error: " + err);
  })
}

function acceptMediaConnection(mediaConnection)
{
  myMediaConnection = mediaConnection;

  mediaConnection.on("stream", function(remoteStream){

    document.getElementById("remoteVideo").setAttribute("src",
    URL.createObjectURL(remoteStream));
    document.getElementById("remoteVideo").play();
  })

  mediaConnection.on("close", function(data){
```

```
      alert("MediaConnecion closed");
   })

   mediaConnection.on("error", function(err){
      alert("Error occured on MediaConnection. Error: " + err);
   })

   navigator.getUserMedia({video: true, audio: true},
   function(mediaStream) {
      mediaConnection.answer(mediaStream);
   }, function(e){ alert("Error with MediaStream: " + e); });
}
```

This is how the preceding code works:

- In the `acceptDataConnection()` function, we attached three event handlers to `DataConnection`. The `data` event is triggered when the other peer sends us data. The `close` event is triggered when `DataConnection` is closed. Finally, the `error` event is triggered when an error occurs on `DataConnection`. We can manually close `DataConnection` using the `dataConnection.close()` method.

- In the `acceptMediaConnection()` function, we attached three event handlers and transferred our `MediaStream` to the other peer. The `stream` event is triggered when other peer sends us `MediaStream`. The `close` event is triggered when `MediaConnection` is closed. Finally, we activated `MediaConnection` using the `mediaConnection.answer()` method by passing our `MediaStream`. After `MediaConnection` is activated, the `stream` event will be triggered.

We finished writing the code to handle `MediaConnection` or `DataConnection` established by another peer with us. Now we need to write a code to create `MediaConnection` and `DataConnection` that a user clicks on the **connect** button. Here is the code:

```
function connect()
{
   var id = prompt("Please enter other peer ID");
   establishDataConnection(id);
   establishMediaConnection(id);
}

function establishDataConnection(id)
```

```
{
  var dataConnection = peer.connect(id, {reliable: true, ordered:
  true});

  myDataConnection = dataConnection;

  dataConnection.on("open", function(){
    alert("DataConnecion Established");
  });

  dataConnection.on("data", function(data){
    alert("Message from " + dataConnection.peer + ".\n" + data)
  })

  dataConnection.on("close", function(data){
    alert("DataConnecion closed");
  })

  dataConnection.on("error", function(err){
    alert("Error occured on DataConnection. Error: " + err);
  })
}

function establishMediaConnection(id)
{
  var mediaConnection = null;

  navigator.getUserMedia({video: true, audio: true},
  function(mediaStream) {
    mediaConnection = peer.call(id, mediaStream);

    myMediaConnection = mediaConnection;

    mediaConnection.on("stream", function(remoteStream){
      document.getElementById("remoteVideo").setAttribute("src",
      URL.createObjectURL(remoteStream));
      document.getElementById("remoteVideo").play();
    })

    mediaConnection.on("error", function(err){
      alert("Error occured on MediaConnection. Error: " + err);
    })

    mediaConnection.on("close", function(data){
```

```
      alert("MediaConnecion closed");
    })
  }, function(e){ alert("Error with MediaStream: " + e); });
}
```

Here is how the code works:

- First we asked the user to input another user's ID.

- Then we established `DataConnection`. To establish a `DataConnection` with another user, we need to invoke the `connect()` method of the `Peer` instance with other peer's ID. We also made `DataConnection` reliable and ordered. Then, we attached the event handlers. We also saw how `data`, `close`, and `error` events work. The `open` event is triggered when `DataConnection` is established.

- After establishing the `DataConnection`, we established `MediaConnection`. To establish `MediaConnection`, we need to call the `call()` method of the `Peer` instance. We need to pass `MediaStream` to the `call()` method. Finally, we attached the event handlers. The `stream` event will be triggered when the other user calls the `answer()` method of the `MediaConnection` instance, that is, when the MediaConnection is activated.

Now the last thing we need to do is write the code to send the message when a user clicks on the send message button. Here is the code for this:

```
function send_message()
{
  var text = document.getElementById("message").value;

  myDataConnection.send(text);
}
```

To send data via `MediaConnection`, we need to call the `send()` method of the `MediaConnection` instance. Here, we are sending a string, but you can pass any type of data including blobs and objects.

Now, to test the application, open the `index.html` page URL in two different browsers, devices, or tabs. I am assuming that you have opened the URL in two different devices. In each device, provide a different ID to identify the user. Then click on the connect button in any one device and enter the other peer's ID. Now accept the request on the other device. Once this is done, both the devices will be able to display each other's webcam video and microphone audio. You can also send messages between them.

You can find the official documentation of PeerJS API at `http://peerjs.com/docs/#api`.

Miscellaneous

At the time of writing this book, the WebRTC specifications were still not finalized. The overall idea of what WebRTC does and how WebRTC works has been finalized. It's just that the APIs are still under development.

For example, WebRTC has introduced an alternative to the `navigator.getUserMedia()` method, that is, the `navigator.mediaDevices.getUserMedia()` method. At the time of writing this book, `navigator.mediaDevices.getUserMedia()` is not supported in any browsers. The difference between them is that the `navigator.mediaDevices.getUserMedia()` method is based on the promise pattern, whereas `navigator.getUserMedia()` is based on the callback pattern. At present, there is no plan to get rid of `navigator.getUserMedia()` due to the backward compatibility reason, but in future, `navigator.getUserMedia()` may be removed as WebRTC wants to implement all APIs using the promise pattern, therefore, it's difficult to maintain multiple APIs that do the same thing. Similarly, `navigator.mediaDevices.enumerateDevice()` is an alternative to `MediaStreamTrack.getSources()`, that is, `navigator.mediaDevices.enumerateDevice()` is based on the promise pattern.

 You can find the official specification of WebRTC at `http://www.w3.org/TR/#tr_Web_Real_Time_Communication`.

Due to the fact that there are multiple APIs for the same feature, each with a different browser support, WebRTC provides a script called `adapter.js`, which is a shim to insulate websites from specification changes and prefix differences. You can find the shim at `https://github.com/webrtc/adapter`.

WebRTC has a GitHub repository where it puts a lot of example projects showing some of the things that can be built using WebRTC. You can find the repository at `https://github.com/webrtc/samples`. Just by looking at the examples and their source code, you can learn a lot more about WebRTC.

Summary

In this chapter, we discussed the fundamentals of WebRTC and PeerJS by creating a simple app. We discussed the various protocols, techniques, and other technologies that WebRTC uses to enable real-time peer-to-peer communication and read streams of physical media sources. We also saw an overview of PeerServer. Now you must be comfortable with building any type of WebRTC app using PeerServer cloud.

In the next chapter, we will build an advanced WebRTC app using a custom PeerServer.

4
Building a Chatroulette

The best way to master MediaStream and PeerJS is by building real-world applications, which is what we will do in this chapter. A chatroulette is a website that pairs random site visitors together for webcam and text-based conversation. Discussing how to build a chatroulette will help us to study PeerJS and PeerServer in depth, as it requires us to integrate PeerServer with Express. We will also add media controls to our site in order to pause/resume local MediaStream and allow the user to choose their desired microphone/webcam, which will help us to study MediaStream even more in depth. We will be actually creating a chatroulette that only allows the users of a particular country to chat, which would require an extra step of verification before connecting to the PeerServer; therefore, taking us even deeper into the integration of PeerServer into Express.

In this chapter, we will cover the following topics:

- Running your own instance of PeerServer
- Creating a custom PeerServer
- Integrating PeerServer with Express
- Verify users for connecting to PeerServer
- Finding the IP address and country of a user connected to the server
- Allowing the user to use a microphone and webcam directly on the webpage
- Discussing the requirements for building a completely working chatroulette

Creating your own PeerServer

Before we start building a chatroulette, let's see how to run our own instance of PeerServer.

PeerServer is available as an npm package on npm cloud. Let's create a custom PeerServer and use it with the PeerJS application that we built in our previous chapter.

First create a directory named Custom-PeerServer and place app.js and package. json files in it.

In the package.json file, place the following code and run the npm install command to download the PeerServer package:

```
{
  "name": "Custom-PeerServer",
  "dependencies": {
    "peer": "0.2.8",
    "express": "4.13.3"
  }
}
```

At the time of writing, the latest version of PeerServer is 0.2.8. Here, we will also download the express package, as we will need to demonstrate how to integrate PeerServer with Express.

PeerServer package provides a library to create a custom PeerServer or integrate PeerServer with Express and also an executable file to directly create our own instance of PeerServer without any customization.

Run PeerServer from shell

If you want to directly run your own instance of PeerServer from shell without any customization, then run the following command in the Custom-PeerServer/node_ modules/peer/bin directory:

```
./peerjs –port 8080
```

It should now print the following command:

```
Started PeerServer on ::, port: 8080, path: / (v. 0.2.8)
```

This confirms that `PeerServer` is running. To test whether the `PeerServer` instance is working or not, go to the `index.html` file of the application that we created in our previous chapter and replace the following code:

```
peer = new Peer(id, {key: ""});
```

The preceding code will be replaced with the following code:

```
peer = new Peer(id, {host: "localhost", port: 8080});
```

Now run the application and it should work as usual.

Using PeerServer library

PeerServer library is used to create a custom PeerServer. The PeerServer library also allows us to integrate PeerServer with the Express server.

Creating custom PeerServer

Here is an example code that demonstrates how to create your own custom PeerServer. Place the following code in the `app.js` file and run the `node app.js` command to start the server:

```
var PeerServer = require("peer").PeerServer;
var server = PeerServer({port: 8080});

server.on("connection", function(id) {
  console.log(id + " has connected to the PeerServer");
});

server.on("disconnect", function(id) {
  console.log(id + " has disconnected from the PeerServer");
});
```

Here, the first two lines of the code create the custom PeerServer. We then attached event handlers that will be triggered when a user connects or disconnects from PeerServer. A custom PeerServer doesn't provide an API to check whether a peer is allowed to connect to PeerServer or not. It just allows us to do something after the peer is connected or when the peer disconnects.

To test whether the custom PeerServer is working or not, go to the `index.html` file of the application that we created in the previous chapter and replace the following code:

```
peer = new Peer(id, {key: ""});
```

The preceding code will be replaced with the following code:

```
peer = new Peer(id, {host: "localhost", port: 8080});
```

Now run the application and it should work as usual.

Integrating PeerServer with the Express server

We can also integrate PeerServer with the Express server, that is, a particular path of the Express server will provide the signaling service. The main advantage of integrating PeerServer with the Express server is that we can check whether a peer is allowed to connect to PeerServer or not, and if it is not allowed, then we can stop the peer from using it.

Here is an example code that demonstrates how to integrate PeerServer with the Express server. Place the following code in the app.js file and run the node app.js command to start the server:

```
var express = require("express");
var app = express();

var server = app.listen(8080);

app.use("/signaling", function(httpRequest, httpResponse, next){
  //check whether peer is allowed to connect or not.

  next();
});


var ExpressPeerServer = require("peer").ExpressPeerServer(server,
{debug: true});

app.use("/signaling", ExpressPeerServer);

ExpressPeerServer.on("connection", function(id){

});

ExpressPeerServer.on("disconnect", function(id){

});
```

Here we are using a middleware provided by the `PeerServer` library to integrate PeerServer with Express. Here, PeerServer is made available on the `/signaling` path. You can use any path you want to.

The `PeerServer` library doesn't provide any way to check whether the peer is allowed to connect to PeerServer or not, so we are using our own technique, that is, we are attaching another middleware on top of the `ExpressPeerServer` middleware, which performs this check. Although this technique may seem fine, if our custom middleware stops the request from proceeding further, then PeerServer fires the `connection` and `disconnect` events and destroys the `Peer` instance on the frontend.

 You can learn more about PeerServer at `https://www.npmjs.com/package/peer`.

Creating a chatroulette

The chatroulette that we will build is only for people residing in India, that is, a peer cannot connect to the PeerServer if the IP address of the peer doesn't resolve to India. We added this filter to make the website a little more complex to code so that you can learn how to check whether a user is allowed to connect to PeerServer or not.

We will use a single server that will serve webpages and also act as a PeerServer, that is, we will integrate PeerServer with the Express server.

We won't get into designing the frontend of our chatroulette. We will only be concentrating on building the architecture and functionalities.

The exercise files for this chapter contain two directories: `Chatroulette` and `Custom-PeerServer`. In the `Chatroulette` directory, there are two directories: `Initial` and `Final`. In the `Final` directory, you will find the complete chatroulette source code. In the `Initial` directory, you will only find the HTML code for our chatroulette. The `Initial` directory is to help you quickly get started with building the chatroulette.

You will place the code related to the frontend functionality of the site in the `Initial/public/js/main.js` file and you will place the code related to the server side functionality in the `Initial/app.js` file.

Building the backend

Our site will basically contain three URL end points: a root path for serving the home page, the /find path to find the ID of a free user for chatting, and finally the /signaling path that serves as the end point for PeerServer.

Every user will have a unique ID that is generated by PeerServer. For a user to retrieve the ID of another free user using the /find URL, they must be first be connected to PeerServer.

The server will maintain two different arrays, that is, the first array contains IDs of the users connected to PeerServer and the second array contains IDs of the users that need a partner to chat.

Let's get started with building our backend. Place the following code in the app.js file to create our web server and serve the home page of our site:

```
var express = require("express");
var app = express();

app.use(express.static(__dirname + "/public"));

app.get("/", function(httpRequest, httpResponse, next){
  httpResponse.sendFile(__dirname + "/public/html/index.html");
})

var server = app.listen(8080);
```

Here we are serving the index.html file as our home page. Run the node app.js command to start the server. I am assuming that you are running node.js on the localhost, so open the http://localhost:8080/ URL on the browser to see the home page. The home page should look similar to the following image:

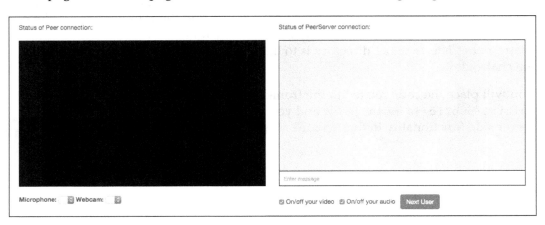

The following are the different elements of the home page:

- At the top of the home page, we will display the status of the `PeerServer` connection, `DataConnection`, and `MediaConnection`.

- Then we will display a video element and message box. `MediaStream` of the remote peer will be rendered on the video element.

- Then we have drop-down boxes for the user to select a microphone and webcam that they want to use if they have multiple microphones or webcams connected to their computer.

- Then we have checkboxes that allow the users to pause or resume their audio and video.

- Finally, we have a button that allows the user to disconnect from the current user and chat with another user.

Every interactive element in the HTML page has an ID associated with it. While coding the frontend of the website, we will be using their IDs to get their reference.

Now let's create our signaling server. Here is the code for this. Place it in the `app. js` file:

```
var requestIp = require("request-ip");
var geoip = require("geoip-lite");

app.use("/signaling", function(httpRequest, httpResponse, next){

  var clientIp = requestIp.getClientIp(httpRequest);
  var geo = geoip.lookup(clientIp);

  if(geo != null)
  {
    if(geo.country == "IN")
    {
      next();
    }
    else
    {
      httpResponse.end();
    }
  }
  else
  {
    next();
  }
```

```
});

var ExpressPeerServer = require("peer").ExpressPeerServer(server);

app.use("/signaling", ExpressPeerServer);

var connected_users = [];

ExpressPeerServer.on("connection", function(id){
  var idx = connected_users.indexOf(id);
  if(idx === -1) //only add id if it's not in the array yet
  {
    connected_users.push(id);
  }
});

ExpressPeerServer.on("disconnect", function(id){
  var idx = connected_users.indexOf(id);
  if(idx !== -1)
  {
    connected_users.splice(idx, 1);
  }

  idx = waiting_peers.indexOf(id);
  if(idx !== -1)
  {
    waiting_peers.splice(idx, 1);
  }
});
```

The following is how the code works:

- Before the user can connect to PeerServer, we will find the country to which the IP address of the user belongs. We will find the IP address using the request-ip module and resolve the IP address to the country using the geoip-lite module. If the country is IN or the country name couldn't be resolved, then we will allow the user to connect to PeerServer by triggering the next middleware, otherwise we will stop them by sending an empty response.

- When a user connects to PeerServer, we will add the ID of the user in the connected_users array that maintains a list IDs if the users that are connected to PeerServer. Similarly, when the user disconnects from the PeerServer, we will remove the ID of the user from the connected_users array.

Now let's define route for the /find path using which a user can find another user who is free to chat. The following is the code for this. Place this code in the app. js file:

```
var waiting_peers = [];

app.get("/find", function(httpRequest, httpResponse, next){

  var id = httpRequest.query.id;

  if(connected_users.indexOf(id) !== -1)
  {

    var idx = waiting_peers.indexOf(id);
     if(idx === -1)
     {
       waiting_peers.push(id);
     }

     if(waiting_peers.length > 1)
     {
       waiting_peers.splice(idx, 1);
       var user_found = waiting_peers[0];
       waiting_peers.splice(0, 1);
       httpResponse.send(user_found);
     }
     else
     {
       httpResponse.status(404).send("Not found");
     }
  }
  else
  {
    httpResponse.status(404).send("Not found");
  }
})
```

Here is how the code works:

- The waiting_users array holds the IDs of the users who are free and looking for a partner to chat to.

- When a user makes a request to the /find path, the route handler first checks whether the user is connected to PeerServer or not by checking whether the user ID is present in the connected_users array.

- If the user is not connected to PeerServer, then it sends an HTTP 404 error. If the user is connected to PeerServer, then it checks whether the user's ID is present in the `waiting_list` array. If not, it adds in the array and proceeds.

- Now it checks whether any other user ID is also present in the `waiting_list` array, and if yes, then it sends the first user ID in the list and then removes all user IDs from the `waiting_list` array. If it doesn't find any other user ID in the `waiting_list` array, then it simply sends `404 error`.

Now we are done building the backend of our website. Before we get into building the frontend of our site, make sure that you restart the server with the latest code.

Building the frontend

First of all, as soon as the home page loads, we need to find the microphones and webcams connected to the user computer and list them so that the user can choose the desired device. The following is the code to do this. Place this code in the `main.js` file:

```
window.addEventListener("load", function(){
  MediaStreamTrack.getSources(function(devices){
    var audioCount = 1;
    var videoCount = 1;

    for(var count = 0; count < devices.length; count++)
    {
      if(devices[count].kind == "audio")
      {
        var name = "";

        if(devices[count].label == "")
        {
          name = "Microphone " + audioCount;
          audioCount++;
        }
        else
        {
          name = devices[count].label;
        }

        document.getElementById("audioInput").innerHTML =
        document.getElementById("audioInput").innerHTML + "<option
        value='" + devices[count].id + "'>" + name + "</option>";
      }
      else if(devices[count].kind == "video")
```

```
      {
        var name = "";

        if(devices[count].label == "")
        {
          name = "Webcam " + videoCount;
          videoCount++;
        }
        else
        {
          name = devices[count].label;
        }

        document.getElementById("videoInput").innerHTML =
        document.getElementById("videoInput").innerHTML + "<option
        value='" + devices[count].id + "'>" + name + "</option>";
      }
    }
  });
});
```

Here we are retrieving the audio and video input devices using `MediaStream.getSources` and populating the `<select>` tags so that the user can choose an option.

As soon as the home page loads, we also need to create a `Peer` instance. Here is the code to do this. Place this code in the `main.js` file:

```
var peer = null;
var dc = null;
var mc = null;
var ms = null;
var rms = null;

window.addEventListener("load", function(){
  peer = new Peer({host: "localhost", port: 8080, path:
  "/signaling", debug: true});

  peer.on("disconnected", function(){

    var interval = setInterval(function(){
      if(peer.open == true || peer.destroyed == true)
      {
        clearInterval(interval);
      }
      else
```

```
      {
        peer.reconnect();
      }
    }, 4000)
})

peer.on("connection", function(dataConnection){
  if(dc == null || dc.open == false)
  {
    dc = dataConnection;

    dc.on("data", function(data){
      document.getElementById("messages").innerHTML =
      document.getElementById("messages").innerHTML + "<li><span
      class='right'>" + data + "</span><div
      class='clear'></div></li> ";
      document.getElementById("messages-container").scrollTop =
      document.getElementById("messages-
      container").scrollHeight;
    })

    dc.on("close", function(){
      document.getElementById("messages").innerHTML = "";
    })
  }
  else
  {
    dataConnection.close();
  }
})

peer.on("call", function(mediaConnection){
  if(mc == null || mc.open == false)
  {
    mc = mediaConnection;
    navigator.getUserMedia = navigator.getUserMedia ||
    navigator.webkitGetUserMedia || navigator.mozGetUserMedia;
    navigator.getUserMedia({video: true, audio: true},
    function(mediaStream) {
      ms = mediaStream;
      mc.answer(mediaStream);
      mc.on("stream", function(remoteStream){
        rms = remoteStream;
        document.getElementById("peerVideo").setAttribute("src",
        URL.createObjectURL(remoteStream));
```

```
        document.getElementById("peerVideo").play();
    })

  }, function(e){ alert("An error occured while retrieving
  webcam and microphone stream"); })
}
else
{
  mediaConnection.close();
}
    })
});
```

Here is how the code works:

- First we declared five global variables. peer will hold reference for the Peer instance, dc will hold reference for DataConnection, mc will hold reference for MediaConnection, ms will hold reference for the local MediaStream, and rms will hold reference for the remote MediaStream.

- Then, as soon as the page finished loading, we connected to PeerServer, creating a Peer instance and attaching event handlers for the disconnected, connection, and call event handlers.

- Then we made sure that in case a peer gets disconnected from PeerServer due to some reason, then it automatically tries to connect to PeerServer.

- If another peer tries to establish DataConnection with us, then we will only accept it if there is no other DataConnection currently established, otherwise we will reject it. After accepting DataConnection, we attached the event handlers for the data and close events to print the incoming messages in the chat box, and clear all messages in the chat box if DataConnection is closed.

- Similarly, if another peer tries to establish MediaConnection with us, we will only accept it if there is no other MediaConnection currently established, otherwise we will reject it. After accepting the MediaConnection, we will attach the event handler for the stream event so that when remote MediaStream arrives, we can display it.

In the preceding code, we are waiting for another peer to establish DataConnection and MediaConnection with us.

Now let's write a code to find a free peer and establish `DataConnection` and `MediaConnection` with it. The following is the code for this. Place this code in the `main.js` file:

```
function ajaxRequestObject()
{
  var request;
  if(window.XMLHttpRequest)
  {
    request = new XMLHttpRequest();
  }
  else if(window.ActiveXObject)
  {
    try
    {
      request = new ActiveXObject('Msxml2.XMLHTTP');
    }
    catch (e)
    {
      request = new ActiveXObject('Microsoft.XMLHTTP');
    }
  }

  return request;
}

function connectToNextPeer()
{
  var request = ajaxRequestObject();

  var url = "/find?id=" + peer.id;

  request.open("GET", url);

  request.addEventListener("load", function(){
    if(request.readyState === 4)
    {
      if(request.status === 200)
      {
        dc = peer.connect(request.responseText, {reliable: true,
        ordered: true});

        dc.on("data", function(data){
          document.getElementById("messages").innerHTML =
          document.getElementById("messages").innerHTML +
```

```
  "<li><span class='right'>" + data + "</span><div
  class='clear'></div></li>";
  document.getElementById("messages-container").scrollTop
  = document.getElementById("messages-
  container").scrollHeight;
})

dc.on("close", function(){
  document.getElementById("messages").innerHTML = "";
})

navigator.getUserMedia = navigator.getUserMedia ||
navigator.webkitGetUserMedia || navigator.mozGetUserMedia;

var audioInputID = document.getElementById("audioInput")
.options[document.
getElementById("audioInput").selectedIndex].value;
var videoInputID =
document.getElementById("videoInput").options[document.
getElementById("videoInput").selectedIndex].value;

navigator.getUserMedia({video: {mandatory: {sourceId:
videoInputID}}, audio: {mandatory: {sourceId:
audioInputID}}}, function(mediaStream) {
  ms = mediaStream;

  if(document.getElementById("audioToggle").checked)
  {
    var tracks = ms.getAudioTracks();
    if(document.getElementById("audioToggle").checked)
    {
      tracks[0].enabled = true;
    }
    else
    {
      tracks[0].enabled = false;
    }
  }

  if(document.getElementById("videoToggle").checked)
  {
    var tracks = ms.getVideoTracks();
    if(document.getElementById("videoToggle").checked)
    {
      tracks[0].enabled = true;
```

```
        }
        else
        {
          tracks[0].enabled = false;
        }
      }

      mc = peer.call(request.responseText, ms);

      mc.on("stream", function(remoteStream){
        rms = remoteStream;
        document.getElementById("peerVideo").
        setAttribute("src",
        URL.createObjectURL(remoteStream));
        document.getElementById("peerVideo").play();
      })

    }, function(e){ alert("An error occured while retrieving
    webcam and microphone stream"); });

    }
  }
}, false);

request.send(null);
}

function communication()
{
  if(peer != null && peer.disconnected == false && peer.destroyed
  == false)
  {
    if(dc == null || mc == null || dc.open == false || mc.open ==
    false)
    {
      connectToNextPeer();
    }
  }
}

setInterval(communication, 4000);
```

This code is long but easy to understand. Here is how the code works:

- First we defined a `ajaxRequestObject()` function that just returns an AJAX object and hides browser differences by creating an AJAX object.
- Then we defined the `connectToNextPeer()` method that makes requests for a free ID from the `/next` path, and if found, it establishes `DataConnection` and `MediaConnection` with this peer. It also attaches the necessary event handlers that are same as the previous code.
- While retrieving `MediaStream`, it uses the device selected by the user in the dropdown.
- Before calling the other peer, it sets the `enabled` property to `true` or `false`, depending on whether the checkbox is checked or not respectively.
- Finally, we set a timer that calls the `connectToNext()` peer once in every four second if the peer is connected to PeerServer, and `MediaConnection` or `DataConnection` is currently not established with another peer.

Now we need to write code to send the message to a connected peer when the user presses the *Enter* key on the text input fields of the message box. Here is the code to do this. Place this code in the `main.js` file:

```
document.getElementById("message-input-
box").addEventListener("keypress", function(){
  if(dc != null && dc.open == true)
  {
    var key = window.event.keyCode;
    if (key == 13)
    {
      var message = document.getElementById("message-input-
      box").value;
      document.getElementById("message-input-box").value = "";
      dc.send(message);
      document.getElementById("messages").innerHTML =
      document.getElementById("messages").innerHTML + "<li><span
      class='left'>" + message + "</span><div
      class='clear'></div></li> ";
      document.getElementById("messages-container").scrollTop =
      document.getElementById("messages-container").scrollHeight;
    }
    else
    {
      return;
    }
  }
})
```

Here, at first, we are checking whether DataConnection is established or not. If DataConnection is currently established, then we will send a message to the connected peer and also display the message in the message box.

Now we need to write the code to pause or resume audio and video when the user toggles the checkboxes. The following is the code to do this. Place this code in the main.js file:

```
document.getElementById("videoToggle").addEventListener("click",
function(){
  if(ms !== null)
  {
    var tracks = ms.getVideoTracks();

    if(document.getElementById("videoToggle").checked)
    {
      tracks[0].enabled = true;
    }
    else
    {
      tracks[0].enabled = false;
    }
  }
});

document.getElementById("audioToggle").addEventListener("click",
function(){
  if(ms !== null)
  {
    var tracks = ms.getAudioTracks();

    if(document.getElementById("audioToggle").checked)
    {
      tracks[0].enabled = true;
    }
    else
    {
      tracks[0].enabled = false;
    }
  }
});
```

Here we are achieving this functionality by assigning true or false to the enabled property of the tracks.

We need to close `MediaConnection` and `DataConnection` and find another user for chatting when the user clicks on the **Next User** button. The following is the code to do this. Place this code in the `main.js` file:

```
document.getElementById("next").addEventListener("click",
function(){
  if(mc != null)
  {
    mc.close();
  }

  if(dc != null)
  {
    dc.close();
  }

  connectToNextPeer();
})
```

If there is any `MediaConnection` or `DataConnection` currently established, then we are closing it. Then we will call the `connectToNextPeer()` method to establish `MediaConnection` and `DataConnection`.

Now we finally need to display the status of the peer-to-peer connection and PeerServer connection. Here is the code to do this. Place this code in the `main.js` file:

```
setInterval(function(){
  if(dc == null || mc == null || dc.open == false || mc.open ==
  false)
  {
    document.getElementById("peerStatus").innerHTML = "Waiting for
    a free peer";
  }
  else
  {
    document.getElementById("peerStatus").innerHTML = "Connected
    to a peer";
  }

  if(peer != null && peer.disconnected == false && peer.destroyed
  == false)
  {
    document.getElementById("peerServerStatus").innerHTML =
    "Connected to PeerServer";
  }
  else
```

```
  {
    document.getElementById("peerServerStatus").innerHTML = "Not
    connected to PeerServer";
  }
}, 4000);
```

Here we are checking and updating the status every 4 seconds.

Testing the website

To test the chatroulette website we just created, first make sure that the server is running and then open the `http://localhost:8080/` URL in two different tabs, browsers, or devices.

Now you will see that both of them automatically get connected and are able to chat with each other.

Summary

In this chapter, we saw how to build a chatroulette using our own instance of PeerServer that is integrated with Express. The website we build had almost all the features that a chatroulette should have. You can now add features such as screen sharing, connecting users of particular a gender with each other, connecting users of a particular age, integrating captcha to prevent spam, and other features of your choice.

At the time of writing, the WebRTC team is working on an API that allows you to retrieve a stream from a screen for screen sharing. As this API is still under development, you can use browser plugins to retrieve a stream from a screen. You can find more about retrieving a stream from a screen using the plugins at `https://www.webrtc-experiment.com/Pluginfree-Screen-Sharing/` and `http://hancke.name/webrtc/screenshare/#/`.

In the next chapter, we will discuss bidirectional communication between the client and the server in real time using WebSockets.

Bidirectional Communication in Real Time

5

We have been using COMET techniques to implement bidirectional communication between a web browser and web server. Long polling is the most popular technique of achieving bidirectional communication between a web browser and web server because it works without compromising user experience and without any extra server configuration, and it works on all web browsers that support AJAX. Long polling can easily be implemented in any existing HTTP server. But the problem with long polling and other comet techniques is that none of them are suitable for building real-time apps because of HTTP overhead. This means that every time an HTTP request is made, a bunch of headers and cookie data is transferred to the server, which in turn increases the latency, therefore making it unsuitable for creating applications such as multiplayer games, chat apps, social networks, and live score websites, which require bidirectional communication in real time. Therefore, a new protocol called **WebSocket** was introduced, which was designed to enable bidirectional communication in real time between a web browser and WebSocket server.

In this chapter, we'll cover the following:

- An overview of WebSocket
- The relationship between WebSocket and HTTP
- The interaction of WebSocket with proxy servers and firewalls
- Implementing WebSocket using Socket.IO
- The Socket.IO API in depth
- Many other important things related to WebSocket and Socket.IO

Introducing WebSocket

WebSocket is an application-layer protocol designed to facilitate bidirectional (either the client or server can send a message to the other party whenever a message is available) and full-duplex communication (both the client and server can send messages to each other simultaneously) between a web browser and WebSocket server in real time.

WebSocket is a binary protocol; therefore, it is faster than the HTTP protocol, which is a text-based protocol.

WebSocket has gained popularity and is already being used by many websites due to its real-time and full-duplex features. Due to overhead caused by comet techniques, it was not suitable for real-time bidirectional message transfer, and it was also not possible to establish a full-duplex communication system between a web browser and web server using comet. That is, comet techniques let us achieve only half-duplex communication system (only the client or server can send messages to the other party at a given time).

WebSocket is designed to facilitate bidirectional communication between a web browser and WebSocket server, but it can be used by any client. In this chapter, we will only concentrate on how it's implemented in a web browser.

What is the WebSocket API?

Web browsers provide an API for creating and managing a WebSocket connection to a WebSocket server as well as for sending and receiving data on the connection. We won't use this API for implementing WebSocket; instead, we will use the Socket.IO library.

The relationship between WebSocket and HTTP

The only relationship between WebSocket and HTTP is that a WebSocket handshake between a web browser and WebSocket server is done using HTTP. Therefore, a WebSocket server is also an HTTP server. Once the handshake is successful, the same TCP connection is used for WebSocket communication, that is, communication switches to the bidirectional binary protocol, which does not conform to the HTTP protocol. The default port number for WebSocket is 80, same as for HTTP.

Why is the default WebSocket port 80?

The main reason for integrating HTTP and WebSocket so tightly and making WebSocket share the HTTP port is to prevent firewalls from blocking non-web content.

Although you can implement your own WebSocket handshake mechanism if you are using WebSocket outside a web browser environment, the official WebSocket documentation only states the HTTP handshake mechanism because WebSocket is designed to enable bidirectional communication between web browsers and WebSocket servers.

You can integrate a WebSocket server into your main web server that serves your HTML pages, or you can use a separate web server for WebSocket communication.

Sending and receiving data on a WebSocket connection

Data is transferred through a WebSocket connection as messages, each of which consists of one or more frames containing the data you are sending (called the payload). In order to ensure that the message can be properly reconstructed when it reaches the other party, each frame is prefixed with 4-12 bytes of data about the payload. Using this frame-based messaging system helps reduce the amount of non-payload data that is transferred, leading to significant reductions in latency, therefore making it possible to build real-time components.

We won't get into the exact data format and other details of the WebSocket handshake, data framing, and sending and receiving data as this is only required if you are planning to create your own WebSocket server. We will use Socket.IO JavaScript library to implement WebSocket in our application, which takes care of all the internal details of WebSocket and provides an easy-to-use API.

WebSocket schemes

WebSocket protocol specifications have introduced two new URL schemes, called **ws** and **wss**.

ws represents an unencrypted connection whereas wss represents an encrypted connection. Encrypted connections use TLS to encrypt messages.

So, when making a WebSocket handshake request using HTTP, we need to use ws or wss instead of http or https, respectively.

Why ws and wss instead of `http` and `https`?

You must be wondering what the point of introducing a new scheme instead of just using `http`. Well, the reason behind this is that WebSocket can also be used outside a web browser environment, and a handshake can be negotiated via a non-HTTP server. Therefore, a different scheme is required when not using HTTP for the handshake.

The interaction of WebSocket with proxy servers, load balancers, and firewalls

The WebSocket protocol is unaware of proxy servers by itself. When a WebSocket connection is established behind a proxy server, the WebSocket connection can fail or work properly, depending on whether the proxy server is transparent or explicit and also whether we have established a secure or unsecure connection.

If the browser is configured to use an explicit proxy server, then it will first issue an `HTTP CONNECT` method to that proxy server when establishing the WebSocket connection. The `CONNECT` method is used to tell a proxy to make a connection to another host and simply reply with the content, without attempting to parse or cache it. A browser issues the `HTTP CONNECT` method regardless of whether the connection is encrypted or unencrypted.

If we are using a transparent proxy server (that is, a proxy server that the web browser is unaware of) and the connection is encrypted, then the browser doesn't issue an `HTTP CONNECT` method because it's unaware of the proxy server. But as the connection is encrypted, the proxy server will most probably let all the encrypted data through, therefore causing no problems to the WebSocket connection.

If we are using a transparent proxy server and the connection is unencrypted, then the browser doesn't issue an `HTTP CONNECT` method because it's unaware of the proxy server. But as the connection is unencrypted, the proxy server is likely to try to cache, parse, or block the data, therefore causing issues for the WebSocket connection. In this case, the proxy server should be upgraded or explicitly configured to support WebSocket connections.

The WebSocket protocol is unaware of load balancers by itself. If you are using a TCP load balancer, it is unlikely to cause any problems for a WebSocket connection. But if you are using an HTTP load balancer, it's likely to cause problems; therefore, it needs to be upgraded or explicitly configured to handle WebSocket connections.

The WebSocket protocol is unaware of firewalls by itself. Firewalls are unlikely to cause any problems for a WebSocket connection.

The same-origin policy for WebSocket

Browsers as well as WebSocket instances can perform cross-domain communication, that is, they are not restricted by any same-origin policy.

While making an HTTP request for a handshake, the browser sends an `Origin` header assigned to the webpage origin.

If a WebSocket server wants to restrict communication to a particular domain, it can read the `Origin` HTTP header of the handshake HTTP request and block or allow the handshake accordingly.

Introduction to Socket.IO

Socket.IO is a combination of the client-side JavaScript library and Node.js library used to integrate bidirectional communication between a browser and Node.js backend.

The Socket.IO client-side library is used to create a Socket.IO client whereas the Socket.IO Node.js library is used to create a Socket.IO server. The Socker.IO client and server can communicate with each other bidirectionally. Socket.IO primarily uses WebSocket to achieve bidirectional communication.

The main reason for using the Socket.IO client-side library instead of using the WebSocket API is that WebSocket is a relatively new protocol at the time of writing and not all browsers support the API. If Socket.IO sees that the browser doesn't support WebSocket, then it jumps to one of the other mechanisms, such as Flash sockets, long polling, multipart streaming, iframes, or JSONP polling, to implement bidirectional communication between browsers and servers. Therefore, we can say that Socket.IO is guaranteed to work on every browser. The Socket.IO backend library provides APIs to create namespaces and rooms, broadcast messages, and so on, which are very useful in some cases. Therefore, Socket.IO is the best way to implement bidirectional communication between a browser and Node.js server.

Setting up your project

Before we start learning about the Socket.IO API, let's first set up our project directory and files. Create a directory named `SocketIO-Example`. Inside the directory, create files called `package.json`, `app.js`, and `socket.js`, and a directory called `public`. Inside the `public` directory, create two directories, `html` and `js`. Inside the `html` directory, create a file called `index.html`. Finally, in the `js` directory, download and place the Socket.IO library from `https://cdn.socket.io/socket.io-1.3.7.js`. At the time of writing, the latest version of Socket.IO is 1.3.7; therefore, we will be using that version.

Inside the `app.js` file, we will write code for the web server, and inside the `socket.js` file, we will write code for the Socket.IO server. For now, we will run two different servers, that is, a separate web server serving the website, and another server for bidirectional communication. In the next chapter, we will learn how to integrate the Socket.IO server with the Express server.

Inside the `package.json` file, place this code:

```
{
    "name": "SocketIO-Example",
    "dependencies": {
      "express": "4.13.3",
      "socket.io": "1.3.7"
    }
}
```

Now, run the `npm install` command inside the `SocketIO-Example` directory in order to download and install Express and the Socket.IO Node.js library.

Now, inside the `index.html` file, place this HTML code:

```
<!doctype html>
<html>
  <head>
    <title>SocketIO-Example</title>
  </head>
  <body>
    <script src="js/socket.io-1.3.7.js"></script>
    <script>
      //place JavaScript code here
    </script>
  </body>
</html>
```

Inside the second `<script>` tag, you will be placing the Socket.IO client-side code.

Now, place this code in the `app.js` file to serve the `index.html` file:

```
var express = require("express");
var app = express();

app.use(express.static(__dirname + "/public"));

app.get("/", function(httpRequest, httpResponse, next){
  httpResponse.sendFile(__dirname + "/public/html/index.html");
```

```
})

app.listen(8080);
```

Here, we are listening on port `8080`. Run the `app.js` file and visit the `http://localhost:8080/` URL to load the `index.html` page.

We are done with setting up the files and directories. Now, let's learn about the Socket.IO client-side and server-side APIs.

Diving into the Socket.IO API

Let's first look at an overview of the Socket.IO API. After that, we will get into the advanced features one by one.

Let's first build a Socket.IO server. The following is the code to create a Socket.IO server instance and listen to new Socket.IO client handshake requests. Place it in the `socket.js` file:

```
var Server = require("socket.io");
var io = new Server({path: "/websocket"});
io.listen(3000);
```

Here is how the code works:

1. First, we import the Socket.IO Node.js library.
2. Then, we create a new instance of the Socket.IO server using the `Server` constructor.
3. Then, while creating a new instance, we pass the HTTP path to which the Socket.IO client will make a handshake request. If we don't pass the path, it defaults to `/socket.io`
4. Finally, we listen on port `3000`.

I created a single Socket.IO server in the code, but we have the freedom to create multiple servers listening on different ports.

Now, Socket.IO clients can send a handshake request, and the Socket.IO server can establish a Socket.IO connection with its clients. Let's write some code to do something on a Socket.IO server after a Socket.IO connection has been established. Place this code in the `socket.js` file:

```
io.on("connection", function(socket){

    socket.send("Hi, from server");
```

```
   socket.on("message", function(message){
     console.log(message);
   });

   socket.on("disconnect", function(){
     console.log("User Disconnected");
   });

   socket.emit("custom-event", "parameter1", "parameter2");

   socket.on("custom-event", function (parameter1, parameter2) {
     console.log(parameter1, parameter2);
   });
});
```

Let's see how this code works and what the `send()`, `on()`, and `emit()` methods do:

- The `on()` method of the `io` object is used to attach event handlers to events triggered on the Socket.IO server by itself.

- We first attach an event handler for the `connection` event. As soon as a Socket.IO connection has been established, the `connection` event is fired. The event handler has a single parameter, which is an object representing the Socket.IO client. Here, we've named the parameter `socket`.

- The `on()` method of the `socket` object is used to attach event handlers to the events emitted by the Socket.IO client to the server.

- The `send()` method of the `socket` object is used to send a message to the Socket.IO client. We are sending a string here, but you can also send an instance of `ArrayBuffer`, `Blob Node.js Buffer`, and even `File`. You can also send a simple JavaScript object.

- Then, we attached an event handler for the `message` event, which is triggered when the Socket.IO client sends a message to the Socket.IO server.

- After that, we attached an event handler to the `disconnect` event, which is triggered when the Socket.IO client disconnects from the Socket.IO server.

- The `emit` method of the `socket` object is used to send custom events to the Socket.IO client. It can take an infinite number of arguments. The first argument it takes is the event name, and the rest of the arguments are the parameters of the event handler, which is triggered on the Socket.IO client.

- Finally, we use the `on()` method of the `socket` object to register an event handler for a custom event named `custom-event`.

So now, we have finished creating a very simple Socket.IO server that lets Socket.IO clients establish a connection with it. It is also listening to `message` and `custom-event` events. It also sends a message and emits a custom event to the Socket.IO clients as soon as they are connected.

 As every Socket.IO client gets a separate `socket` object on the Socket.IO server, if we want a `socket` object to be able to access the `socket` object of another Socket.IO client, then we can keep a reference to the `socket` objects of every Socket.IO client in a global array. This can be useful if we are creating a chat app in which a `socket` object needs to access another `socket` object to send messages to it.

You can now run the Socket.IO server using the `node socket.js` command.

Now, let's build the Socket.IO client. The following is the code to create a Socket.IO client instance and establish a Socket.IO connection with the Socker.IO server. Place this code in the `<script>` tag of the `index.html` file:

```
var socket = io("http://localhost:3000", {path: "/websocket"});
```

Here, we are first creating a Socket.IO client instance and establishing a connection with the Socket.IO server using the `io` constructor. The first argument is the base URL of the Socket.IO server. The second argument is an optional object to which we have passed the URL path that the handshake request should be made to. If we don't pass the path, then the default path will be `/socket.io`.

We created a single Socket.IO client instance here, but we have the freedom to create multiple Socket.IO client instances if we want to connect to multiple Socket. IO servers.

We are using the `http` scheme instead of the `ws` scheme here because Socket.IO can use any technique or protocol other than WebSocket to achieve bidirectional communication. If Socket.IO chooses to use WebSocket, then it will automatically replace `http` with `ws`.

Let's write some code to do something on a Socket.IO client after a Socket.IO connection has been established.
Place this code in the `<script>` tag of `index.html` file:

```
socket.on("connect", function () {

  socket.send("Hi, from client");

  socket.on("message", function (msg) {
    console.log(msg)
```

```
  });

  socket.on("disconnect", function(){
    console.log("I am disconnected");
  });

  socket.on("custom-event", function (parameter1, parameter2) {
    console.log(parameter1, parameter2);
  });

  socket.emit("custom-event", "parameter1", "parameter2");
});
```

Let's understand how this code works and what the `send()`, `on()`, and `emit()` methods do:

- The `on()` method of the `socket` object is used to attach event handlers to the events triggered on the Socket.IO client by itself.

- We first attach an event handler to the `connect` event. As soon as a Socket.IO connection has been established, the `connect` event is fired.

- The `send()` method's `socket` object is used to send a message to the Socket.IO server. We are sending a string here, but you can also send an instance of `ArrayBuffer`, `Blob`, or even `File`. You can also send a simple JavaScript object.

- Then, we attached an event handler to the `message` event, which is triggered when the Socket.IO server sends a message to the Socket.IO client.

- We then attached an event handler to the `disconnect` event, which is triggered when the Socket.IO client disconnects from the Socket.IO server. As soon as a Socket.IO connection breaks, the Socket.IO client keeps trying to connect again automatically.

- After that, we use the `on()` method of the `socket` object to register an event handler for a custom event named `custom-event`.

- The `emit` method of the `socket` object is used to send custom events to the Socket.IO server. It can take an infinite number of arguments. The first argument it takes is the event name, and the rest of the arguments are the parameters of the event handler, which is triggered in the Socket.IO client.

Now, open the URL `http://localhost:8080/` in your browser, and you should see the following console output:

```
Hi, from server
parameter1 parameter2
```

And you will see the following output in the shell running the Socket.IO server:

```
Hi, from client
parameter1 parameter2
```

Restricting connections based on origin

By default, a Socket.IO server lets Socket.IO clients from any origin establish a Socket.IO connection with it. Socket.IO provides a way to restrict connections to a particular origin.

To restrict connections to a particular origin or set of origins, we can use the `origins` method of the `Server` instance.

Place this code in the `socket.js` file to only allow Socket.IO clients running on the `localhost` domain and port number `8080` to connect to the Socket.IO server:

```
io.origins("localhost:8080");
```

We cannot simply pass any `origin` to the `origins` method. Here are examples of some valid `origins`:

- `testsite.com:80`
- `http://testsite.com:80`
- `http://*:8080` (* is a wildcard)
- `*:8080`
- `testsite.com:* http://someotherdomain.com:8080` (multiple origins separated by spaces)
- `testsite.com:*/somepath` (Socket.IO will ignore /somepath)
- `*:*`

In the previous list, every origin has a port number associated with it because it is compulsory to provide a port number or * in place of the port number, indicating any port.

Here are some examples of invalid origins:

- `testsite.com`
- `http://testsite.com`
- `http://testsite.com/somepath`

These are invalid because they don't have port numbers associated with them.

Also note that if you specify sub.testsite.com as the origins value, testsite.com will be a valid origin.

Namespaces in Socket.IO

A Socket.IO server is actually divided into child servers called **namespaces**. A Socket.IO client always connects to a namespace. Every namespace has a name, which looks like an HTTP path.

In the previous code, when we created a Socket.IO server, a default namespace was created. The default namespace is identified by the / path. If we don't mention a namespace when creating a Socket.IO client, then it connects to the default namespace. So, the connection event is specific to a particular namespace, that is, for every namespace, we have to register a different connection event handler.

What is the benefit of namespaces?

You must be wondering what the point of introducing namespaces is. Well, namespaces make writing complex code easier. Let's look at an example to understand this.

Suppose you have a web page that has multiple components that update in real time. You would then either create multiple Socket.IO servers for a component or use a single Socket.IO server and rely on the data format of a message or custom event to find which data belongs to which component. Both of these techniques have demerits, that is, creating multiple Socket.IO servers occupies multiple ports, so it's not suitable for a large number of components, and relying on the data formats of messages and custom events make it difficult to move frontend components to a separate application, as the new application will get a lot of unnecessary messages and events, causing bandwidth issues on both sides. Therefore, namespaces were introduced, which combine the benefits of both techniques while omitting their demerits.

Here is how to create a custom namespace. Place this code in the socket.js file:

```
var nsp = io.of("/custom-namespace");

nsp.on("connection", function(socket){
  socket.send("Hi, from custom-namespace");

  socket.on("message", function(message){
    console.log(message);
  });
```

```
socket.on("disconnect", function(){
  console.log("User Disconnected");
});

socket.on("custom-event", function (parameter1, parameter2) {
  console.log(parameter1, parameter2);
});

socket.emit("custom-event", "parameter1", "parameter2");
});
```

On adding this code to the `socket.js` file, we will have two namespaces, that is, the default one, which we created earlier, and this one, called `/custom-namespace`. Here, you can see that we registered a new connection event handler for this namespace.

Now, let's create another Socket.IO client, one which connects to the `/custom-namespace` namespace. Place this code in the `<script>` tag of `index.html` file:

```
var socket1 = io("http://localhost:3000/custom-namespace", {path:
"/websocket"});

socket1.on("connect", function () {

  socket1.send("Hi, from client");

  socket1.on("message", function (msg) {
    console.log(msg)
  });

  socket1.on("disconnect", function(){
    console.log("I am disconnected");
  });

  socket1.on("custom-event", function (parameter1, parameter2) {
    console.log(parameter1, parameter2);
  });

  socket1.emit("custom-event", "parameter1", "parameter2");
});
```

Here, we are creating another Socket.IO client; this one connects to the `/custom-namespace` namespace.

Now, rerun the `socket.js` file and visit `http://localhost:8080/`. This will be the browser console output:

```
Hi, from server
parameter1 parameter2
Hi, from custom-namespace
parameter1 parameter2
```

And this will be the new shell output:

```
Hi, from client
parameter1 parameter2
Hi, from client
parameter1 parameter2
```

 When we restrict access based on origin using the `origins()` method, it is applied to all namespaces.

Referring to all connected Socket.IO clients

The Socket.IO server API also provides us with a way of sending a message or custom event to everyone in a namespace.

Let's look at an example of how to do this. Place the following code in the `socket.js` file:

```
setInterval(function(){
  //sending message and custom-event-2 to all clients of default
  namespace
  io.emit("custom-event-2");
  io.send("Hello Everyone. What's up!!!");

  //sending message and custom-event-2 to all clients of /custom-
  namespace namespace
  nsp.emit("custom-event-2");
  nsp.send("Hello Everyone. What's up!!!");
}, 5000)
```

Here, to send a message or custom event to all the Socket.IO clients connected to the default namespace, we use the `io` object. And to send to Socker.IO clients connected to a custom namespace, we use the object returned by the `of()` method.

Here, we are simply sending a message and custom event to everyone in both the namespaces every 5 seconds.

Rooms in Socket.IO

A **room** simply represents a group of Socket.IO clients connected to a particular namespace. A room belongs to a particular namespace.

A namespace cannot have two rooms with the same name, but two different namespaces can have rooms with the same name. Rooms with the same name on different namespaces are different rooms entirely.

Every Socket.IO client connected to a namespace must belong to one or more groups. By default, when a Socket.IO client is connected, a new group is created and the client is added to it. Therefore, every Socket.IO client belongs to a unique group by default.

Here is the code that prints the unique group name of a Socket.IO client after it has connected. Place it inside the default and `/custom-namespace` namespaces' `connection` event handlers:

```
console.log(socket.id);
```

The `id` property of the `socket` object holds the unique room name.

Joining and leaving a room

To add a Socket.IO client to a custom room, we need to use the `socket.use()` method. To remove a Socket.IO client from a custom room, we need to use the `socket.leave()` method.

The following code adds every Socket.IO client connected to the default and `/custom-namespace` servers to a room called `my-custom-room`. Place it inside the default and `/custom-namespace` namespaces' `connection` event handlers:

```
socket.join("my-custom-room");
```

Similarly, to remove a user from `my-custom-room`, you can use this code:

```
socket.leave("my-custom-room");
```

Referring to all connected Socket.IO clients in a room

The Socket.IO server API also provides us with a way to send a message or custom event to everyone in a room.

Let's look at an example of how to do this. Place the following code in the `socket.js` file:

```
setInterval(function(){
  //sending message and custom-event-3 to all clients in my-
  custom-room room of default namespace
  io.to("my-custom-room").send("Hello to everyone in this group");
  io.to("my-custom-room").emit("custom-event-3");

  //sending message and custom-event-3 to all clients in my-
  custom-room room of /custom-namespace namespace
  nsp.to("my-custom-room").send("Hello to everyone in this
  group");
  nsp.to("my-custom-room").emit("custom-event-3");
}, 5000)
```

Here, to send a message or custom event to all the Socket.IO clients in the `my-custom-room` room of the default namespace, we need to use the `io.to().send()` method. And to send a message or custom event to all the Socket.IO clients in the `my-custom-room` room of the `/custom-namespace` namespace, we need to use the `nsp.to().send()` method.

Broadcasting messages and custom events to namespaces and rooms

Broadcasting is a feature of the Socket.IO server API that lets a `socket` object send a message or custom event to everyone in the namespace or room except itself.

Broadcasting to a namespace

To broadcast a message to all Socket.IO clients in a namespace, we need to use the `socket.broadcast.send()` method, and to broadcast a custom event, we need to use the `socket.broadcast.emit()` method.

Let's look at an example. Place the following code in the `connection` event handler of the default namespace to broadcast a message every time a new Socket.IO client joins:

```
socket.broadcast.send("A new user have joined");
```

Now, open `http://localhost:8080/` in two different tabs. In the first tab's console, you will see this output:

```
Hi, from server
parameter1 parameter2
```

```
Hi, from custom-namespace
parameter1 parameter2
A new user have joined
```

In the second tab's console, you will see this output:

```
Hi, from server
parameter1 parameter2
Hi, from custom-namespace
parameter1 parameter2
```

Broadcasting to a room

To broadcast a message to all Socket.IO clients in a room, we need to use the `socket.broadcast.to().send()` method, and to broadcast a custom event, we need to use the `socket.broadcast.to.emit()` method.

Place this code inside the default and `/custom-namespace` namespaces' `connection` event handlers:

```
socket.broadcast.to("my-custom-room").send("Hi everyone. I just
joined this group");
```

Here, as soon as a Socket.IO client is connected, it sends a message to everyone else in the room.

 Remember that a Socket.IO client doesn't have to be a member of a room to broadcast a message to its Socket.IO clients.

Middleware in Socket.IO

Middleware in Socket.IO server is a callback that's executed when a Socket.IO client makes a handshake request, before the Socket.IO server replies to it. Middleware allows us to allow or reject handshakes.

The middleware concept of Socket.IO is similar to that of Express, but the difference is that the middleware doesn't get access to the HTTP response object; also, the `parameter` signature is different. Therefore, Express middleware cannot be used in Socket.IO.

An instance of middleware is attached to a specific namespace. Here is a basic example that demonstrates how to register a middleware instance with all namespaces. Place this code in the `Socket.IO` file:

```
io.use(function(socket, next) {
  //request object
  //socket.request

  //to reject
  //next(new Error("Reason for reject"));

  //to continue
  next();
});
```

Here, we can see that we need to use the `io.use()` method to register a middleware instance with all namespaces. To attach middleware to the `/custom-namespace` namespace, we can use the `nsp.use()` method.

Disconnecting manually

You can also manually disconnect a Socket.IO connection. To disconnect from the client side, you need to use the `disconnect()` method of the `io` instance. To disconnect from the server side, you need to use the `socket.disconnect()` method.

Summary

In this chapter, we learned the fundamentals of the WebSocket protocol. We learned about its relationship with HTTP and how it behaves with proxies, load balancers, and firewalls. Then, we jumped into the Socket.IO library, which primarily uses WebSocket to achieve bidirectional full-duplex communication in real time. You should be comfortable with implementing bidirectional communication between a browser and a Node.js server.

In the next chapter, we will build a real-world application using Socket.IO. You will learn more advanced things, such as integrating a Socket.IO server with an Express server and checking authentication before connecting to a WebSocket server.

6
Building a Live Score Site

The best way to master socket.io is by building a real-world application, which is what we will be doing in this chapter. A live score website shows score changes in real time to the user as soon as the administrator updates the scores. We will create a football live score website. Discussing how to build a live score website will help us study socket.io in depth, as it requires socket.io authentication, and optionally, integrating socket.io with Express. Our live score website will provide an admin panel for the administrators to update the score.

In this chapter, we will cover the following topics:

- Accessing cookies in the socket.io middleware
- Discussing HTTP basic authentication
- Integrating socket.io with Express
- Discussing socket.io authentication

Building the backend

Before we start building the backend of our live score site, let's first set up our directory and files.

We will only write code for the backend and frontend architecture and functionality, not any HTML and CSS design code.

The exercise files of this chapter contain two directories: Initial and Final. In both the directories, you will find a directory named Live-Score. In the Final/Live-Score directory, you will get the complete live score website source code. In the Initial/Live-Score directory, you will only find HTML and CSS files for our live score site. The Initial/Live-Score directory is to help you quickly get started with building the live score site.

In the `Initial/LiveScore` directory, you will find the `public` directory, `app.js` file, and `package.json` file. Inside the `public` directory, you will find `css`, `html`, and `js` directories. In the `css` and `html` directories, you will find HTML files and CSS files for our user and administrator pages. In the `js` directory, you will find `admin.js` and `index.js` files, inside which you will place the socket.io client code for the administrator and users, respectively. Similarly, in the `html` directory, you will find `index.html` and `admin.html` files that will be served to the users and administrator respectively.

Inside the `package.json` file, place the following code:

```
{
  "name": "Live-Score",
  "dependencies": {
    "express": "4.13.3",
    "socket.io": "1.3.7",
    "basic-auth": "1.0.3",
    "socket.io-cookie": "0.0.1"
  }
}
```

Now run the `npm install` command inside the `Initial/Live-Score` directory to download `express`, `socket.io`, `basic-auth`, and `socket.io-cookie` npm packages.

Integrating socket.io server with the Express server

We can integrate the socket.io server with the Express server with just a few lines of code. Here is the code to integrate the socket.io server with the Express server.

Create an `app.js` file and place the following code in it:

```
var express = require("express");
var app = express();
var server = require("http").createServer(app);
var io = require("socket.io")(server, {path: "/socket-io"});

server.listen(8080);
```

The fourth line is where the main integration happens. Here we are using the `/socket-io` path for socket.io handshaking.

Finally, we are listening on port number `8080`. That is, both Express server and socket.io server will listen on port number `8080`.

Serving static files and HTML to the users

Now we need to write the code to server HTML, CSS, and JavaScript files to the site users. The following is the code to do this. Place this code in the app.js file right after the previous snippet:

```
app.use(express.static(__dirname + "/public"));

app.get("/", function(httpRequest, httpResponse, next){
  httpResponse.sendFile(__dirname + "/public/html/index.html");
})
```

Here, the first line of the code is serving static files. The rest of the code is serving index.html to the site users when they visit the root path.

Serving HTML to the administrator and protecting the admin panel

We only want the administrators to access the admin panel to update the scores. So, for visitors to access the admin panel, they must enter the username and password. We will use the HTTP basic authentication to protect the admin panel.

The following is the code to authenticate and serve HTML to the administrator:

```
var basicAuth = require("basic-auth");

function uniqueNumber() {
  var date = Date.now();

  if (date <= uniqueNumber.previous) {
    date = ++uniqueNumber.previous;
  } else {
    uniqueNumber.previous = date;
  }

  return date;
}

uniqueNumber.previous = 0;

var authenticated_users = {};
```

```
var auth = function (req, res, next){
  var user = basicAuth(req);

  if(!user || user.name !== "admin" || user.pass !== "admin")
  {
    res.statusCode = 401;
    res.setHeader("WWW-Authenticate", "Basic realm='Authorization
    Required'");
    res.end("Access denied");
  }
  else
  {
    var id = uniqueNumber();
    authenticated_users[id] = id;
    res.cookie("authentication_id", id);
    next();
  }
}

app.get("/admin", auth, function(httpRequest, httpResponse, next){
  httpResponse.sendFile(__dirname + "/public/html/admin.html");
})
```

Here is how the code works:

- First, we imported the `basic-auth` library, which is used to implement basic authentication in Express.

- Then, we wrote a custom function to generate a unique number whenever it's called.

- We also created a function with the name `auth`, which will be used to check whether the visitor is authenticated. If not, then we will send an HTTP status code 404, asking the visitor to provide the username and password. If the visitor is authenticated, then we will generate a unique number and store it as a cookie in the administrator's browser. Later on, this cookie will be used by the socket.io server to check whether the administrator is authenticated.

- Finally, we created a route with the `/admin` path, which has two route handlers attached to it. The first one is the `auth` function to check for authentication and the second serves the `admin.html` file.

Socket.IO cookie authentication and broadcasting messages to a namespace

We will have two namespaces in our socket.io server: the default namespace where users will connect and the /admin namespace where the administrator will connect.

A socket.io client will not require authentication to connect to the default namespace. However, to connect to the /admin namespace, the socket.io will need authentication.

Updates made by the administrator will be broadcasted to all the users in the default namespace.

Here is the code for creating the /admin namespace, broadcasting messages to the default namespace, and implementing authentication for the /admin namespace. Place this code in the app.js file:

```
var cookieParser = require("socket.io-cookie");

var admin = io.of("/admin");

admin.use(cookieParser);

admin.use(function(socket, next) {
  if(socket.request.headers.cookie.authentication_id in
  authenticated_users)
  {
    next();
  }
  else
  {
    next(new Error("Authentication required"));
  }
});

admin.on("connection", function(socket){
  socket.on("message", function(message){
    io.send(message);
  });
})
```

Here is how the code works:

- First, we imported the socket.io-cookie middleware, which is used to parse the HTTP `Cookie` header
- Then, we created the `/admin` namespace
- We also parsed the cookie using the socket.io-cookie middleware
- Then, we wrote our own middleware to check whether `authentication_id` exists, and if yes, then whether it was valid
- Finally, we listened to the `message` event and broadcasted the message to the users in the default namespace

Now we are done with our backend. Run the `node app.js` command inside the initial directory. Then visit `http://localhost:8080` and `http://localhost:8080/admin` in any browser. Here, I am assuming that you are running the Express server locally.

When you visit `http://localhost:8080`, you will see the following screen:

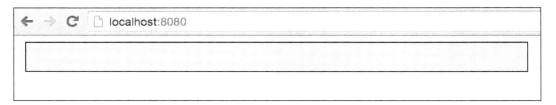

There is nothing inside the box yet as the user hasn't received any messages.

When you visit `http://localhost:8080/admin`, you will see the following screen:

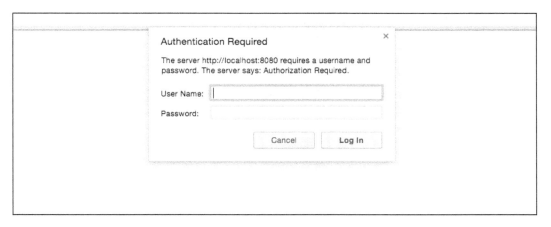

Now enter `admin` as **User Name** and **Password** and click on **Log In**. You will see the following screen:

Building the frontend

Let's write the frontend code for the users and administrators. socket.io client instances of users will listen to incoming messages from the server and display them. Whereas, socket.io client instances of administrator will send messages to the server so that the messages can be broadcasted to the users.

The following is the socket.io client code for the users. Place this code inside the `index.js` file:

```
var socket = io("http://localhost:8080", {path: "/socket-io"});

socket.on("connect", function () {
    socket.on("message", function (msg) {
    document.getElementById("messages").innerHTML =
    "<li><div><h4>" + msg.team1_name + "(" + msg.team1_goals + ")
    : " + msg.team2_name + "(" + msg.team2_goals + ")" +
    "</h4><p>" + msg.desc + "</p></div></li>" +
    document.getElementById("messages").innerHTML;
    });
});
```

This code is self-explanatory.

Here is the socket.io client code for the administrators. Place this code inside the `admin.js` file:

```
var socket = io("http://localhost:8080/admin", {path: "/socket-io"});

document.getElementById("submit-button").addEventListener("click",
function(){
  var team1_name = document.getElementById("team1-name").value;
  var team2_name = document.getElementById("team2-name").value;
  var team1_goals = document.getElementById("team1-goals").value;
  var team2_goals = document.getElementById("team2-goals").value;
  var desc = document.getElementById("desc").value;

  if(team1_goals == "" || team2_goals == "" || team1_name == "" ||
  team2_name == "")
  {
    alert("Please enter all details");
  }

  socket.send({
    team1_name: team1_name,
    team2_name: team2_name,
    team1_goals: team1_goals,
    team2_goals: team2_goals,
    desc: desc
  });
}, false)
```

This is how the preceding code works:

- In the first line, we connected to the socket.io /admin namespace. If the cookie is invalid in any case, then the connection will fail.

- We also made sure that the team names and their scores are filled, otherwise we will display an alert message asking them to enter all the details.

- Then, we sent the message to the socket.io server.

Testing the website

Now we are done building our live score website. To test the site, refresh the `http://localhost:8080/` and `http://localhost:8080/admin` pages.

Now, in the `admin` panel, fill the form with some sample data, and click on the **Send** button:

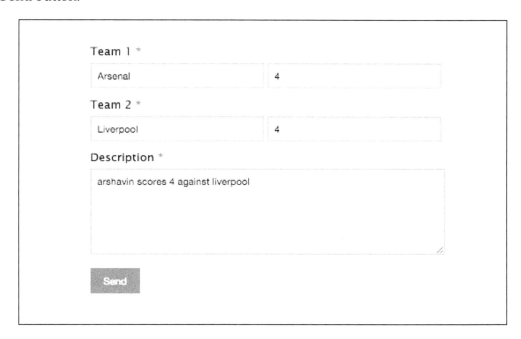

On the user page, you should see something similar to the following image:

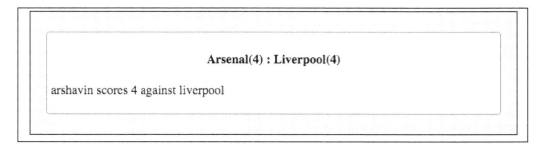

Summary

In this chapter, we saw how to build a live score website using socket.io and Express. You should now be comfortable with building any kind of application that requires bidirectional communication in real time. You should now try building a chat application, multiplayer game, or something else where socket.io would be very useful.

So, overall you learned socket.io in depth, WebSockets, and bidirectional communication.

7
Functional Reactive Programming

If you are a frontend or backend JavaScript developer who works on large and complex JavaScript applications and deals with a lot of code that responds to asynchronous data updates, user activities, and system activities, then it's perhaps the best time to explore **functional reactive programming** (**FRP**), as it's a time-saving, bug-preventing, easy-to-read, and modularized style of writing code. You don't need to know any functional programming language or be a hardcore functional language programmer; rather, you just need to know the basics of functional programming. In this chapter, we will learn how to use FRP using `Bacon.js`, which is an FRP library for both frontend and backend JavaScript.

We'll cover the following:

* Reactive programming in a nutshell
* Problems with writing reactive code in JavaScript
* Introduction to functional programming
* What FRP is
* The building blocks of FRP
* The advantages of FRP
* All the APIs provided by Bacon.js

Introduction to reactive programming

Before we get into FRP, we need to understand what it is. I will be explaining reactive programming with respect to JavaScript. The concept of reactive programming is the same in every programming language.

Reactive programming is writing code to look for asynchronous data updates, user activities, and system activities and propagate changes onto the dependent parts of the application. Reactive programming is not something new; believe it or not, you have already been doing reactive programming without realizing it. For example, the code you write to handle a button's click event is reactive code. There are various approaches to reactive programming, such as event-driven, callback, promise patterns and FRP.

Not every snippet of asynchronous code we write is reactive code. For example, uploading analytics data to a server asynchronously after a page load is not reactive code. But uploading a file to a server asynchronously and displaying a message to the user after the upload is complete is reactive code because we are reacting to the completion of the file upload.

A more complex example of reactive programming is in the MVC architecture, where reactive programming is what reacts to a change in the model and updates the view accordingly, and vice versa.

Problems with writing reactive code

There are basically three patterns natively supported by JavaScript for writing reactive code: **event-driven**, **callback**, and **promise**.

Anyone who knows a bit of JavaScript is familiar with event-driven and callback patterns. Although these two patterns are the most popular way of writing reactive code, they make it difficult to catch exceptions and result in nested function calls, which makes the code harder to read and debug.

Due to the problems caused by event-driven and callback patterns, ES6 (`https://www.packtpub.com/web-development/learning-ecmascript-6`) introduced the promise pattern. The promise pattern makes the code look more like synchronous code, therefore making it easy to read and debug. The pattern also makes exception handling easier. A promise represents an asynchronous operation.

But the promise pattern has a problem, that is, a promise can be resolved only once. The promise pattern can only respond to a single activity or data update of an asynchronous operation. For example, if we make an AJAX request using a promise pattern, then we can handle only *request success* and *failure* activities and not the states of the request and response cycle, such as weather server connections that have been established and response headers received. Similarly, if we handle a user click activity using a promise pattern, then we can handle only the first click, not the ones occurring after it, because the promise gets resolved in the first click.

You may or may not be familiar with the promise pattern, so let's look at some sample code of what a promise pattern looks like:

```
$http("http://example.com/data.json").then(function(){
  //do something
}).then(function(){
  //do something more here
}).then(function(){
  //do something more here
}).catch(function(){
  //handle error
})
```

Here, the `$http()` method makes an HTTP request asynchronously and returns a promise. The promise is resolved if the request is successful, and the callback passed to the first `then()` method is invoked, that is, the promise is resolved. If the request fails, then the callback is passed to the `catch()` method, which is invoked, and the promise is rejected. The `then()` method always returns a promise, making it possible to run multiple asynchronous operations one after another. In the code, you can see how asynchronous operations are chained. What's important here is that the `then()` methods are invoked only once, that is, the promise returned by the `$http()` method can be resolved only once, and multiple attempts to resolve a promise will be ignored. Therefore, we cannot use promise patterns to write reactive code when we have to deal with multiple activities or data updates of an asynchronous operation.

 Some developers create a new promise for every activity and data update. This technique may seem fine since you are able to write reactive code involving multiple activities and data updates using promise patterns, but it's an anti-pattern.

Due to the problems with the event-driven, callback, and promise patterns, there was a need for another pattern, and functional reactive programming came to the rescue.

FRP is simply reactive programming using functional programming style. We will learn more about functional programming in the next section. Actually, the drawbacks of the event-driven, callback, and promise patterns weren't the real reason for the invention of FRP; rather, FRP was actually invented because there were demands for a functional pattern for reactive programming, as functional code is easy to write, test, debug, reuse, update, and read. But as FRP solves the problems caused by the event-driven, callback, and promise patterns, we can say that FRP is an alternative to the other patterns.

In this chapter, we will learn about FRP, which is considered the modern way of writing reactive code.

Functional programming in a nutshell

Before we get into FRP, it's necessary to have basic knowledge about functional programming.

In a nutshell, functional programming is a style of writing code in which we use only pure function calls (including recursion) instead of loops and conditionals, and data is immutable.

Functional programming falls under the criterion of declarative programming. Declarative programming is a style of writing code where we write code to tell the system what we would like to happen instead of how to do it. Some other examples of declarative programming are SQL and regular expressions.

So what is a pure function? A **pure function** is a function that depends only on its input arguments and that always provides the same output for a particular input. If it reads anything else outside of its scope, including global variables, then it's not a pure function.

Obviously, it's not always possible to make all the functions pure. For example, a function that fetches a web page or reads from the filesystem cannot guarantee the same return value. We should try to make as many as functions as pure as possible. So, we can say that 100% purity is impossible to achieve, but 85% purity is still very productive.

Functions without side effects, stateless functions, and pure functions are terms used interchangeably.

As data is immutable in functional programming, you must be wondering how it is possible to write code without modifying data. Well, in practice, we simply create new data structures instead of modifying existing ones. For example, if we have an array with four values and we want to remove the last one, then we simply create a new array, which doesn't have the last value.

The advantages of immutable data

There are several advantages of immutable data. Here are a few of them:

- They are thread-safe, that is, multiple threads operating on them cannot modify/corrupt their state. Learn more about thread safety at https://en.wikipedia.org/wiki/Thread_safety.

- They object copying can be shared easily. One doesn't have to employ a strategy such as defensive copying, like in mutable data structures. Learn more about object copying at https://en.wikipedia.org/wiki/Object_copying.

- They help avoid temporal coupling. More about temporal coupling can be found at https://en.wikipedia.org/wiki/Coupling_(computer_programming)#Object-oriented_programming.

Functional data structures

As data is immutable, there are several problems you are likely to face. Here are a few:

- If an immutable array has millions of values, then creating a new array and copying all the values from the previous array is CPU and memory intensive

- If two threads need to write to the same variable, coordinating the final value of the variable will be difficult

There are many other issues. These issues led to the idea of functional data structures. Functional data structures are a different type of data structure that aim to solve these kinds of issue. But you don't need to know about functional data structures to follow this chapter or write functional reactive code in JavaScript.

The advantages of pure functions

Here are a few advantages of pure functions:

- They increase reusability and maintainability, as each function is independent

- Easier testing and debugging is possible, as each function can be tested and debugged separately

- Functional programs are easy to understand as they are written in a declarative manner, that is, the code says what is to be done instead of how it's done.

 The style of writing code using loops, conditionals, and function calls is called imperative programming. Imperative programming and functional programming are considered opposites of each other. JavaScript, C++, Java, Python, Ruby, are examples of imperative programming languages.

Functional programming with JavaScript

You don't have to use a functional programming language such as Erlang, Haskell, and so on to write functional code. Most imperative programming languages allow us to write functional code.

Due to the fact that functions in JavaScript are first-class (we will learn more about first-class functions later), it is possible to write functional code in JavaScript.

 "First-class" and "high-order" are terms used interchangeably.

A function is said to be first-class when it can be passed as an argument to another function, can return another function, and be assigned to a variable.

In JavaScript, functions are first-class because they are objects. Because an object can be passed as an argument to another function, a function can return an object, and an object can be assigned to a variable, functions can be first-class.

What is the difference between a closure and a first-class function?

Closures are the most misunderstood topic in JavaScript. In a nutshell, a closure is a function returned by another function, and when the function is invoked, it has access to the lexical scope in which it was defined. A function returned by a first-class function may or may not be a closure. Here is an example to demonstrate closures:

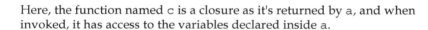

```
function a()
{
  var b = 12;
  function c()
  {
    console.log(b);
  }

  return c;
}

var d = a();

d(); //Output "12"
```

Here, the function named c is a closure as it's returned by a, and when invoked, it has access to the variables declared inside a.

Functional programming helper functions

Functional programming languages provide a lot of in-built functions called helper functions to make it easy to write functional code. For example, as we cannot use loops for iteration in functional code, we need some sort of function to take a collection and map each value of the collection to a function. Functional programming languages provide the map helper function for this purpose. Similarly, there are a lot of other helper functions for different purposes.

As JavaScript is not a functional programming language, it doesn't come with functional helper functions. However, ES6 introduced some helper functions, such as Array.from(), Array.prototype.from(), and Array.prototype.find(). Still, this list is not enough to write functional code. Therefore, developers use libraries such as Underscore.js to write functional code.

Getting started with FRP

FRP is simply reactive programming using functional programming style.

EventStreams and properties (don't get these confused with object properties) are the building blocks of FRP. Let's look at an overview of what both these terms mean.

EventStreams

An EventStream represents a stream of events. Events in an EventStream may happen at any time and need not occur synchronously.

Let's understand EventStreams by comparing them to events in an event-driven pattern. Just like we subscribe to events in an event-driven pattern, we subscribe to EventStreams in FRP. Unlike events in event-driven programming, the power of EventStreams is that they can be merged, concatenated, combined, zipped, filtered, or transformed in any number of ways before you handle and act on the events.

In functional programming, data is immutable, so merging, concatenating, combining, zipping, filtering, or transforming an EventStream creates a new EventStream instead of modifying the existing one.

Here is a diagram that shows how an EventStream representing the click event of a UI element would look:

This EventStream can be merged with any other stream. Here is a diagram that shows how it looks when two EventStreams are merged:

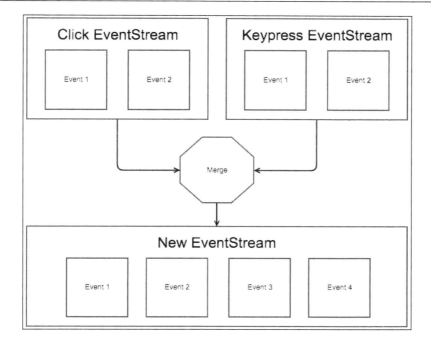

Merging can be useful when we want to apply the same action when an event occurs to two different EventStreams. Instead of subscribing and attaching a callback to two different EventStreams, we can now subscribe to a single EventStream, eliminating duplicate code and making it easy to update code. Merging can be useful in various other cases as well.

Properties

A property represents a value that changes over time. Properties can be used as an alternative to JavaScript variables whose values change in response to asynchronous activities and data updates. For example, you can use properties to represent the total number of times a button was clicked, the total number of logged-in users, and so on.

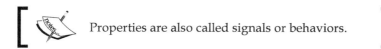

Properties are also called signals or behaviors.

The advantage of using properties instead of JavaScript variables is that you can subscribe to properties, that is, whenever the value of a property changes, a callback is fired to update the parts of the system that depend on it. This prevents code duplication and has many other benefits.

 You can create a property from another property as well as merge, combine, zip, sample, filter, or transform properties.

We've just looked at the basics of FRP. Creating EventStreams and properties, their methods, and other things to work with them differ depending on the library we use to write functional reactive code. Now, let's explore how to write functional reactive code using the Bacon.js library.

FRP using Bacon.js

Bacon.js is a JavaScript library that helps us write functional reactive code in JavaScript. It can be used for both frontend and backend JavaScript. The official website of Bacon.js library is `https://baconjs.github.io/`.

Let's create a basic website project to demonstrate FRP with Bacon.js.

Setting up the project

Let's learn how to download and install Bacon.js for use with frontend and backend JavaScript. On the frontend, Bacon.js depends on jQuery.

Create a directory named `baconjs-example`. Inside it, create files called `package.json` and `app.js` and a directory called `public`. Inside the `public` directory, create directories called `html` and `js`. Inside the `html` directory, create a file called `index.html`. Finally, inside the `js` directory, create a file called `index.js`.

Download the frontend Bacon.js library from `http://cdnjs.cloudflare.com/ajax/libs/bacon.js/0.7.73/Bacon.js` and jQuery from `https://code.jquery.com/jquery-2.2.0.min.js`, and place them in the `js` directory.

At the time of writing this book, 0.7.73 was the latest version of the frontend Bacon.js library, and 2.2.0 was the latest version of jQuery.

In the `index.html` file, place this code to enqueue jQuery and the frontend Bacon.
js library:

```
<!doctype html>
<html>
  <head>
    <title>Bacon.js Example</title>
  </head>
  <body>
    <script type="text/javascript" src="js/jquery-2.2.0.min.js"></
script>
    <script type="text/javascript" src="js/Bacon.js"></script>
    <script type="text/javascript" src="js/index.js"></script>
  </body>
</html>
```

In the `package.json` file, place this code:

```
{
  "name": "Baconjs-Example",
  "dependencies": {
    "express": "4.13.3",
    "baconjs": "0.7.83"
  }
}
```

Now, run `npm install` inside the `baconjs-example` directory to download the
npm packages.

At the time of writing this book, 0.7.83 was the latest version of backend
Bacon.js library.

In the `app.js` file, place the following code to import the backend Bacon.js and
Express modules. It also starts our webserver in order to serve the web page and
static files:

```
var Bacon = require("baconjs").Bacon;
var express = require("express");
var app = express();

app.use(express.static(__dirname + "/public"));

app.get("/", function(httpRequest, httpResponse, next){
  httpResponse.sendFile(__dirname + "/public/html/index.html");
})

app.listen(8080);
```

We have now set up a basic Bacon.js project. Run `node app.js` to start the web server. Now, let's explore Bacon.js APIs.

Bacon.js APIs

Bacon.js provides APIs to do almost anything that's possible using EventStreams and properties. The method of importing and downloading Bacon.js for the backend and frontend is different, but the APIs are the same for both. Let's look at the most important APIs provided by Bacon.js.

Creating EventStreams

There are various ways of creating EventStreams, depending on how an asynchronous API is designed, that is, which pattern an asynchronous API follows. An asynchronous API follows the event-driven, promise, or callback pattern. We need to wrap these patterns with Bacon-provided APIs to connect their data updates or activity updates to event streams, that is, convert them to functional reactive patterns.

If we want to create an EventStream for a UI element on a web page, we can use the `$.asEventStream()` method. Let's look at an example of how it works. Place the following code in the `<body>` tag of the `index.html` file to create a button:

```
<button id="myButton">Click me!!!</button>
```

In an event-driven pattern, to print something whenever a button is clicked, we would write something like this:

```
document.getElementById("myButton").addEventListener("click",
function(){
  console.log("Button Clicked");
}, false)
```

But in Bacon.js, we will write it this way. Place this code in the `index.js` file:

```
var myButton_click_stream = $("#myButton").asEventStream("click");
myButton_click_stream.onValue(function(e){
  console.log("Button Clicked");
})
```

Here, we use a jQuery selector to point to the button, and we then use the `$.asEventStream` method to connect its click events to an EventStream. The `$.asEventStream` method takes the name of the event as its first parameter.

The `onValue` method is used to add subscribers to an EventStream. The `onValue` method of an EventStream takes a callback, which is executed every time a new event is added to the EventStream. The callback has a single parameter, which represents the current event that has been added to the EventStream. In this case, it's of the event interface. We can call the `onValue` method multiple times to add multiple callbacks.

A subscriber can be used to update the UI, perform logging, and so on. But the logic code for handling the event should be written using the helper functions and not be inside the subscriber. This is how functional reactive code is supposed to be written.

The subscriber callback will not be invoked for events that occurred before the subscriber was registered.

Similarly, there are lots of other APIs provided by Bacon.js to create EventStreams. Here are a few of them:

- `Bacon.fromPromise`: This is used to create an EventStream from a promise object.

- `Bacon.fromEvent`: This is used to create an EventStream from events of an EventTarget or Node.js EventEmitter object.

- `Bacon.fromCallback`: This is used to create an EventStream from a function that accepts a callback.

- `Bacon.fromNodeCallback`: This is the same as `Bacon.fromCallback`, but it requires the callback to be called in Node.js convention.

- `Bacon.fromBinder`: If none of the previous APIs are fitting well, then you can use this one.

Creating properties

A property is created from an EventStream, that is, a stream whose events the value of the property depends on. Whenever an event occurs in the EventStream, a callback is executed to update the property value.

You can create a property for an EventStream using either the `toProperty` or `scan` methods. The `scan` method is used instead of `toProperty` when we want to give an initial value as well as an accumulator function to the property. You may or may not provide an initial value when creating a property using `toProperty()`.

Calling `scan` or `toProperty` multiple times create multiple properties.

Let's create a property to hold the total number of times a button is clicked. Here is the code to do this; place it in the `index.js` file:

```
var button_click_counter = myButton_click_stream.scan(0,
function(value, e){
  return ++value;
})

button_click_counter.onValue(function(value){
  console.log("Button is clicked " + value + " number of times");
})
```

Here, we created a property using the `scan` method and initialized it to 0. The second argument is a callback, which is invoked to update the property value whenever an event happens in the EventStream to which the property is attached. This callback should return the new property value. The callback has two parameters, that is, the current value of the property and the event.

The `onValue` method of a property takes a callback that is executed every time the property value changes. We can call the `onValue` method multiple times to register multiple callbacks.

When we register a subscriber for a property, the subscriber is executed with the current value as soon as it's registered, but not for the values that occurred before it had been registered. If the property has not yet been assigned to anything, then the callback is not executed.

Here, whenever the property value changes, we log a statement informing us about the total number of times the button was clicked.

A property can also be created from another property. This is useful when a property's value depends on another property. Let's create a property from the previous property, which holds the time at which the property was last clicked and the button click count at that time. Here is the code to do this; place it in the `index.js` file:

```
var button_click_time = button_click_counter.scan({}, function(value,
count){
  return {time: Date.now(), clicks: count};
})

button_click_time.onValue(function(value){
  console.log(value);
})
```

Everything here is self-explanatory. The only thing you need to know is that the second parameter of the second argument passed to the `scan` method represents the value of the property we used to create this property.

A property holds a stream that has all of its previous and current values internally; therefore, we can also merge, combine, zip, sample, filter, and transform properties. Merging, combining, zipping, sampling, filtering, or transforming properties gives us new properties. This feature is useful for writing code for the more complex situation of a property's value depending on another property. For example, if we want to ignore some values of a property while calculating the value of another property based on it, then we can use filter feature.

Bacon.js also allows us to create EventStreams based on properties, that is, the events of an EventStream represent the values of a property. Events in these EventStreams occur when their respective property value is changed. This feature has many benefits, one of which is that it can prevent code duplication when we have to trigger the same action in response to several properties changing their values.

To create EventStreams based on properties, we can use the `toEventStream` method of a property.

Retrieving the latest value of a property

There is no method to obtain the latest value of a property, and there will be. You obtain the value by subscribing to the property and handling the values in your callback. If you need the value of more than one source, use one of the `combine` methods. This is how functional reactive code using Bacon.js is supposed to be written.

Merging, filtering, and transforming EventStreams and properties

Bacon.js provides various helper functions to work with EventStreams and properties. Let's look at some of the most useful helper functions.

Merging

Merging streams or properties gives us a new stream or property that delivers all the events or values of all the streams or properties. To merge EventStreams or properties, we can use their `Bacon.mergeAll` method instances. Here is some example code to demonstrate this. Place it in the `index.js` file:

```
var merged_property = Bacon.mergeAll([button_click_counter, button_click_time]);

merged_property.onValue(function(e){
  console.log(e);
})
```

Here, we merge two properties. `Bacon.mergeAll` takes an array of either EventStreams or properties. Whenever the value of either of the two properties changes, the value is made the current value of the resultant property.

There are various other helper functions available for merging properties and EventStreams.

Filtering

Filtering is removing specific events or values from EventStreams or properties, respectively, that we don't need.

Bacon.js provides a lot of helper functions to filter EventStreams and properties, depending on what you want to filter. Let's look at the `filter` method for EventStreams and properties that lets us filter based on a predicate function; that is, if the function returns `true`, then the value is accepted; otherwise, it is rejected.

Let's look at example code to demonstrate this. In the `index.js` file, find this code:

```
var myButton_click_stream = $("#myButton").asEventStream("click");
myButton_click_stream.onValue(function(e){
  console.log(e);
  console.log("Button Clicked");
})
```

Replace that with this code:

```
var myButton_click_stream = $("#myButton").asEventStream("click").
filter(function(e){
  return e.shiftKey === true;
});
```

```
myButton_click_stream.onValue(function(e){
  console.log(e);
  console.log("Button Clicked");
})
```

Here, we are filtering all those click events in which we didn't press the *Shift* key. So, for the click event to be accepted, we need to press the *Shift* key while clicking on the button.

You can think of filtering as an alternative to using the `if...else` conditional.

Transforming

Transforming is creating an EventStream or property from another EventStream or property, respectively, whose events are transformed to something else. For example, a property whose value represents a URL can be transformed to another property, whose value represents the response of the URL. Transforming EventStreams and properties actually creates new EventStreams and properties, respectively.

You can think of transforming as an alternative to loops, that is, to using `for` loops.

There are several helper functions provided by Bacon.js for transformation depending on how and what you want to transform.

One popular transformation function is `map()`, which maps events or values of EventStreams or properties to a function. Let's look at a code sample to demonstrate this. Find this code in the `index.js` file:

```
var button_click_time = button_click_counter.scan({},
function(value, count){
  return {time: Date.now(), clicks: count};
})
```

Replace it with this code:

```
var button_click_time = button_click_counter.scan({},
function(value, count){
  return {time: Date.now(), clicks: count};
}).map(function(value){
  var date = new Date(value.time);
  return (date).getHours() + ":" + (date).getMinutes();
})
```

Here, we are using map() to transform the Unix timestamp to the HH:MM format, which is easy to understand.

There is another, vital transformation helper function provided by Bacon.js called flatMap. There are basically two differences between flatMap and map:

- The flatMap function always returns an EventStream regardless of whether it was called on a EventStream or property.

- If the callback passed to flatMap returns an EventStream or property, then the events of the EventStream returned by the flatMap function are events and values of the streams and properties returned by the callback passed to flatMap. Whenever an event or value is added to the streams and properties returned by the callback passed to flatMap, the event and value will automatically be added to the EventStream returned by the flatMap function.

You need to use flatMap instead of map when retrieving the return value of a callback passed to a network, disk drive, or somewhere else asynchronous. For example, in the previous example, where I talked about transforming a URL to a URL response, we need to use flatMap instead of map as instead of a callback, we need to make an AJAX request, and its response will be captured as a stream, and the stream will be returned. When the AJAX request completes, the event will be put inside the stream returned by the flatMap function.

Let's look at an implementation of this example. First, create an input text field and place it in the index.html file, as follows:

```
<input id="url" type="url">
```

Now, let's write code using Bacon.js to log the output of the URL entered in the field when a user hits the *Enter* key. Here is the code to do this. Place it in the index.js file:

```
var enter_key_click_stream = $("#url").asEventStream("keyup").
filter(function(e){
  return e.keyCode == 13;
})

var url = enter_key_click_stream.scan("", function(value, e){
  return e.currentTarget.value;
})
```

```
var response = url.flatMap(function(value){
 return Bacon.fromPromise($.ajax({url:value}));
}).toProperty();

response.onValue(function(value){
  console.log(value);
})
```

This is how the code works:

- First, we create an EventStream for the keyup event.
- Then, we filter only *Enter*-key events because we will take action only if the *Enter* key is pressed.
- Then, we create a variable to hold the value of the text field.
- Then, we use flatMap to fetch the response of the URL using jQuery AJAX. We are using Bacon.fromPromise to create an EventStream from a promise.
- When the AJAX request finishes, it adds the response to the EventStream returned by the callback passed to flatMap. Then, flatMap adds the same response to the EventStream returned by the flatMap function itself. As soon as it's added, we log the response using onValue.

Here, if we had used map instead of flatMap, then we would have ended up logging EventStream objects instead of the events of the EventStream returned by the map function.

Although we can have both url and response properties directly created from the enter_key_click_stream, it is likely to cause code repetition and make the code difficult to understand.

When you call a method to transform, filter, or do something else with EventStreams, then the events that occurred before the method call are not taken into account. However, in the case of a property, the current value is taken into account, but not the values that occurred before the method call. If the property has not yet been assigned to anything, nothing is taken into account.

Summary

We looked at reactive programming, functional programming, FRP, and finally an overview of Bacon.js. You should now be comfortable with writing basic functional reactive code and have a clear idea of its benefits.

We will learn about more of the APIs provided by Bacon.js and build a real-world project using Bacon.js in the next chapter.

8
Building an Advanced Profile Search Widget

The best way to master FRP using Bacon.js is by building a real world application, which is what we will do in this chapter. We will build an advanced profile search widget, just like the ones you would usually find on social networking or dating sites. To keep the chapter short and to the point, we will work with some sample data instead of building registration functionality. We will also learn some more advanced concepts of functional programming and Bacon.js.

In this chapter, we will cover the following:

- Error events in Bacon.js
- Handling exceptions in FRP
- Lazy evaluation
- Buses in Bacon.js
- Join patterns
- Finally, we will build an advanced profile search widget

Errors in Bacon.js

Bacon provides the `Bacon.Error` constructor to explicitly mark events or values of EventStreams or properties respectively as errors so that Bacon can identify them and open up a wide variety of other APIs to work with those errors specifically.

Depending on how we create a stream, Bacon.js can sometimes identify whether an event is a success or error event, and if it's an error event, then it can convert it to `Bacon.Error`. For example, if we use `Bacon.fromPromise` to create an EventStream, then Bacon can identify an error easily, since when an error occurs in a promise pattern, the second callback of the `then()` method or the callback passed to the `catch()` method is executed.

In case Bacon cannot identify whether an event is an error or success event while creating a stream, then we need to explicitly create instances of `Bacon.Error` and replace the error events with them. For example, when using `Bacon.fromCallback`, there is no way for Bacon.js to know whether an event is a success or error event, so we need to explicitly convert error events to instances of `Bacon.Error`.

Subscribing to errors

A callback passed to `onValue` is not invoked for `Bacon.Error` events or values; instead, we need to use `onError`.

To see it in action, open the `index.js` file that we created in our previous chapter, and add this code:

```
response.onError(function(error){
  console.log("An error occured while fetching the page",
error);
})
```

Now, if you enter an URL that cannot be fetched, a custom error message is displayed on the console.

Mapping errors

The `map()` function doesn't map `Bacon.Error` instances; therefore, Bacon provides us with `mapError ()`, which works the same way as `map` but maps only `Bacon.Error` instances.

Similarly, `flapMap()` doesn't map `Bacon.Error` instances. Therefore, Bacon provides us with `flatMapError()`, which works the same way as `flatMap` but maps only `Bacon.Error` instances.

Aside from `flatMap` and `map`, `Bacon.Error` instances can pass through everything.

Retrying a function call

Sometimes, we might want to retry an operation if it fails. For example, if we fail to retrieve a web page using AJAX due to a server timeout error, then we might want to try retrieving it again after some time.

Bacon provides the `Bacon.retry` function, using which we can make a function call again and again as long as we want to.

`Bacon.retry` returns an EventStream, and it takes an object with four properties, as follows:

- `source`: This is a function that is to be reinvoked. This function must return a property or EventStream.
- `retries`: This is a number representing the total number of times to retry the source function for in addition to the initial attempt. When a `Bacon.Error` instance is pushed to the property or stream returned by the source function, then an attempt to retry is made.
- `isRetryable`: This is an optional property. It needs to be assigned to a function. The function should return either `true` or `false`. When something is pushed into the property or EventStream returned by the source function, then `isRetryable` is invoked to find our whether an attempt to retry should be made.
- `delay`: This is an optional property. It's assigned to a function that returns the time in milliseconds to wait for before retrying. The default value is `0`.

The EventStream returned by `Bacon.retry` has the event or value that was present in the last EventStream or property returned by the last call to the source function.

Let's see the `Bacon.retry` function in action. Find this code in the `index.js` file:

```
var response = url.flatMap(function(value){
  return Bacon.fromPromise($.ajax({url:value}));
}).toProperty();
```

Replace it with this code:

```
var response = url.flatMap(function(value){
  return Bacon.retry({
    source: function(){ return
    Bacon.fromPromise($.ajax({url:value})); },
    retries: 5,
    isRetryable: function (error) { return error.status !== 404;
    },
    delay: function(context) { return 2000; }
  })
}).toProperty();
```

Here, we are retrying the AJAX request 5 times after every 2 seconds for any error other than 404.

Ending an EventStream or property on error

An EventStream or property is said to have ended when you cannot push anything to it.

If you want to end an EventStream or property when a `Bacon.Error` instance is pushed, then you need to call the `endOnError` method of the EventStream or property. The `endOnError` method returns a new EventStream or property, which is ended when a `Bacon.Error` instance is pushed.

Handling exceptions

If an exception is encountered inside a callback passed to a Bacon helper function, then it's not caught automatically; rather, we have to use a `try...catch` statement to handle it. A common practice is to return a `Bacon.Error` instance after catching an exception so that we can handle it just like an error.

Here is an example of how to handle exceptions. In the `index.js` file, find the following code:

```
var response = url.flatMap(function(value){
  return Bacon.retry({
    source: function(){ return
    Bacon.fromPromise($.ajax({url:value})); },
    retries: 5,
    isRetryable: function (error) { return error.status !== 404;
    },
    delay: function(context) { return 2000; }
  })
}).toProperty();
```

Replace it with this:

```
var response = url.flatMap(function(value){
  try
  {
    return Bacon.retry({
      source: function(){ return
      Bacon.fromPromise($.ajax({url:value})); },
```

```
      retries: 5,
      isRetryable: function (error) { return error.status !== 404;
      },
      delay: function(context) { return 2000; }
    })
  }
  catch(e)
  {
    return new Bacon.Error(e);
  }

}).toProperty();
```

Here, we are catching exceptions and creating a new `Bacon.Error` instance with the exception as the details of the error, that is, we are passing the exception as an argument to the constructor.

Constant properties

Bacon also provides us ways to create constant properties. Constant properties are initialized at the time of creation and cannot be reinitialized, that is, new values cannot be pushed.

A constant property is created using the `Bacon.constant()` constructer. We need to pass the value of the property to the constructor. A constant property can be merged, concatenated, combined, zipped, sampled, filtered, and transformed.

Here is an example of how to create a constant property. Place this code in the `index.js` file:

```
var script_start_time =
Bacon.constant(Date.now()).map(function(value){
  var date = new Date(value);
  return (date).getHours() + ":" + (date).getMinutes() + ":" +
  (date).getSeconds();
});

script_start_time.onValue(function(value){
  console.log("This script started running at : " + value);
})
```

Here, the `constant` property stores the time at which the script was started and prints the time.

An overview of buses

A **bus** is just like an EventStream, but it lets us push values into the stream manually instead of attaching it to a source, and it also allows plugging other EventStreams and properties into the bus on the fly.

Here is an example that demonstrates how to create a bus and various methods provided by a `Bacon.Bus` instance. Place this code in the `index.js` file:

```
var bus1 = new Bacon.Bus();

bus1.onValue(function(event){
  console.log(event);
})

bus1.push(1);
bus1.push(2);
var bus2 = new Bacon.Bus();
bus1.plug(bus2);
bus2.push(3);
bus1.error("Unknown Error"); //pushed an Bacon.Error
bus1.end();
bus2.push(4); //this will not be pushed as bus has ended
```

The code is self explanatory. The output of the above code is as follows:

```
1
2
3
```

Subscribing to the end of EventStreams and properties

Bacon provides the `onEnd` method to subscribe to callbacks that will be executed when an EventStream or property ends.

Here is some example code, which shows you how to use the `onEnd` callback. Place it in the `index.js` file:

```
script_start_time.onEnd(function(){
  console.log("Script start time has been successfully calculated
  and logged");
})
```

Here, we are attaching an onEnd callback to the constant property, which we created previously. After initialization, the property is ended; therefore, the onEnd callback is invoked. We can register multiple subscribers as well.

Actually, to end an EventStream or property, Bacon internally pushes an instance of the Bacon.End constructor. So, we can also use the Bacon.End constructor to end an EventStream or property.

Let's look at an example of how to use Bacon.End. Place this code in the index.js file:

```
var custom_stream = Bacon.fromBinder(function(sink) {
  sink(10);
  sink(20);
  sink(new Bacon.End()); //event stream ends here
  sink(30); //this will not be pushed
});

custom_stream.onValue(function(event){
  console.log(event);
});
```

The output of the code is this:

```
10
20
```

A Bacon.End instance doesn't pass through helper functions.

Unplugging subscribers

We saw how to subscribe to an EventStream and property using onValue, onError, and onEnd. We can also unsubscribe the subscribers if we don't need them anymore.

These functions return a function for unsubscribing. To unsubscribe, we need to call the function returned by the subscriber function.

Combining and zipping

Bacon provides certain methods to combine and zip properties and EventStreams. There is a significant difference between combining and zipping.

When we combine properties, we always get a property, which will have an array of all source properties as its value. If we try to combine EventStreams, then they are first converted to properties before combining takes place. When there is a push in any one of the source properties, a new value is pushed into the resultant property. **Combining** starts after each of the source properties has a value pushed.

Here is an example to demonstrate combining. Place this code in the `index.js` file.

```
var x1 = new Bacon.Bus();
var x2 = new Bacon.Bus();
var x3 = new Bacon.Bus();

Bacon.combineAsArray(x1, x2, x3).onValue(function(value){
  console.log(value);
})

x1.push(0);
x1.push(1);
x2.push(2);
x3.push(3);
x3.push(4);
x1.push(5);
```

Here is the output of the code:

```
[1, 2, 3]
[1, 2, 4]
[5, 2, 4]
```

Zipping is different from combining. **Zipping** means that events from each source are combined pairwise so that the first event from each source is published first, then the second event, and so on. The results will be published as soon as there is a value from each source. When we zip properties and EventStreams, we always get an EventStream.

Here is an example to demonstrate zipping. Place this code in the `index.js` file:

```
var y1 = new Bacon.Bus();
var y2 = new Bacon.Bus();
var y3 = new Bacon.Bus();

Bacon.zipAsArray(y1, y2, y3).onValue(function(value){
  console.log(value);
})

y1.push(0);
```

```
y1.push(1);
y2.push(2);
y3.push(3);
y3.push(4);
x1.push(5);
```

Here is the output of the code:

```
[0, 2, 3]
```

Lazy evaluation

In programming, **lazy evaluation** is a strategy that delays the evaluation of values until they're needed. There are two means by which lazy evaluation is implemented by Bacon.js.

Type 1

A stream or property will not be attached to its data source until it has subscribers. Let's look at an example to understand this. Place this code in the index.js file:

```
var myButton_click_stream1 =
$("#myButton").asEventStream("click").map(function(event){
  console.log(event);
  return event;
});
```

Here, when you click on the myButton button, nothing will be logged. Now, place this code in the index.js file:

```
myButton_click_stream1.onValue(function(event){})
```

Now when you click on the button, the event will be logged.

The log method is also considered as a subscriber.

Type 2

Methods such as map and combine* use lazy evaluation to avoid evaluating events and values that aren't actually needed. Lazy evaluation results in huge performance benefits in some cases.

But how do map and combine* know whether an event or value is not needed? Well, there are a few methods that give a hint about this to map and combine*, for example, sampledBy.

What is the `sampledBy` method?

The `sampledBy` method is used for sampling a property based on a property or EventStream. It returns a property or EventStream, respectively, by sampling the property value at each event from the given property or EventStream. The returned property or EventStream will contain the property value at each push in the source property or EventStream.

Let's look at an example of how `map` implements lazy evaluation. Place this code in the `index.js` file:

```
var myBus_1 = Bacon.Bus();
var myBus_2 = Bacon.Bus();

var myProperty_1 = myBus_1.map(function(event){
  console.log(""Executing 1"");
  return event;
}).toProperty();

var myStream_1 = myProperty_1.sampledBy(myBus_2);

myStream_1.onValue(function(event){
  console.log(""Logged"", event);
})

myBus_1.push(1);
```

Here is what we are doing in the previous code:

1. We first create two buses.
2. Then, we map events in the first bus using the `map` method, and it is then transformed into a property.
3. We then create an EventStream by sampling the property value at each event in the second bus.
4. We then add a subscriber to the EventStream.
5. Finally, we push a value to the first bus.

The previous code looks like it should log the following output:

```
Executing 1
Logged 1
```

Unfortunately, it doesn't log anything. That's because lazy evaluation is taking place here. The `sampledBy` function takes the current value of the property, not the ones that were generated from previous events. Therefore, `map` decides to generate the property value when an event occurs in the second bus, therefore preventing unnecessary calls to the callback passed to the `map` function. In short, here, `map` simply prevents calculating property values until it's actually needed. Now, add this code to the `index.js` file:

```
myBus_1.push(2);
myBus_2.push();
```

Now, when you run the code, you will get this output:

```
Executing 1
Logged 2
```

Here, you can see that `map` prevented calculating for the first event pushed inside the first bus. It calculated the property value for second event because sampling was done after that.

> If you want to prevent lazy evaluation when using the `map()` method, then use `flatMap` instead of `map`. The `flatMap` method doesn't use lazy evaluation. There is no way to prevent lazy evaluation when using `combine*` methods, but if you need it badly, then you can try to rewrite the code using other methods, which may or may not be possible depending on what you are trying to achieve.

Building the profile search widget

We've covered almost all the important APIs and concepts of Bacon.js. Now, it's time to build the profile search widget. We will also learn some more APIs and concepts in the process.

We will build the profile search widget to learn how to write reactive code using Bacon for both the frontend and backend in real-world projects. Let's get started.

Understanding project directories and files

In the exercise files of this chapter, you will find a directory named `profile-search-widget`. Inside that directory, you will find two other directories named `final` and `initial`. The `final` directory contains the final code for the profile search widget whereas the `initial` directory contains the files and code for you to quickly get started with building the profile search widget. You will now work with the `initial` directory.

You are supposed to put the server-side code inside the `app.js` file and the frontend code inside the `public/js/index.js` file. Currently, the `app.js` file imports Bacon, Express, and filesystem modules and also has basic code to run the web server and serve static files.

Inside the `public/html/index.html` file, you will find HTML code. We will not be writing any HTML or CSS.

Let's first build the backend and then the frontend.

Converting Express.js routes to a functional reactive pattern

Express.js routes are written using a callback pattern. We need a wrapper to convert the callback pattern to a functional reactive pattern.

Bacon doesn't provide any direct method for doing this — there are various other custom methods. The easiest and shortest way to do this is by creating a bus for every route, and whenever a request to a route is made, pushing an event into its respective bus. Let's create a route this way for serving the `index.html` file for requests to the root URL. Place this code in the `app.js` file:

```
function route_eventstream(path)
{
    var bus = new Bacon.Bus();

    app.get(path, function(req, res) {
      bus.push({
          req: req,
          res: res
      });
    });
```

```
      return bus;
  }

  var root_stream = route_eventstream("/");

  root_stream.onValue(function(event){
    event.res.sendFile(__dirname + ""/public/html/index.html"");
  })
```

This is how the code works:

1. At first, we define a function named `route_eventstream`, which acts as a wrapper to convert callback patterns to EventStream patterns. It takes a path and returns a bus. Whenever a request is made to the route, an event is pushed into the bus. The event is a connection object, that is, it holds the request and response objects for that client request.

2. Then, we create an EventStream for root path requests.

3. Finally, we register a subscriber that returns the `index.html` file whenever an event is pushed into the root EventStream.

Now, run the `node app.js` command and visit `localhost:8080` in your browser. This is the output you will see:

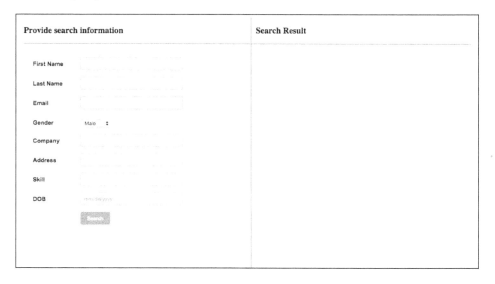

Making the user experience better

In the previous screenshot, you can see that there are eight fields based on which a user can perform a search.

Instead of a user just filling some of the fields and clicking on the **Search** button to get the result, we can add some more features to make the user experience better. Here are the extra things we are going to add:

- Whenever a user uses the *Enter* key in any of the fields, we need fetch the search result

- While a user types the company name, we will show a drop-down menu with suggestions

- At least one of the fields except the gender field should have some value in order for us to fetch a search result.

- If the entered e-mail is of invalid format, then we should display an error message.

These features will make the frontend code more complex, which will give us a chance to explore how to write complex logic using Bacon.

The company suggestions route

Let's create a route that responds with an array of company name suggestions based on a given value. Later on, to populate the company name text field drop-down menu, we will make a request to this route.

We will not build functionality to add profiles; instead, we will simply retrieve profiles from a JSON file that has some random profiles. In the `initial` directory, you will find a file named `data.json`, which has some profiles in it.

Let's first read the data from the `data.json` file. Here is the code for this. Place it in the `app.js` file.

```
var data = Bacon.fromNodeCallback(fs.readFile, "data.json",
"utf8").map(function(event){
  return JSON.parse(event);
}).toProperty();
```

Here, we are reading the data in functional reactive style and then converting the EventStream to a property, which represents the data.

Here is the code for the company suggestion route. Place it in the `app.js` file:

```
function findMatchingCompanyName(list, companyName)
{
  return list.filter(function(value){
    return companyName != "" &&
    value.company.toLowerCase().indexOf(companyName.toLowerCase()) ==
0;
```

```
    })
}

var company_dropdown_list_stream =
route_eventstream(""/company/dropdown"");

var company_dropdown_list_data_stream = Bacon.combineAsArray([data,
company_dropdown_list_stream]).map(function(event){
    return findMatchingCompanyName(event[0],
    event[1].req.query.companyName);
}).toEventStream();

Bacon.zipAsArray(company_dropdown_list_stream, company_dropdown_list_
data_stream).onValues(function(event1, event2) {
    event1.res.send(event2);
});
```

Here is how the code works:

1. At first, we define a method that takes an array of profiles and a company name. It checks for the profiles that have the same company and returns the filtered list. We are using the ES6 filter method, as Bacon doesn't provide any filter method for arrays. If the company name string is empty, then it returns an empty array.

2. Then, we create an EventStream for /company/dropdown path requests.

3. Then, we combine company_dropdown_list_stream and the data property. The resultant property is then mapped, and the filtered result is the transformed value.

4. We cannot simply use a subscriber here for company_dropdown_list_ stream to respond to, as we have lost the reference to the connection object. Therefore, we zip company_dropdown_list_stream and company_ dropdown_list_data_stream so that we get the reference to the connection object as well as the final result. We then attach a subscriber to the zipped EventStream, which sends the response.

5. One more thing to notice here is that we are using onValues instead of onValue. The difference between them is that onValues splits the value (assuming it's an array) as function arguments.

The search result route

Let's create a route that responds with an array of profiles based on a given parameter. This will be used to find the search result. Later on, from the frontend, we will make a request to this route.

Here is the code for this route. Place it in the app.js file:

```
function findMatchingProfilesForEmail(list, email)
{
  return list.filter(function(value){
    return value.email == email;
  })
}

function findMatchingProfiles(list, firstName, lastName, gender,
skill, company, dob, address)
{
  var firstName_matches = list.filter(function(value){
    return firstName == "" || value.first_name.toLowerCase() ==
    firstName.toLowerCase();
  })

  var lastName_matches = firstName_matches.filter(function(value){
    return lastName == "" || value.last_name.toLowerCase() ==
    lastName.toLowerCase();
  })

  var gender_matches = lastName_matches.filter(function(value){
    return gender == "" || value.gender.toLowerCase() ==
    gender.toLowerCase();
  })

  var skill_matches = gender_matches.filter(function(value){
    return skill == "" || value.skill.toLowerCase() ==
    skill.toLowerCase();
  })

  var company_matches = skill_matches.filter(function(value){
    return company == "" || value.company.toLowerCase() ==
    company.toLowerCase();
  })
```

```
var dob_matches = company_matches.filter(function(value){
  return dob == "" || value.dob == dob;
})

var address_matches = dob_matches.filter(function(value){
  return address == "" || value.address.toLowerCase() ==
  address.toLowerCase();
})

return address_matches;
}

var profile_search_stream = route_eventstream("/search");

var profile_search_data_stream_for_email =
Bacon.combineAsArray([data,
profile_search_stream.filter(function(event){
  return event.req.query.email != "";
})]).map(function(event){
  return findMatchingProfilesForEmail(event[0],
  event[1].req.query.email);
}).toEventStream();

var profile_search_data_stream_for_others =
Bacon.combineAsArray([data,
profile_search_stream.filter(function(event){
  return event.req.query.email == "";
})]).map(function(event){
  return findMatchingProfiles(event[0],
  event[1].req.query.firstName, event[1].req.query.lastName,
  event[1].req.query.gender, event[1].req.query.skill,
  event[1].req.query.company, event[1].req.query.dob,
  event[1].req.query.address);
}).toEventStream();

Bacon.zipAsArray(profile_search_stream,
Bacon.mergeAll([profile_search_data_stream_for_email,
profile_search_data_stream_for_others])).onValues(function(event1,
event2) {
  event1.res.send(event2);
});
```

This is how the code works:

1. At first, we define two methods, which take a list of profiles and search data and filter based on the data. The first one only filters based on e-mail whereas the second one filters based on other search data. We have done it this way because e-mail is unique for every profile, and if a user provides an e-mail ID, then we don't need to use other data and waste computation. When there is a lot of data, you will get a big performance advantage this way.

2. Then, we create an EventStream for the `/search` path.

3. After that, we create two streams, namely, `profile_search_data_stream_form_email` and `profile_search_data_stream_form_others`. The `profile_search_data_stream_form_email` stream is the final result if an e-mail is provided, and `profile_search_data_stream_form_others` is the final result if an e-mail is not provided.

4. Finally, we merge `profile_search_data_stream_form_email` and `profile_search_data_stream_form_others`, zip that with `profile_search_stream`, and return the response.

Building the frontend

We are done building the backend part of our profile search widget. Now, we need to write the frontend part.

Before we get into it, it's worth looking at the code in the `index.html` file:

```
<!doctype html>
<html>
  <head>
    <title>Advanced Profile Search Widget</title>

    <link rel="stylesheet" type="text/css" href="css/style.css">
  </head>
  <body>
    <div class="container">
      <div class="section-1">
        <h3>Provide search information</h3>
        <hr>
        <div class="form-style">
            <form action="" method="post">
                <label><span>First Name</span><input type="text"
                class="input-field" id="first-name" value=""
                /></label>
                <label><span>Last Name </span><input type="text"
```

```
            class="input-field" id="last-name" value=""
            /></label>
            <label>
              <span>Email</span>
              <input type="email" class="input-field"
              id="email" value="" />
              <br><small class="hide" id="email-error">Email
              address is invalid</small>
            </label>
            <label>
                <span>Gender</span>
                <select id="gender" class="select-field">
                    <option value="male">Male</option>
                    <option value="female">Female</option>
                </select>
            </label>
            <label><span>Company</span><input list="companies"
            type="text" class="input-field" value=""
            id="company" /></label>
            <label><span>Address</span><input type="address"
            class="input-field" value="" id="address"
            /></label>
            <label><span>Skill</span><input type="text"
            class="input-field" value="" id="skill" /></label>
            <label><span>DOB</span><input
            placeholder="mm/dd/yyyy" type="text" class="input-
            field" value="" id="dob" /></label>
            <label><span> </span><input type="button"
            value="Search" id="search" /></label>

            <datalist id="companies"></datalist>
        </form>
      </div>
    </div>
    <div class="section-2">
      <h3>Search Result</h3>
      <hr>
      <ul id="search-result">
      </ul>
    </div>
    <div class="clear"></div>
</div>

<script type="text/javascript" src="js/jquery-
2.2.0.min.js"></script>
<script type="text/javascript" src="js/Bacon.js"></script>
```

```
    <script type="text/javascript" src="js/index.js"></script>
  </body>
</html>
```

Most of the code is self-explanatory. Here are a few things you need to pay special attention to:

- Here, every input element has an `id` value attached to it. We will use the `id` value to create an EventStream.

- We have displayed an error message below the e-mail field. It has a class `hide`, which hides it. Removing the class will unhide it.

- We also have a `datalist` element, which is the drop-down menu for the `company` field. We just need to add `option` tags to the `datalist` element to show the drop-down menu.

- Finally, we have a section to display the search result.

Now, let's create EventStreams for `keyup` events on the input fields and store the current value of the fields in properties. Here is the code for this. Place it in the `index.js` file:

```
var first_name_keypress_stream = $("#first-
name").asEventStream("keyup");

var first_name = first_name_keypress_stream.scan("",
function(value){
  return $("#first-name").val();
});

var last_name_keypress_stream = $("#last-
name").asEventStream("keyup");

var last_name = last_name_keypress_stream.scan("",
function(value){
  return $("#last-name").val();
});

var email_keypress_stream = $("#email").asEventStream("keyup");

var is_email_valid = email_keypress_stream.scan("",
function(value){
  return $("#email").val();
}).map(function(value){
  var re = /^(([^<>()[\]\\.,;:\s@"]+(\.[^<>()
[\]\\.,;:\s@"]+)*)|(".+"))@((\[[
0-9]{1,3}\.[0-9]{1,3}\.[0-9]{1,3}\.[0-9]{1,3}])|(([a-zA-Z\-0-
9]+\.)+[a-zA-Z]{2,}))$/;
  return re.test(value);
```

```
});

var email = Bacon.mergeAll(is_email_valid.filter(function(value){
  return value == true;
}).map(function(value){
  $("#email-error").addClass("hide");
  return $("#email").val();
}), is_email_valid.filter(function(value){
  return value == false;
}).map(function(value){
  $("#email-error").removeClass("hide");
  return "";
}))

var gender_select_stream = $("#gender").asEventStream("change");

var gender = gender_select_stream.scan("male", function(value){
  return $("#gender option:selected").val()
})

var company_keypress_stream  =
$("#company").asEventStream("keyup");

var company = company_keypress_stream.scan("", function(value){
  return $("#company").val();
});

var address_keypress_stream  =
$("#address").asEventStream("keyup");

var address = address_keypress_stream.scan("", function(value){
  return $("#address").val();
});

var skill_keypress_stream  = $("#skill").asEventStream("keyup");

var skill = skill_keypress_stream.scan("", function(value){
  return $("#skill").val();
});

var dob_keypress_stream  = $("#dob").asEventStream("keyup");

var dob = dob_keypress_stream.scan("", function(value){
  return $("#dob").val();
});
```

Most of the above code is self-explanatory. The only thing that you need to understand is that instead of directly assign the e-mail field value to the e-mail property, we first validate whether the e-mail is valid. If the e-mail is invalid, then we display the error message and don't assign anything to the e-mail property. If the e-mail is valid, then we hide the error message and assign the current value of the e-mail field to the e-mail property.

Now, let's write code to display the suggestions drop-down menu for the company field. Here is the code for this. Place it in the `index.js` file:

```
company.flatMap(function(event){
    return Bacon.fromPromise($.ajax({url:"/company/
dropdown?companyName=" +
encodeURIComponent(event)}));
}).flatMap(function(event){
    $("#companies").empty();
    return Bacon.fromArray(event);
}).onValue(function(event){
    $("#companies").append("<option value='" + event.company +
    "'>");
});
```

Here, whenever the value of company property changes, we make a request to the `/company/dropdown` path, retrieve the suggestions, and append them to the `datalist`.

Finally, we need to make a `search` request whenever a user clicks on the **Search** button or hits *Enter* while in any of the input fields. Here is the code for this. Place it in the `index.js` file:

```
var search_button_click_stream =
$("#search").asEventStream("click");

var search_result_request_stream =
Bacon.mergeAll(Bacon.mergeAll([first_name_keypress_stream,
last_name_keypress_stream, email_keypress_stream,
company_keypress_stream, address_keypress_stream,
skill_keypress_stream, search_button_click_stream,
dob_keypress_stream]).filter(function(event){
    return event.keyCode == 13;
}), search_button_click_stream);
```

```
var search_result_request_data = Bacon.combineAsArray([first_name,
last_name, email, gender, company, skill, dob,
address]).sampledBy(search_result_request_stream).flatMap(function
(event){
  return event;
});
var search_result_request_cancel =
search_result_request_data.filter(function(event){
  return event[0] == "" && event[1] == "" && event[2] == "" &&
  event[4] == "" && event[5] == "" && event[6] == "" && event[7]
  ==
  "";
}).onValue(function(){
  $("#search-result").empty();
  alert("Enter enter some data");
});


var search_result_response =
search_result_request_data.filter(function(event){
  return event[0] != "" || event[1] != "" || event[2] != "" ||
  event[4] != "" || event[5] != "" || event[6] != "" || event[7]
  !=
  "";
}).flatMap(function(event){
  return Bacon.fromPromise($.ajax({url:"/search?firstName=" +
  encodeURIComponent(event[0]) + "&lastName=" +
  encodeURIComponent(event[1]) + "&email=" +
  encodeURIComponent(event[2]) + "&gender=" +
  encodeURIComponent(event[3]) + "&company=" +
  encodeURIComponent(event[4]) + "&address=" +
  encodeURIComponent(event[7]) + "&skill=" +
  encodeURIComponent(event[5]) + "&dob=" +
  encodeURIComponent(event[6]) }));
}).toProperty();


search_result_response.onError(function(){
  $("#search-result").empty();
  alert("An error occured");
})


search_result_response.flatMap(function(value){
  $("#search-result").empty();
  return Bacon.fromArray(value);
}).onValue(function(value){
  var html = "<li>";
```

```
html = html + "<p><b>Name: </b> <span>" + value.first_name + " "
+ value.last_name + "</span></p>";
html = html + "<p><b>Email: </b> <span>" + value.email +
"</span></p>";
html = html + "<p><b>Gender: </b> <span>" + value.gender +
"</span></p>";
htmt = html + "<p><b>Company: </b> <span>" + value.company +
"</span></p>";
html = html + "<p><b>Address: </b> <span>" + value.address +
"</span></p>";
html = html + "<p><b>DOB: </b> <span>" + value.dob +
"</span></p>";
html = html + "<p><b>Skill: </b> <span>" + value.skill +
"</span></p>";
html = html + "</li>";

  $("#search-result").append(html);
});

search_result_response.filter(function(value){
  return value.length == 0;
}).onValue(function(value){
  $("#search-result").empty();
  alert("Nothing found")
})
```

Here is how the code works:

- At first, we create a click stream for the **Search** button.

- Then, we create the `search_result_request_stream` stream, in which an event is pushed whenever we click on the **Search** button or press the *Enter* key inside any of the fields.

- Then, we make a request to the `/search` path if any of the fields along with the gender field has a value; otherwise, we display an alert message asking the user to enter some data.

- And then, if the we get an AJAX error, then we display an alert with the error message; if the AJAX response isn't empty, then we display the result; and finally, if the AJAX request is empty, we displaying an alert with a message stating that nothing was found.

Testing the widget

To test the widget, rerun the `node app.js` command. Now, refresh the `localhost:8080` URL.

To test whether the search widget is working, enter `Robert` in the **First Name** field and press *Enter*. You will see this output:

Provide search information	Search Result
First Name Robert	**Name:** Robert Carpenter
	Email: rcarpenteru@theguardian.com
Last Name	**Gender:** Male
Email	**Address:** 1954 Westridge Parkway
Email address is invalid	**DOB:** 6/21/1934
Gender Male ⬍	**Skill:** SDLC
Company	**Name:** Robert Long
Address	**Email:** rlong10@digg.com
Skill	**Gender:** Male
DOB mm/dd/yyyy	**Address:** 45 Eastlawn Circle
Search	**DOB:** 11/15/2007
	Skill: Farms
	Name: Robert Washington
	Email: rwashington2u@pen.io
	Gender: Male
	Address: 25244 Oak Valley Center
	DOB: 11/24/1956
	Skill: FBT
	Name: Robert Fisher
	Email: rfisher3u@issuu.com
	Gender: Male
	Address: 8172 Memorial Point
	DOB: 6/23/1999
	Skill: Graphic Illustrations

To test the company suggestions drop-down menu, enter a in the **Company** field, and you will see this output:

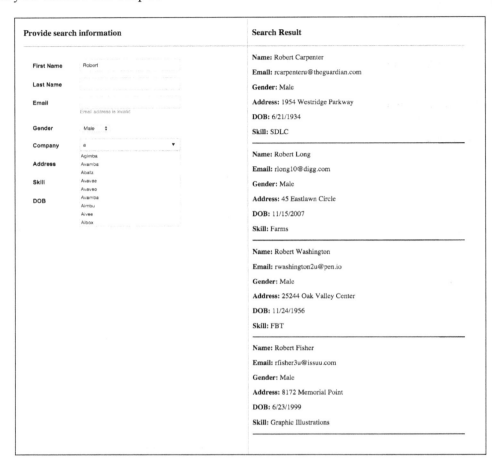

So now, we have finished building and testing our advanced profile search widget.

Summary

In this chapter, we explored the advanced APIs and concepts of Bacon.js and built a real-world project using them. You should now be comfortable with writing reactive code in a functional manner using Bacon.js and should try integrating Bacon.js into your existing and future projects.

You can also learn more about Bacon.js APIs at `https://baconjs.github.io/api.html`.

New Features of Bootstrap 4

Bootstrap 4 is the latest version of Bootstrap at the time of writing. This version makes Bootstrap more powerful and easy to customize and use. In this chapter, you will learn about the new features of Bootstrap 4 with examples. I will assume that you already have some knowledge of Bootstrap and know how to create responsive websites using it. If you are new to Bootstrap or responsive web design, you can find good books to learn Bootstrap from scratch from the Packt catalog. We will use Bootstrap 4 to design all the projects we will be building from this chapter onwards.

In this chapter, we'll cover the following topics:

- Various ways to download Bootstrap 4
- The compatibility of Bootstrap 4
- Support for Flexbox
- Customizing Bootstrap 4
- Responsive CSS units

Downloading Bootstrap 4

To download Bootstrap 4, first visit `http://v4-alpha.getbootstrap.com/getting-started/download/`. Here, you will find various ways to download Bootstrap 4, depending on the package manager you use. You can also directly download the compiled version if the package manager you use is not listed or if you don't use a package manager at all. This page also provides you with a link to download the source files.

It also provides custom builds, which are just parts of Bootstrap 4 that can be used when you just need a few features of Bootstrap 4 but not the whole library.

All major CDN services also support Bootstrap 4, so in case you want to enqueue it from a CDN, you can easily find CDN URLs.

For this chapter, directly download the compiled version and place it in a new directory named bs4. In the same directory, create a file named index.html, and place the following code in it:

```
<!DOCTYPE html>
<html lang="en">
  <head>
    <!-- Required meta tags always come first -->
    <meta charset="utf-8">
    <meta name="viewport" content="width=device-width, initial-
    scale=1, shrink-to-fit=no">
    <meta http-equiv="x-ua-compatible" content="ie=edge">

    <!-- Bootstrap CSS -->
    <link rel="stylesheet" href="bootstrap.min.css">
  </head>
  <body>

    <!-- jQuery first, then Bootstrap JS. -->
    <script src="https://ajax.googleapis.com/ajax/libs/
    jquery/2.1.4/jquery.min.js"></script>
    <script src="bootstrap.min.js"></script>
  </body>
</html>
```

Browser and device support

Bootstrap 4 supports the latest stable releases of all major browsers and platforms.

In terms of compatibility, the only change Bootstrap 4 has brought in is that it drops support for Internet Explorer 8. Everything else remains the same as in Bootstrap 3.

Understanding the rem and em CSS units

Bootstrap 4 has switched from px to rem and em wherever possible. This is the main reason why Bootstrap 4 is not supported in IE 8 as IE 8 doesn't support the em and rem units. Bootstrap 4 switched to rem and em because they make responsive typography and component sizing easier.

If you are not familiar with the `rem` and `em` CSS units, then it's the right time to learn it.

The `em` unit is relative to the font size of the parent element. `1em` is equal to the current font size of the parent element. `2em` means two times the size of the current font. For example, if an element is displayed with a font size of `10 px`, then `2em` is `20 px`. We can achieve responsive typography and components by just changing the parent element's font size using CSS media queries for different viewport or device width sizes.

As `em` sizing is nested (it depends on parent element), if you have elements with `1.5em` sizing and then nest some HTML with elements that also have an `em` declaration, their sizing multiplies.

The `rem` unit is similar to `em` but is relative to the font size of the HTML tag (root element). Therefore, it's not nested.

 Bootstrap 4 uses a base font size of 16 pixels.

The grid system

The only change made in the Bootstrap 4 grid system is that a new extra-large breakpoint has been added. The class prefix for this breakpoint is `.col-xl-`. Here are the Bootstrap 4 grid breakpoints after this new addition:

	Extra Small	Small	Medium	Large	Extra Large
	<544px	≥544px	≥768px	≥992px	≥1200px
Container width	Auto	576px	720px	940px	1140px
Class prefix	.col-xs-	.col-sm-	.col-md-	.col-lg-	.col-xl-
Gutter width	1.875rem / 30px (15px on each side of a column)				

The `.col-xl-` breakpoint targets screen sizes of **1200px** or larger, which was targeted by `.col-lg-` in Bootstrap 3. Therefore, this makes other breakpoints compress to target smaller screen sizes than they used to in Bootstrap 3. Here, you can see that `.col-xs-` now targets a screen width of less than **544px** instead of the **768px** it did in Bootstrap 3, making it easier to target mobile devices and have different layouts for tablets and mobile devices, which was lacking in Bootstrap 3.

While Bootstrap uses em or rem for defining most sizes, px is used for grid breakpoints and container widths. This is because viewport width is in pixels and does not change with font size.

Here is an example of the new grid system. Place this code in the <body> tag of the index.html file:

```
<div class="container">
  <div class="row">
    <div class="col-xs-12 col-sm-6 col-md-4 col-lg-3 col-xl-2">
      <p>
        Lorem ipsum dolor sit amet, consectetur adipiscing elit.
        Vivamus arcu nunc, lobortis et lacinia ut, pellentesque
        quis lacus. Aliquam non dapibus erat
      </p>
    </div>

    <div class="col-xs-12 col-sm-6 col-md-4 col-lg-3 col-xl-2">
      <p>
        Lorem ipsum dolor sit amet, consectetur adipiscing elit.
        Vivamus arcu nunc, lobortis et lacinia ut, pellentesque
        quis lacus. Aliquam non dapibus erat
      </p>
    </div>

    <div class="col-xs-12 col-sm-6 col-md-4 col-lg-3 col-xl-2">
      <p>
        Lorem ipsum dolor sit amet, consectetur adipiscing elit.
        Vivamus arcu nunc, lobortis et lacinia ut, pellentesque
        quis lacus. Aliquam non dapibus erat
      </p>
    </div>

    <div class="col-xs-12 col-sm-6 col-md-4 col-lg-3 col-xl-2">
      <p>
        Lorem ipsum dolor sit amet, consectetur adipiscing elit.
        Vivamus arcu nunc, lobortis et lacinia ut, pellentesque
        quis lacus. Aliquam non dapibus erat
      </p>
    </div>

    <div class="col-xs-12 col-sm-6 col-md-4 col-lg-3 col-xl-2">
      <p>
        Lorem ipsum dolor sit amet, consectetur adipiscing elit.
        Vivamus arcu nunc, lobortis et lacinia ut, pellentesque
        quis lacus. Aliquam non dapibus erat
```

```
        </p>
      </div>

      <div class="col-xs-12 col-sm-6 col-md-4 col-lg-3 col-xl-2">
        <p>
          Lorem ipsum dolor sit amet, consectetur adipiscing elit.
          Vivamus arcu nunc, lobortis et lacinia ut, pellentesque
          quis lacus. Aliquam non dapibus erat
        </p>
      </div>
    </div>
  </div>
```

A Bootstrap row can have 12 columns at the most. As here we have more than 12 columns in the row in some cases, the columns are wrapped, that is, columns are wrapped to a new line.

On mobile screens, the previous code will look like this:

Lorem ipsum dolor sit amet, consectetur adipiscing elit. Vivamus arcu nunc, lobortis et lacinia ut, pellentesque quis lacus. Aliquam non dapibus erat

Lorem ipsum dolor sit amet, consectetur adipiscing elit. Vivamus arcu nunc, lobortis et lacinia ut, pellentesque quis lacus. Aliquam non dapibus erat

Lorem ipsum dolor sit amet, consectetur adipiscing elit. Vivamus arcu nunc, lobortis et lacinia ut, pellentesque quis lacus. Aliquam non dapibus erat

Lorem ipsum dolor sit amet, consectetur adipiscing elit. Vivamus arcu nunc, lobortis et lacinia ut, pellentesque quis lacus. Aliquam non dapibus erat

Lorem ipsum dolor sit amet, consectetur adipiscing elit. Vivamus arcu nunc, lobortis et lacinia ut, pellentesque quis lacus. Aliquam non dapibus erat

Lorem ipsum dolor sit amet, consectetur adipiscing elit. Vivamus arcu nunc, lobortis et lacinia ut, pellentesque quis lacus. Aliquam non dapibus erat

On small tablets, it will look like this:

Lorem ipsum dolor sit amet, consectetur adipiscing elit. Vivamus arcu nunc, lobortis et lacinia ut, pellentesque quis lacus. Aliquam non dapibus erat

Lorem ipsum dolor sit amet, consectetur adipiscing elit. Vivamus arcu nunc, lobortis et lacinia ut, pellentesque quis lacus. Aliquam non dapibus erat

Lorem ipsum dolor sit amet, consectetur adipiscing elit. Vivamus arcu nunc, lobortis et lacinia ut, pellentesque quis lacus. Aliquam non dapibus erat

Lorem ipsum dolor sit amet, consectetur adipiscing elit. Vivamus arcu nunc, lobortis et lacinia ut, pellentesque quis lacus. Aliquam non dapibus erat

Lorem ipsum dolor sit amet, consectetur adipiscing elit. Vivamus arcu nunc, lobortis et lacinia ut, pellentesque quis lacus. Aliquam non dapibus erat

Lorem ipsum dolor sit amet, consectetur adipiscing elit. Vivamus arcu nunc, lobortis et lacinia ut, pellentesque quis lacus. Aliquam non dapibus erat

It will look like this on regular tablets:

Lorem ipsum dolor sit amet, consectetur adipiscing elit. Vivamus arcu nunc, lobortis et lacinia ut, pellentesque quis lacus. Aliquam non dapibus erat

Lorem ipsum dolor sit amet, consectetur adipiscing elit. Vivamus arcu nunc, lobortis et lacinia ut, pellentesque quis lacus. Aliquam non dapibus erat

Lorem ipsum dolor sit amet, consectetur adipiscing elit. Vivamus arcu nunc, lobortis et lacinia ut, pellentesque quis lacus. Aliquam non dapibus erat

Lorem ipsum dolor sit amet, consectetur adipiscing elit. Vivamus arcu nunc, lobortis et lacinia ut, pellentesque quis lacus. Aliquam non dapibus erat

Lorem ipsum dolor sit amet, consectetur adipiscing elit. Vivamus arcu nunc, lobortis et lacinia ut, pellentesque quis lacus. Aliquam non dapibus erat

Lorem ipsum dolor sit amet, consectetur adipiscing elit. Vivamus arcu nunc, lobortis et lacinia ut, pellentesque quis lacus. Aliquam non dapibus erat

Laptops users will see this:

> Lorem ipsum dolor sit amet, consectetur adipiscing elit. Vivamus arcu nunc, lobortis et lacinia ut, pellentesque quis lacus. Aliquam non dapibus erat
>
> Lorem ipsum dolor sit amet, consectetur adipiscing elit. Vivamus arcu nunc, lobortis et lacinia ut, pellentesque quis lacus. Aliquam non dapibus erat
>
> Lorem ipsum dolor sit amet, consectetur adipiscing elit. Vivamus arcu nunc, lobortis et lacinia ut, pellentesque quis lacus. Aliquam non dapibus erat
>
> Lorem ipsum dolor sit amet, consectetur adipiscing elit. Vivamus arcu nunc, lobortis et lacinia ut, pellentesque quis lacus. Aliquam non dapibus erat
>
> Lorem ipsum dolor sit amet, consectetur adipiscing elit. Vivamus arcu nunc, lobortis et lacinia ut, pellentesque quis lacus. Aliquam non dapibus erat
>
> Lorem ipsum dolor sit amet, consectetur adipiscing elit. Vivamus arcu nunc, lobortis et lacinia ut, pellentesque quis lacus. Aliquam non dapibus erat

Finally, on desktop monitors, it will look like this:

> Lorem ipsum dolor sit amet, consectetur adipiscing elit. Vivamus arcu nunc, lobortis et lacinia ut, pellentesque quis lacus. Aliquam non dapibus erat
>
> Lorem ipsum dolor sit amet, consectetur adipiscing elit. Vivamus arcu nunc, lobortis et lacinia ut, pellentesque quis lacus. Aliquam non dapibus erat
>
> Lorem ipsum dolor sit amet, consectetur adipiscing elit. Vivamus arcu nunc, lobortis et lacinia ut, pellentesque quis lacus. Aliquam non dapibus erat
>
> Lorem ipsum dolor sit amet, consectetur adipiscing elit. Vivamus arcu nunc, lobortis et lacinia ut, pellentesque quis lacus. Aliquam non dapibus erat
>
> Lorem ipsum dolor sit amet, consectetur adipiscing elit. Vivamus arcu nunc, lobortis et lacinia ut, pellentesque quis lacus. Aliquam non dapibus erat
>
> Lorem ipsum dolor sit amet, consectetur adipiscing elit. Vivamus arcu nunc, lobortis et lacinia ut, pellentesque quis lacus. Aliquam non dapibus erat

So, in Bootstrap 4, we are able to precisely target all types of device.

Global margin reset

For all elements, Bootstrap 4 resets `margin-top` to `0` while keeping a consistent `margin-bottom` value on all elements.

For example, headings have `margin-bottom: .5rem` added, and paragraphs have `margin-bottom: 1rem` for easy spacing.

Spacing utility classes

Bootstrap 4 adds a new set of utility classes called **spacing utility classes**. These classes allow you to quickly add spacing in any direction of an element via margin or padding.

The format of these classes is `[margin or padding]-[direction]-[size]`.

For margin or padding, use the following:

- m for margin
- p for padding

For direction, you can use these:

- a for all
- t for top
- r for right
- l for left
- b for bottom
- x for left and right
- y for top and bottom

You can use these for sizes:

- 0 for zero
- 1 for 1rem
- 2 for 1.5rem
- 3 for 3rem

Here is an example to demonstrate the spacing utility classes. Place this code at the end of the container element of index.html:

```
<hr>
<div class="row">
  <div class="col-xs-12 m-t-2">
    <p>
      Lorem ipsum dolor sit amet, at suscipit sodales eget ante
      ultricies mauris. Etiam dolor felis morbi nibh, mollit
      porttitor tempor, dignissim magna pellentesque dictumst
      bibendum dictum integer. Justo mattis dapibus in diam. Quis
      arcu mauris mattis, orci est magna arcu scelerisque, integer
      gravida sit volutpat tellus, nulla enim quis. In non, in et,
      nec mauris in eu nec, nostra pellentesque nulla sodales,
      tempor neque ultrices lorem.

    </p>
  </div>

  <div class="col-xs-12 m-b-2">
    <p>
```

```
        Lorem ipsum dolor sit amet, at suscipit sodales eget ante
        ultricies mauris. Etiam dolor felis morbi nibh, mollit
        porttitor tempor, dignissim magna pellentesque dictumst
        bibendum dictum integer. Justo mattis dapibus in diam. Quis
        arcu mauris mattis, orci est magna arcu scelerisque, integer
        gravida sit volutpat tellus, nulla enim quis. In non, in et,
        nec mauris in eu nec, nostra pellentesque nulla sodales,
        tempor neque ultrices lorem.
      </p>
    </div>
  </div>
  <hr>
```

Here is how the page looks now:

Lorem ipsum dolor sit amet, consectetur adipiscing elit. Vivamus arcu nunc, lobortis et lacinia ut, pellentesque quis lacus. Aliquam non dapibus erat	Lorem ipsum dolor sit amet, consectetur adipiscing elit. Vivamus arcu nunc, lobortis et lacinia ut, pellentesque quis lacus. Aliquam non dapibus erat	Lorem ipsum dolor sit amet, consectetur adipiscing elit. Vivamus arcu nunc, lobortis et lacinia ut, pellentesque quis lacus. Aliquam non dapibus erat	Lorem ipsum dolor sit amet, consectetur adipiscing elit. Vivamus arcu nunc, lobortis et lacinia ut, pellentesque quis lacus. Aliquam non dapibus erat	Lorem ipsum dolor sit amet, consectetur adipiscing elit. Vivamus arcu nunc, lobortis et lacinia ut, pellentesque quis lacus. Aliquam non dapibus erat	Lorem ipsum dolor sit amet, consectetur adipiscing elit. Vivamus arcu nunc, lobortis et lacinia ut, pellentesque quis lacus. Aliquam non dapibus erat

Lorem ipsum dolor sit amet, at suscipit sodales eget ante ultricies mauris. Etiam dolor felis morbi nibh, mollit porttitor tempor, dignissim magna pellentesque dictumst bibendum dictum integer. Justo mattis dapibus in diam. Quis arcu mauris mattis, orci est magna arcu scelerisque, integer gravida sit volutpat tellus, nulla enim quis. In non, in et, nec mauris in eu nec, nostra pellentesque nulla sodales, tempor neque ultrices lorem.

Lorem ipsum dolor sit amet, at suscipit sodales eget ante ultricies mauris. Etiam dolor felis morbi nibh, mollit porttitor tempor, dignissim magna pellentesque dictumst bibendum dictum integer. Justo mattis dapibus in diam. Quis arcu mauris mattis, orci est magna arcu scelerisque, integer gravida sit volutpat tellus, nulla enim quis. In non, in et, nec mauris in eu nec, nostra pellentesque nulla sodales, tempor neque ultrices lorem.

Here, you can see the top and bottom margin space created by the spacing utility classes.

Display headings

Traditional heading elements, namely h1, h2, and so on, are designed to work best in the meat of your page content. When you need a heading to stand out, consider using a display heading—a larger, slightly more opinionated heading style. Display heading classes can be applied to any element of a page.

Here is an example to demonstrate display heading. Place this code at the end of the container element of `index.html`:

```
<h1 class="display-1">Display-1</h1>
<h1 class="display-2">Display-2</h1>
<h1 class="display-3">Display-3</h1>
<h1 class="display-4">Display-4</h1>
<hr>
```

`display-1`, `display-2`, `display-3`, and `display-4` are the display heading classes.

Here is the output of the code:

Inverse tables

A new class for tables has been introduced, named `table-inverse`. This is just another variation of `table` in terms of looks.

Here is how to create an inverse table. Place this code at the end of the container element of `index.html`:

```
<table class="table table-inverse">
  <thead>
    <tr>
      <th>#</th>
      <th>First Name</th>
      <th>Last Name</th>
      <th>Username</th>
    </tr>
  </thead>
```

```
<tbody>
  <tr>
    <th scope="row">1</th>
    <td>Ramesh</td>
    <td>Kumar</td>
    <td>@ramesh</td>
  </tr>

  <tr>
    <th scope="row">2</th>
    <td>Sudheep</td>
    <td>Sahoo</td>
    <td>@sudheep</td>
  </tr>

  <tr>
    <th scope="row">3</th>
    <td>Abhinash</td>
    <td>Singh</td>
    <td>@abhi</td>
  </tr>
</tbody>
</table>
<hr>
```

Here is how the table looks:

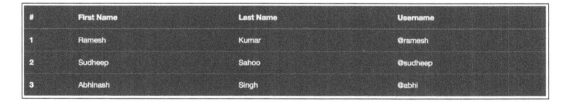

#	First Name	Last Name	Username
1	Ramesh	Kumar	@ramesh
2	Sudheep	Sahoo	@sudheep
3	Abhinash	Singh	@abhi

The card component

Cards are a new component in Bootstrap 4 that replaces wells, panels, and thumbnails. A card is a flexible and extensible content container. It includes options for headers and footers, a wide variety of content, contextual background colors, and powerful display options.

Here is an example that demonstrates how to create a card and all of its subparts and styles. Place this code at the end of the container element of index.html:

```
<div class="row">
  <div class="col-md-4">
    <div class="card">

      <div class="card-header">
        Featured
      </div>
      <div class="card-block">
        <h4 class="card-title">Card title</h4>
        <h6 class="card-subtitle">Support card subtitle</h6>
      </div>

      <img class="img-fluid" src="https://placehold.it/800x400"
      alt="Card image cap">

      <div class="card-block">
        <p class="card-text">
          Lorem ipsum dolor sit amet, at suscipit sodales eget
          ante ultricies mauris. Etiam dolor felis morbi nibh,
          mollit porttitor tempor, dignissim magna pellentesque
          dictumst bibendum dictum integer.
        </p>
      </div>

      <div class="card-block">
        <a href="#" class="card-link">Card link</a>
        <a href="#" class="card-link">Another link</a>
      </div>

      <div class="card-footer">
        2 days ago
      </div>
    </div>

  </div>
  <div class="col-md-4">
    <div class="card">
      <img class="card-img-top img-fluid"
      src="https://placehold.it/800x400" alt="Card image cap">

      <div class="card-block">
        <blockquote class="card-blockquote">
```

```
          <p>Lorem ipsum dolor sit amet, consectetur adipiscing
          elit. Integer posuere erat a ante.</p>
          <footer>Someone famous in <cite title="Source
          Title">Source Title</cite></footer>
        </blockquote>
      </div>
    </div>
  </div>

  <div class="col-md-4">
    <div class="card">
      <div class="card-block">
        <p class="card-text">
          Lorem ipsum dolor sit amet, at suscipit sodales eget
          ante ultricies mauris. Etiam dolor felis morbi nibh,
          mollit porttitor tempor, dignissim magna pellentesque
          dictumst bibendum dictum integer.
        </p>
      </div>

      <img class="card-img-bottom img-fluid"
      src="https://placehold.it/800x400" alt="Card image cap">
    </div>
  </div>

  <div class="col-md-4">
    <div class="card">
      <img class="card-img img-fluid"
      src="https://placehold.it/800x400" alt="Card image cap">

      <div class="card-img-overlay">
        <h4 class="card-title">Card title</h4>
        <p class="card-text">Lorem ipsum dolor sit amet, at
        suscipit.</p>
      </div>
    </div>
  </div>

  <div class="col-md-4">
    <div class="card card-inverse" style="background-color:
    black">
      <div class="card-block">
        <h3 class="card-title">Card Title</h3>
        <p class="card-text">Lorem ipsum dolor sit amet, at
        suscipit sodales eget ante ultricies mauris. </p>
```

```
      </div>
    </div>
  </div>

  <div class="col-md-4">
    <div class="card card-inverse card-primary">
      <div class="card-block">
        <h3 class="card-title">Card Title</h3>
        <p class="card-text">Lorem ipsum dolor sit amet, at
        suscipit sodales eget ante ultricies mauris.</p>
      </div>
    </div>
  </div>

  <div class="col-md-4">
    <div class="card card-inverse card-success">
      <div class="card-block">
        <h3 class="card-title">Card Title</h3>
        <p class="card-text">Lorem ipsum dolor sit amet, at
        suscipit sodales eget ante ultricies mauris.</p>
      </div>
    </div>
  </div>

  <div class="col-md-4">
    <div class="card card-inverse card-info">
      <div class="card-block">
        <h3 class="card-title">Card Title</h3>
        <p class="card-text">Lorem ipsum dolor sit amet, at
        suscipit sodales eget ante ultricies mauris.</p>
      </div>
    </div>
  </div>

  <div class="col-md-4">
    <div class="card card-inverse card-warning">
      <div class="card-block">
        <h3 class="card-title">Card Title</h3>
        <p class="card-text">Lorem ipsum dolor sit amet, at
        suscipit sodales eget ante ultricies mauris.</p>
      </div>
    </div>
  </div>
```

```
<div class="col-md-4">
  <div class="card card-inverse card-danger">
    <div class="card-block">
      <h3 class="card-title">Card Title</h3>
      <p class="card-text">Lorem ipsum dolor sit amet, at
      suscipit sodales eget ante ultricies mauris.</p>
    </div>
  </div>
</div>
</div>
```

Here is how the code looks:

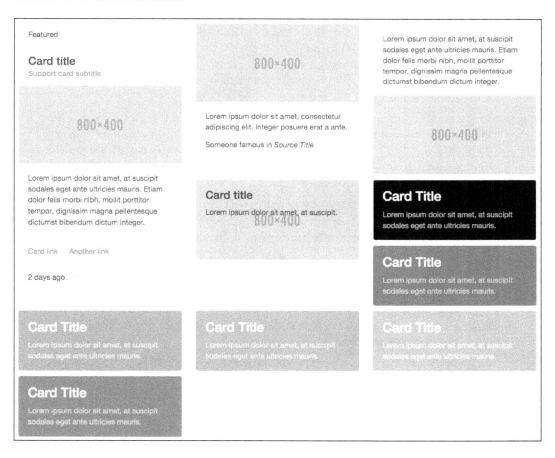

Here, I've created multiple cards so that it is easier to demonstrate all of their subparts and different styles.

Here is how the previous code works:

- To create a card, we need to use the `.card` class.

- By default, card width is 100% of its parent container. Therefore, here we are using a grid system to control width.

- In the first card, we have a header, which is created using the `.card-header` class. Then, we have a card block, inside which we have a title and subtitle. A card block is a part of a card that has padding. Whenever you need padding in any part of the card, simply use the `.card-block` class. A card title is created using `.card-title`, and a card subtitle is created using the `.card-subtitle` class. The `.card-title` and `.card-subtitle` classes simply give appropriate margins. Then, we simply have a responsive image. After that, we have a paragraph using the `.card-text` class. The `.card-text` class makes sure that the last child element doesn't have any bottom margin. Then, we have two links with the `.card-link` class. `.card-link` applies a left margin to all `.card-link` classes from the second one. And finally, we have a card footer, which is created using `.card-footer`.

- In the second card, we have a responsive image and then a block quote. We have added the `.card-img-top` class to the image, which adds a top-right and top-left border radius to the image. We have also added `.card-blockquote` to the block quote to remove the margin, padding, and left border from the block quote.

- In the third card, we simply have some text and a responsive image. We have added the `.card-img-bottom` class to the responsive image, which adds a bottom-right and bottom-left border radius to the image.

- The fourth card we created is for demonstrating card overlays. First, we added a responsive image with the `.card-img` class, which adds a border radius to all the corners. And then, we created an overlay using the `.card-img-overlay` class, which simply makes the position of the element absolute with some padding and no top, right, left, and bottom, thus putting the content on top of the card.

- By default, cards use dark text and assume a light background. Add `.card-inverse` for white text and specify the `background-color` and `border-color` values to go with it. The fifth card is a demonstration of `.card-inverse`. Bootstrap 4 also provides a few classes that add a background color and border color to cards. These classes are demonstrated in the last five cards.

Card groups, decks, and columns

Card groups let you render cards as a single, attached element with equal width and height columns. Card groups only apply to screen sizes greater than 544px.

If you need a set of same-sized cards that aren't attached to one another, then use card decks instead of card groups. Card decks only apply to screen sizes greater than 544px.

Finally, card columns let you organize cards into Masonry-like columns. Card columns only apply to screen sizes greater than 544px.

Here is a code example of card groups, decks, and columns. Place it at the end of the container element of `index.html`:

```
<div class="card-group">
    <div class="card">
        <img class="card-img-top img-fluid"
        src="https://placehold.it/800x400" alt="Card image cap">
        <div class="card-block">
            <p class="card-text">
                Lorem ipsum dolor sit amet, at suscipit sodales
                eget ante ultricies mauris. Etiam dolor felis
                morbi nibh, mollit porttitor tempor, dignissim
                magna pellentesque dictumst bibendum dictum
                integer.
            </p>
        </div>
    </div>
    <div class="card">
        <img class="card-img-top img-fluid"
        src="https://placehold.it/800x400" alt="Card image cap">
    </div>
    <div class="card">
        <img class="card-img-top img-fluid"
        src="https://placehold.it/800x400" alt="Card image cap">
    </div>
    <div class="card">
        <img class="card-img-top img-fluid"
        src="https://placehold.it/800x400" alt="Card image cap">
    </div>
    <div class="card">
        <img class="card-img-top img-fluid"
        src="https://placehold.it/800x400" alt="Card image cap">
    </div>
    <div class="card">
```

```
                <img class="card-img-top img-fluid"
                src="https://placehold.it/800x400" alt="Card image cap">
        </div>
    </div>


    <br>
    <div class="card-deck-wrapper">
        <div class="card-deck">

            <div class="card">
                <img class="card-img-top img-fluid"
                src="https://placehold.it/800x400" alt="Card image
                cap">
                <div class="card-block">
                    <p class="card-text">
                        Lorem ipsum dolor sit amet, at suscipit
                        sodales eget ante ultricies mauris. Etiam
                        dolor felis morbi nibh, mollit porttitor
                        tempor, dignissim magna pellentesque dictumst
                        bibendum dictum integer.
                    </p>
                </div>
            </div>
            <div class="card">
                <img class="card-img-top img-fluid"
                src="https://placehold.it/800x400" alt="Card image
                cap">
            </div>
            <div class="card">
                <img class="card-img-top img-fluid"
                src="https://placehold.it/800x400" alt="Card image
                cap">
            </div>
            <div class="card">
                <img class="card-img-top img-fluid"
                src="https://placehold.it/800x400" alt="Card image
                cap">
            </div>
            <div class="card">
                <img class="card-img-top img-fluid"
                src="https://placehold.it/800x400" alt="Card image
                cap">
            </div>
            <div class="card">
```

```
            <img class="card-img-top img-fluid"
            src="https://placehold.it/800x400" alt="Card image
            cap">
        </div>
    </div>
</div>

<br>
<div class="card-columns">
    <div class="card">
        <img class="card-img-top img-fluid"
        src="https://placehold.it/800x400" alt="Card image cap">
        <div class="card-block">
            <p class="card-text">
                Lorem ipsum dolor sit amet, at suscipit sodales
                eget ante ultricies mauris. Etiam dolor felis
                morbi nibh, mollit porttitor tempor, dignissim
                magna pellentesque dictumst bibendum dictum
                integer.
            </p>
        </div>
    </div>
    <div class="card">
        <img class="card-img-top img-fluid"
        src="https://placehold.it/800x400" alt="Card image cap">
    </div>
    <div class="card">
        <img class="card-img-top img-fluid"
        src="https://placehold.it/800x400" alt="Card image cap">
    </div>
    <div class="card">
        <img class="card-img-top img-fluid"
        src="https://placehold.it/800x400" alt="Card image cap">
    </div>
    <div class="card">
        <img class="card-img-top img-fluid"
        src="https://placehold.it/800x400" alt="Card image cap">
    </div>
    <div class="card">
        <img class="card-img-top img-fluid"
        src="https://placehold.it/800x400" alt="Card image cap">
    </div>
</div>
```

Here is the output of the code:

800×400 800×400 800×400 800×400 800×400 800×400

Lorem ipsum dolor
sit amet, at suscipit
sodales eget ante
ultricies mauris.
Etiam dolor felis
morbi nibh, mollit
porttitor tempor,
dignissim magna
pellentesque
dictumst bibendum
dictum integer.

800×400 800×400 800×400 800×400 800×400 800×400

Lorem ipsum dolor sit amet, at
suscipit sodales eget ante
ultricies mauris. Etiam dolor
felis morbi nibh, mollit porttitor
tempor, dignissim magna
pellentesque dictumst
bibendum dictum integer.

800×400 800×400 800×400

Lorem ipsum dolor sit amet, at suscipit
sodales eget ante ultricies mauris. Etiam
dolor felis morbi nibh, mollit porttitor
tempor, dignissim magna pellentesque
dictumst bibendum dictum integer.

800×400 800×400

800×400

As you can see, we have used the `.card-group` class to create a class group. We have used `.card-deck-wrapper` and `.card-deck` to create a card deck and, finally, `.card-columns` to organize cards into Masonry-like columns.

Outline buttons

Bootstrap 4 has added some new button styles with **outline buttons**. Outline buttons appear hollow or are simply inverses of regular buttons.

Here is example code to demonstrate outline buttons. Place this code at the end of the container element of `index.html`:

```
<hr>
<button type="button" class="btn btn-primary-
outline">Primary</button>
<button type="button" class="btn btn-secondary-
outline">Secondary</button>
<button type="button" class="btn btn-success-
outline">Success</button>
<button type="button" class="btn btn-warning-
outline">Warning</button>
<button type="button" class="btn btn-danger-
outline">Danger</button>
<hr>
```

Here is how the code looks:

Moving from Less to Sass

The Bootstrap 4 source is written in Sass instead of Less. Less was used until Bootstrap 3. This is great because Sass tends to be more favorable by frontend developers. It also compiles faster. Also, it doesn't seem as if there are currently any plans for a Less version. You can find the source files at `https://github.com/twbs/bootstrap/tree/v4-dev`.

Text alignment and float utility classes

Utility classes for floats and text alignment now have responsive ranges. Bootstrap 4 has dropped nonresponsive text alignment and float classes.

Responsive text alignment classes are of the `text-[xs/sm/md/lg/xl]-[left/right/center]` format. For example, the `text-lg-left` class left aligns text on viewports sized `lg` or wider.

Classes of the format `pull-[xs/sm/md/lg/xl]-[left/right/none]` float an element to the left or right or disable floating based on the current viewport size. For example, the `pull-xs-left` class floats the element left on all viewport sizes.

Reboot

Bootstrap 3 used `Normalize.css` as its CSS reset. In Bootstrap 4, the reset and Bootstrap base styles are combined into a single file called `reboot.scss`.

Flexbox support

Flexbox support has finally come to Bootstrap in Bootstrap 4. To enable various components and grid systems to use Flexbox, you can download the Flexbox version of the Bootstrap CSS file, which is available on their download page: `http://v4-alpha.getbootstrap.com/getting-started/download/`.

Remember that Flexbox has poor browser support, so think twice before deciding to use it. Here is a diagram that shows the browser support of Flexbox:

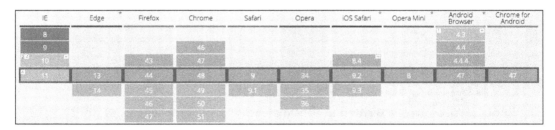

You can also change the value of the `$enable-flex` to `true` Sass variable and compile it to generate the Flexbox version of the Bootstrap CSS.

Learn more about Flexbox support in Bootstrap 4 at `http://v4-alpha.getbootstrap.com/getting-started/flexbox/`.

JavaScript improvements

In the source files, all the JavaScript plugins have been written using ES6, and for distribution, it is compiled with Babel. They also now come with UMD support.

Now that IE 8 support has been dropped, it's safe to always use jQuery 2.0 with Bootstrap. jQuery 2.0 is smaller and faster and has more features.

Adding Tether

Tether is a JavaScript library for efficiently making an absolutely positioned element stay next to another element on the page. For example, you might want a tooltip or dialog to open and remain next to the relevant item on the page.

In Bootstrap 4, Tether is integrated into tooltips and popovers for better auto-placement and performance. So, to make tooltips and popovers work in Bootstrap 4, you have to enqueue `tether.js`.

Add this line of code to the top of the `bootstrap.min.js` file to enqueue tether from a CDN:

```
<script
src="https://cdnjs.cloudflare.com/ajax/libs/tether/1.2.0/js/tether
.min.js"></script>
```

The 21:9 aspect ratio class

A new aspect ratio class has been added to Bootstrap 4: the `.embed-responsive-21by9` class for a `21:9` ratio. Here is an example of it:

```
<div class="embed-responsive embed-responsive-21by9">
        <iframe class="embed-responsive-item"
        src="http://packtpub.com"></iframe>
    </div>
```

Customizing Bootstrap 4

In Bootstrap 4, all the customization variable options are consolidated to a single file called `_variables.scss`, where you can compile your Sass on the fly and with little effort. This used be previously all done in a separate stylesheet.

This file provides a lot more customization options than Bootstrap used to provide earlier.

Glyphicons dropped

Glyphicons have been removed from the build, that is, Boostrap 4 doesn't include an icon pack. You need to manually enqueue a icon pack.

Summary

So, we have seen all the new features of Bootstrap 4. The grid system and cards are the two major additions to Bootstrap 4. It's absolutely fine to switch to Bootstrap 4 now. Although Bootstrap 4 drops support for IE 8, it's still fine as users should also move with the technology. From now on, Bootstrap 4 will be used in all the projects we will create in this book.

10
Building User Interfaces Using React

Writing code for reactive UI is a difficult task, as writing code to manipulate the DOM using JavaScript whenever the application state changes is difficult and it makes understanding the application difficult. Therefore, the MVC architecture was introduced, where we define the UI and application state separately, and the UI is updated automatically as the application state changes. MVC framework views have been concentrating on making the writing of code for reactive UIs easier but not increasing rendering performance, reusability, and ease of debugging. This is what React aims to solve. It not only makes writing code for reactive UI easier but also takes care of rendering performance, reusability, and ease of debugging.

In this chapter, we will cover the following topics:

- What React is
- Virtual DOM technology
- Component-based UI development using React
- One-way dataflow programming
- Using JSX to write React code
- Using React on the server side to build isomorphic apps
- Many other topics to help us get a good hold on React

Introducing React

React is a JavaScript library for building reactive UIs. We usually use jQuery or pure JavaScript to manipulate a reactive UI whenever the application state changes, which makes it difficult to reuse and understand the code. Instead, we can use React, which lets us declare how the UI behaves based on the application state, and it automatically updates the UI whenever the application state changes. There are lots of libraries and technologies, such as web components and templating engines, that aim to make the building of UIs easier, but React stands out from the crowd as it makes it easy to build reusable and high-performance reactive UIs.

React is also used as a view library because it is exactly what a view library is supposed to be. A view holds the UI of the application and defines how the UI changes based on the application state, that is, how the application state is displayed. As it's just a view library, it doesn't tell us how to manage, access, and mutate the application state. It can be used as the view layer in any kind of architecture and framework.

Remember that React is a library and not a framework such as Angular or Ember. Thus, React can be used with Angular to make Angular views better in terms of performance and reusability.

For example, there is an AngularJS module named ngReact that lets React be used as a view in AngularJS.

Even the Flux architecture uses React as its view. We will learn more about Flux in the next chapter.

React is always used with a framework as it only defines the UI but doesn't tell us how to manage the application logic and state, just like a template library or web component is always used with a framework.

Is React a templating engine?

React is not a templating engine. The views of most of the popular MVC frameworks are of a template system. In a templating system, we write HTML with a template language for the UI, and it is processed in order to generate the final HTML. For example, an AngularJS view is a template system that's composed of directives, expressions, and so on. React is not a templating engine because we don't write HTML. Instead, we define the structure of the DOM using JavaScript. React can also do much more than what a templating engine can do. It can also capture user events in the UI. This is how it differs from traditional views. It's just that React works in a different way than a template system.

When building user interfaces using React, we don't write any HTML to build the UI like when using other frameworks and libraries; instead, we declare the DOM structure using JavaScript only. This programming style is what makes React able to implement various algorithms and technologies to achieve high rendering performance and reusability.

Before we get further into learning React, let's first set up a project to use it.

Setting up a basic React project

At the time of writing, the latest version of React was 0.14.7. This is the version this book uses. First, visit `https://facebook.github.io/react/downloads.html` to download React. Here, you will find two types of React builds, namely, production and development builds. The difference between these two build is that the development build is uncompressed and includes extra warnings, whereas the production build is compressed, includes extra performance optimizations, and strips all errors.

You should use the development build when your application is in the development phase. Once your application is ready for deployment, you should change to the production build.

Again, you will find two types of production and development build: one with add-ons and the other without. We will use the development version without add-ons.

You will find CDN links as well as links to download and enqueue React manually. React is composed of two files: `react.js` and `react-dom.js`. Download both of them manually.

Create a folder named `react-demo` and place both the files in it. Then, create a file called `index.html` and put this code in it:

```html
<!DOCTYPE html>
<html>
  <head>
    <meta charset="UTF-8" />
    <title>React Demo</title>

    <script src="react.js"></script>
    <script src="react-dom.js"></script>
  </head>
  <body>
```

```
      <script>
        //place React code here
      </script>
    </body>
  </html>
```

Later on in this chapter, we will learn more about why React is composed of two files and not one. For now, just ignore this.

Virtual DOM

A browser interprets HTML and creates a DOM. A DOM is a tree-like structure that defines the structure of the page. The browser then renders the DOM on the page. The DOM API is what we use to manipulate the DOM. When we manipulate it, the browser re-renders the manipulated parts.

The problem is not with how the DOM works, but how we programmatically alter it. Manipulating nodes of a DOM requires expertise; otherwise, we could often end up re-rendering lots of nodes unnecessarily, which would result in poor rendering performance.

For example, imagine we have a large list of products in an e-commerce website. We also have a filter widget to filter the items. When we change the values in the filter widget, the list items are reloaded and the complete list is re-rendered, which requires a lot of manipulation to the DOM and can result in bad rendering performance. To get better performance, we can actually manipulate only specific parts of the list, such as product titles, image, and cost. But writing code for this is going to be hard.

Let's take another example. If you are using ng-repeat to display a list, then adding a new item to the list will cause the complete re-rending of the list. So, if Facebook or Instagram had used ng-repeat, then whenever we scrolled down, the whole set of posts would have been re-rendered. The solution to this problem is instead of using ng-repeat, which re-renders the whole list, we can append a new post to the end of the list using jQuery or pure JavaScript. But if you want to maintain the posts that are being displayed, then you will end up writing some more complex code.

Due to these kinds of problem, virtual DOM was introduced. Virtual DOM makes sure that anyone can write complex reactive UI code without worrying about performance. Virtual DOM is the secret that React implements to achieve rendering performance.

A virtual DOM is an abstract version of the real DOM, that is, a description of the real DOM. Virtual DOM elements are just JavaScript objects whereas real DOM elements are real UI elements. Virtual DOM is much faster as it's just a JavaScript data structure and manipulating it doesn't automatically re-render the UI. Earlier, I said that in React, you don't write any HTML but instead declare the structure of the DOM. Actually, you declare the structure of the virtual DOM, not the real DOM. React keeps the real DOM in sync with virtual DOM. Whenever the application state changes to update the UI, React uses complex algorithms to compare the real DOM with the virtual DOM and finds as few mutations as possible for the real DOM to sync with the virtual DOM. We will later see how these algorithms actually find the difference and mutate the real DOM. For example, if we have a list in the virtual DOM and we remove the list and add a new list with just an extra item, then, only the new item is rendered when synced with the real DOM, not the whole list.

Let's look at some example code to print **Hello World** using React. Inside the `index.html` body tag, place this code:

```
<div id="container1"></div>
```

We are going to display **Hello World** inside this `div` element. Place this code in the script tag of the `index.html` file to display **Hello World**:

```
var helloBold = React.createElement("b", {}, "Hello");
var worldItalic = React.createElement("i", {}, " World");
var helloWorld = React.createElement("a", {href: "#"}, helloBold,
worldItalic);

ReactDOM.render(helloWorld, document.getElementById("container1"));
```

Here is how the code's output looks:

Let's understand how the code works.

React.createElement is used to create an object of a ReactElement interface. A ReactElement object is a light, stateless, and virtual representation of a real DOM element, but it's not a real DOM element. It's a virtual DOM, basically. ReactElement and real DOM elements are of different interfaces. The first parameter of React.createElement can be an HTML tag name or an object of a ReactClass interface. We will learn more about ReactClass later on. The second argument is an object containing attributes of the HTML tag or properties of the ReactClass object. And then, we can pass an infinite number of arguments, which can be strings, ReactElement objects, or ReactClass objects. All the arguments after the second argument are treated as children of the ReactElement object that's going to be created. If the children are dynamically decided, then you can provide an array as the third argument.

Here, we created three ReactElement objects. helloWorld is an anchor tag with helloBold and worldItalic as its children. We assigned the href attribute of the anchor tag to #.

ReactDOM.render is used to render ReactElement objects in the real DOM. ReactDOM.render takes a ReactElement object as first argument, and the second argument is the reference to the container element in the real DOM inside which we want to add to the ReactElement.

Here, we've rendered the anchor tag inside the container element.

 As a ReactElement object is stateless, we cannot assign any UI event handlers to the properties object. Also, directly mutating the properties passed to the ReactElement object will not have any effect, as React doesn't watch the properties directly.

In the beginning, it may feel as if ReactElement and real DOM elements are just created in different ways and their interface is the same, but this is not true. Here are a few differences:

- Instead of the class attribute, you need to use className
- Instead of the for attribute, you need to use the htmlFor attribute
- The style attribute cannot be a string; it has to be a object

There are many more. We will explore them as we go deeper.

Components

You can use React using only `ReactElement` objects, but to take advantage of React, you have to use React components. `ReactElement` objects are stateless and immutable and therefore useless for building reactive UIs. Also, they don't provide a structured mechanism for UI reusability.

A React component is a reusable custom tag that is mutable and encapsulated with an embedded state, that is, changes to the state or properties will mutate the UI. For example, we can have a component named `clock` that takes the current time as an attribute and displays a clock with the passed time. Another exchange could be a Bitcoin price component that displays Bitcoin prices in real time.

A component state is internal to the component. It's created and mutated inside the component. However, the properties of a component cannot be mutated inside the component; rather, they can be mutated by the code that created the component instance.

You can break your complete UI into components — this is the style of coding that's recommended when building a UI using react. You can use components inside components as well. Before we get further into components, let's rewrite the previous **Hello World** code using components.

Inside the `index.html` body tag, place this code:

```
<div id="container1"></div>
```

We are going to display **Hello World** inside this `div` element. Place this code in the `script` tag of the `index.html` file to display **Hello World**:

```
var anchorWithBoldItalic = React.createClass({
  render: function() {
    return React.createElement(
      "a",
      {href: this.props.href},
      React.createElement("b", {}, this.props.boldText),
      React.createElement("i", {}, this.props.italicText)
    );
  }
});

var HelloWorld = React.createElement(anchorWithBoldItalic, {href:
"#", boldText: "Hello", italicText: " World" });

ReactDOM.render(HelloWorld, document.getElementById("container2"));
```

Here is the output of the previous code:

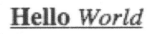

Here is how the code works:

1. A component is created using the `React.createClass` function. This function takes an object, and the object must have a `render` property assigned to a function that returns a `ReactElement` object. The `ReactElement` object returned by the `render` method is said to be the content of the component, that is, it states how the tag is rendered. Whenever we try to display the tag, the contents of the tag are displayed in place.

2. `React.createClass` returns a component. To use the component, we need to create instances of it. Like `React.createElement` is used to create a `ReactElement` object for an HTML tag, it can also create a `ReactElement` object for a component. So, `React.createElement` is used to create instances of a component. `this.props` is used inside the component to access its properties.

3. Here, we created a component called `anchorWithBoldItalic`, which is an anchor element with some text displayed as bold and some displayed as italic.

4. Then, we created a `ReactElement` object for our component and finally rendered it using `ReactDOM.render`.

 Remember that mutating properties after a component instance has been created will re-render the component.

One-way data binding

In the previous subsection, I stated that a component has an enclosing nature. Whenever we make changes to the state, the component is rendered. Components also let you register UI event handlers, and you can mutate the state inside the event handlers too.

React lets you manage, access, and mutate UI state but not application state. The difference between UI state and application state is that the UI state represents the data that's used to manipulate the UI whereas the application state represents the data that's displayed in the UI. For example, let's assume that you have a comment box. The comments in the comment box are the application state, and the **View more comments** button is the UI state, which may or may not be displayed, depending on whether there are any more posts.

Data binding between a UI and its state is only one-way. This means that user actions on the UI cannot alter the UI state directly, but the UI state can alter the UI.

It may seem as if this were a limitation as AngularJS and other popular frameworks provide two-way data binding, but this is actually a feature. This feature makes it easier to understand and debug applications.

Many developers tend to use UI state as application state, but for complex and large apps, this will cause issues and make it difficult to build the application.

Let's look at an example of how to use component state by building a button that hides/shows a box when clicked on.

Place this code in the <body> tag of the index.html file:

```
<div id="container3"></div>
```

We will display the component inside this container element.

Place this code inside the script tag:

```
var hideShowBoxButton = React.createClass({
  getInitialState: function(){
    return {
      display: "inline-block"
    }
  },
  handleClick: function(){
    if(this.state.display == "inline-block")
    {
      this.setState({display: "none"});
    }
    else
    {
```

```
        this.setState({display: "inline-block"});
      }
    },
    render: function(){
      return React.createElement(
        "div",
        {},
        React.createElement(
          "a",
          {href: "#", onClick: this.handleClick},
          "Click to Show/Hide"
        ),
        React.createElement(
          "span",
          {
            style: {
              display: this.state.display,
              height: 30,
              width: 30,
              backgroundColor: "red"
            }
          }
        )
      );
    }
});

ReactDOM.render(React.createElement(hideShowBoxButton),
document.getElementById("container3"));
```

This is the output of the previous code:

This is how the code works:

1. At first, we create a new component.
2. The `getInitialState` method returns the initial state of the component.

3. Then, we create a click handler that toggles the display state. When mutating the state, you must use `this.setState` and not directly mutate the state using `this.state`.

4. Then, we create the `render` method, which displays a button and a small red box. The `render` method sets the display style of the box to the display state. So, whenever the state changes, React renders the component. Instead of rendering the complete component, React re-renders it by comparing the virtual DOM with the real DOM and mutating only the required DOM elements. This is how it achieves rendering performance.

5. Finally, we create a component instance and add it to the container element.

6. Also note that we've only specified a number for height and width without any unit. In such a case, the unit is pixels.

Isomorphic UI development

Isomorphic development is where we can use the same code in both the frontend and backend.

Till now, we've seen how to use React in the frontend to build reactive UI, but the same React code can also be used in the backend. When used in the backend, React outputs HTML and doesn't provide any kind of UI performance advantage or reactivity.

The isomorphic nature of React is one of the things that make it so popular and powerful. It has made many things easier. For example, it makes it easier to prevent FOUC by letting us pre-render the page in the backend, and then in the frontend: the same components will just add event bindings.

React code not only executes in Node.js but can also be executed in PHP, Ruby, .NET, and some other major backend languages.

Due to the fact that React can be used in both the frontend and backend, the React developer team decided to split React into two files: React core and another part that is specific to the executing environment. That's why when we included React in our HTML file earlier, we included two files. The React core contains `React.createElement`, `React.createClass`, and so on whereas the React DOM contains `ReactDOM.render` and so on.

Let's look at an example of how to use React in Node.js by creating and displaying the previous hello world component in Node.js. Create a directory named `React-Server-Demo`. Inside it, create files named `app.js` and `package.json`.

Inside the `package.json` file, place this code:

```
{
  "name": "React-Server-Demo",
  "dependencies": {
    "express": "4.13.3",
    "react": "0.14.7",
    "react-dom": "0.14.7"
  }
}
```

Then, run `npm install` to download the Express and React modules. Now, in the `app.js` file, place the following code and run the `node app.js` command:

```
var React = require("react");
var ReactDOMServer = require("react-dom/server");
var express = require("express");
var app = express();

var anchorWithBoldItalic = React.createClass({
  render: function() {
    return React.createElement(
      "a",
      {href: this.props.href},
      React.createElement("b", {}, this.props.boldText),
      React.createElement("i", {}, this.props.italicText)
    );
  }
});

var HelloWorld = React.createElement(anchorWithBoldItalic, {href:
"#", boldText: "Hello", italicText: " World" });

app.get("/", function(httpRequest, httpResponse, next){
  var reactHtml = ReactDOMServer.renderToString(HelloWorld);
  httpResponse.send(reactHtml)
})

app.listen(8080);
```

Now, open `http://localhost:8080/` in your browser; you'll see this output:

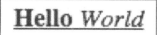

This is how the code works:

1. First, we import the React core module, then the React server-side module, and then Express.
2. We're using the same code we used earlier to create the component.
3. Then, we create a route for the root path.
4. The root path uses the `renderToString` method of the React server-side module to generate the HTML code of the component.
5. Finally, we send the HTML to the client.

 Note that by default, React will be in development mode. To use React in production mode, set the environment variable `NODE_ENV` to `production`.

Getting started with JSX

Writing JavaScript to define a tree-like structure and attributes while building UI using React is difficult and also makes it difficult to understand the UI. So, the React team came up with an alternative syntax to write React code, which is easier to write and understand. This alternate syntax is called JSX. JSX stands for JavaScript syntax extension. It looks similar to XML. Files that contain JSX code have the `.jsx` extension.

Compiling JSX

Of course, browsers and server-side engines cannot understand and interpret JSX; therefore, we need to compile JSX into pure JavaScript before using it.

There are various open source JSX compilers. You can find the list at `https://github.com/facebook/react/wiki/Complementary-Tools#build-tools`. The most popular and recommended compiler for JSX is Babel. Babel can be installed (`https://babeljs.io/docs/setup/`), we can use the Babel compiler online (`https://babeljs.io/repl/`), and we can also embed the Babel compiler in our HTML page so that it compiles in the browser.

For the purpose of demonstration, we will embed the Babel compiler in our HTML page. Compiling takes time, so in production sites, you should never embed the compiler in web pages; instead, you should precompile and serve JSX code.

To embed the Babel compiler in a webpage, visit `https://cdnjs.com/libraries/babel-core` and download the Babel core. These are CDN links, so they can be embedded directly, but let's download and embed them in our webpage. Download the `browser.min.js` file and place it in the `react-demo` directory. And then, embed it in the `index.html` page by placing the following code in the `<head>` tag:

```
<script src="browser.min.js"></script>
```

Now, create a new `<script>` tag at the end of the `body` tag and set the `type` attribute to `text/babel` so that the Babel compiler knows which code to compile. Here is how the code should look:

```
<script type="text/babel">
</script>
```

From now on, all the JSX code will be placed in this script tag.

> **JSX editors**
> There are extensions available for almost all the popular code editors to properly highlight JSX syntax.

JSX syntax

Let's rewrite the data-binding example code using JSX syntax. Place this code in the `body` tag to create a new container element:

```
<div id="container4"></div>
```

Here is the JSX code. Place it in the `script` tag that will be compiled by Babel:

```
var HideShowBoxButton = React.createClass({
  getInitialState: function(){
    return {
      display: "inline-block"
    }
  },
  handleClick: function(){
    if(this.state.display == "inline-block")
    {
```

```
        this.setState({display: "none"});
      }
      else
      {
        this.setState({display: "inline-block"});
      }
    },
    render: function(){
      var boxStyle = {
        display: this.state.display,
        height: 30,
        width: 30,
        backgroundColor: "red"
      };

      return (
        <div>
          <a href="#" onClick={this.handleClick}>Click to
          Show/Hide</a>
          <span style={boxStyle}></span>
        </div>
      )
    }
});

ReactDOM.render(<HideShowBoxButton />,
document.getElementById("container4"));
```

The output of the code is as follows:

Before we see how this code works, let's look at its compiled version:

```
var HideShowBoxButton = React.createClass({
  displayName: "HideShowBoxButton",

  getInitialState: function getInitialState() {
    return {
      display: "inline-block"
    };
  },
```

```
        handleClick: function handleClick() {
          if (this.state.display == "inline-block") {
            this.setState({ display: "none" });
          }
          else
          {
            this.setState({ display: "inline-block" });
          }
        },
        render: function render() {
          var boxStyle = {
            display: this.state.display,
            height: "30px",
            width: "30px",
            backgroundColor: "red"
          };

          return React.createElement(
            "div",
            null,
            React.createElement(
              "a",
              { href: "#", onClick: this.handleClick },
              "Click to Show/Hide"
            ),
            React.createElement("span", { style: boxStyle })
          );
        }
      });

      ReactDOM.render(React.createElement(HideShowBoxButton, null),
      document.getElementById("container4"));
```

This compiled version will give you a basic idea of how JSX syntax works. Let's understand how the previous JSX code works.

In a nutshell, JSX is used to write the `React.createElement` method in XML-like syntax. The XML tag name is the first argument, the attributes are the second argument, and finally, the child elements are the other arguments of `React.createElement`.

If a JSX tag name starts with a lowercase letter, it's an HTML tag, whereas if it starts with a capital letter, it's a component. So here, we made the component name start with a capital H. Had we used a small H, it would have been treated as an HTML tag, and `<hideShowBoxButton></hideShowBoxButton>` would have been inserted into the page, which would have rendered nothing.

In the `HideShowBoxButton` component, except the `render` method code, everything else is the same. We rewrote the `render` method using JSX syntax.

JSX provides {} braces to wrap JavaScript expressions while assigning them to attributes or using them as child elements. Here, we've assigned JavaScript expressions to `onClick` and `style` attributes.

Finally, we created an instance of the component using JSX syntax.

In the compiled code, you will find a `displayName` property in the object passed to `React.createClass`. The `displayName` property is used for debugging. If not set, it's set to the component name while compiling.

Digging into components

Let's dig further into components and master them. We'll look at component composition and ownership. Learning this will help us build complex reactive UIs that are easier to manage.

Component composition

Composability is a feature that lets you use a component inside another component's `render` method.

Let's look at a basic example of component composition. First, create a new container element. To do so, place the following code in the `body` tag:

```
<div id="container5"></div>
```

Here is the component composition example code. Place this code in the `script` tag that's compiled by Babel:

```
var ResponsiveImage = React.createClass({
  render: function(){

    var imgWidth = {
      width: "100%"
    }
```

```
      return (
        <img src={this.props.src} style={imgWidth} />
      )
    }
})

var Card = React.createClass({
  render: function(){
    var CardContainerStyle = {
      maxWidth: 300,
      backgroundColor: "grey"
    }

    return (
      <div style={CardContainerStyle}>
        <h4>{this.props.heading}</h4>
        <ResponsiveImage src={this.props.src} />
      </div>
    )
  }
})

ReactDOM.render(<Card src="http://placehold.it/350x150"
heading="This is a Card Header" />,
document.getElementById("container5"));
```

This is the output of the code:

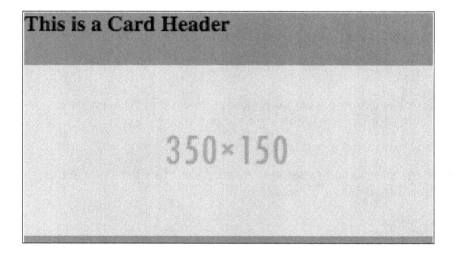

Here, we've created two different components. Inside the Card component, we are using the `ResponsiveImage` component to display a responsive image in it.

Component ownership

When components are used inside other components' `render` methods, they are said to have an owner-ownee relationship and not a parent-child relationship. Component X is said to be the owner of component Y if component X created an instance of component Y in its `render` method.

 Note that component X is not called the parent; rather, it's called the owner of component Y.

For example, in the previous code, the `Card` component is the owner of the `ResponsiveImage` component and `<div>` is the parent of `ResponsiveImage`.

If we place a component instance inside the opening and closing tags of a component instance, then they are said to be in a parent-child relationship. The parent can access its children by using the `this.props.children` object. React also provides utility functions to make working with children easier. You can find the utilities at `https://facebook.github.io/react/docs/top-level-api.html#react.children`.

Reconciliation

Reconciliation is the process by which React updates the DOM whenever the state changes. React doesn't re-render everything from scratch when the state changes; instead, it first finds whether a mutation is required by comparing the new virtual DOM with the old one, and if there is a difference, it compares the new virtual DOM with the real DOM and makes the necessary mutations.

 Note that reconciliation doesn't happen only when you change the component state; it also happens when you call `ReactDOM.render` on the same container element again.

Let's see how exactly reconciliation happens by looking at an example. Suppose this is the initial render:

```
<ul>
  <li>Item 1</li>
  <li>Item 2</li>
</ul>
```

If we remove Item 1 from the state, then the render will change to this:

```
<ul>
  <li>Item 2</li>
</ul>
```

React algorithms compare DOM items one by one, and whenever they find a difference between two nodes, they make mutations. So here, React will remove the Item 1 list item by changing the text of the first list item and removing the last one. This process is much faster than removing both the list items and adding a new list item, which is what ng-repeat does and what we used to do using JavaScript.

If the node type is different, React will treat them as two different subtrees, throw away the first one, and build/insert the second one. For example, if we change <ul> to <ol>, the complete <ul> tree will be deleted.

This behavior is fine until you add new items to the end of the list or modify them. In case you add new items to the beginning or in between the list, you will start facing rendering performance issues. To understand the issue, let's take an example. Let's add Item 0 to the beginning. Now, the render will look like this:

```
<ul>
  <li>Item 0</li>
  <li>Item 1</li>
  <li>Item 2</li>
</ul>
```

Here, while reconciling, React will first change the text of the first list item to Item 0, then change the text of the second list item to Item 1, and finally will add a new list item and assign its text to Item 2 instead of simply adding a new list item to the beginning of the list. This behavior makes the rendering actually slower.

React does provide a way to get around this kind of issue as well. It lets us uniquely identify each child by assigning it a unique key. When React reconciles the keyed children, it will ensure that any child with a key will be reordered (instead of being mutated) or destroyed (instead of being reused). A key is assigned using the key attribute.

Let's look at an example of how to create keyed children. Here is the code to create a new container element. Place this code in the body tag:

```
<div id="container6"></div>
```

Here is the React code for creating keyed children:

```
var DynamicList = React.createClass({
  getInitialState: function(){
    return {
      results: this.props.results
    }
  },
  handleClick: function(){
    var results = this.state.results;
    var firstId = results[0].id - 1;
    var firstValue = results[0].value - 1;

    results.unshift({id: firstId, value: firstValue});
    this.setState({results: results});
  },
  render: function(){
    return (
      <div>
        <a href="#" onClick={this.handleClick}>Click to add new
        item</a>
        <ul>
          {this.state.results.map(function(result) {
            return <li key={result.id}> {result.value} </li>;
          })}
        </ul>
      </div>

    )
  }
})

var results = [{id: 1, value: 1}, {id: 2, value: 2}];

ReactDOM.render(<DynamicList results={results} />,
document.getElementById("container6"));
```

Here is the output of the code:

Click to add new item

- 1
- 2

Here, when the anchor element is clicked on, a new object is added to the beginning of the result array. As the state changes, the list is re-rendered. While rendering, React will reorder the list items and add new list items to the beginning instead of mutating them.

 Remember that when dynamically creating component instances, the key should always be supplied to the components in the array, not to the container element of each component in the array.

Default component property values

React lets you define default values for properties in a very declarative way. The default value is used if the parent does not pass a property.

Default values are returned by a method getDefaultProps, which is a member of the object passed to React.createClass. Here is some sample code:

```
var ComponentWithDefaultProps = React.createClass({
  getDefaultProps: function() {
    return {
      value: 'default value'
    };
  }
});
```

Component life cycle methods

Various methods are executed at specific points in a component's lifecycle. Let's look at them.

componentWillMount()

The `componentWillMount()` method is invoked once immediately before the initial rendering occurs. If you call `setState` within this method, `render()` will see the updated state and will be executed only once despite the state change.

componentDidMount()

The `componentDidMount()` method is invoked only on the client side. It is invoked only once after initial rendering has occurred.

componentWillReceiveProps(nextProps)

Directly mutating the properties passed to a component will have no effect because there is no way for React to find value changes as it doesn't watch the properties directly. But sometimes, it is possible for React to predict property value changes, and in that case, it calls the `componentWillReceiveProps` method, if it exists, with the new property values as its parameters, and it also re-renders the component.

For example, if we change the state of the owner of a component, then that sends a signal that the properties of the components it owns might have changed, so it calls the `componentWillReceiveProps` method and re-renders the components it owns.

Let's look at an example to demonstrate the `componentWillReceiveProps` method. We will create a button whose value increments every second. Here is the code to create a new container element. Place it in the `body` tag:

```
<div id="container7"></div>
```

Here is the code for our example. Place this code in the `script` tag that will be compiled by Babel:

```
var ButtonComponent = React.createClass({
  componentWillReceiveProps: function(nextProps){
    console.log("Text changed to " + nextProps.text);
  },
  render: function(){
    return (
      <button>{this.props.text}</button>
    )
  }
})

var ButtonHolderComponent = React.createClass({
  componentDidMount: function(){
```

```
      setInterval(function(){
        this.setState({
          text: this.state.text + 1
        });
      }.bind(this), 1000)
    },
    getInitialState: function(){
      return {
        text: 1
      }
    },
    render: function(){
      return (
        <ButtonComponent text={this.state.text} />
      )
    }
  })

ReactDOM.render(<ButtonHolderComponent />,
document.getElementById("container7"));
```

Here is the output of the code:

In the code, we are changing the state of the owner every second after the initial rendering has occurred. Whenever the state changes, the componentWillReceieveProps object of ButtonComponent is called. Inside the componentWillReceieveProps object, we can use this.props to access the previous values of the properties. The button is rendered whenever its owner's state changes.

Remember that componentWillReceieveProps is called before the component is re-rendered, so we can make any state changes we want inside it.

shouldComponentUpdate(nextProps, nextState)

The shouldComponentUpdate(nextProps, nextState) method is called before the render method is called, that is, before rendering happens. If this method returns false, then rendering is skipped.

Remember that this method is not called before forced updates or initial rendering.

> **What is a forced update?**
>
> React provides a forceUpdate method inside a component, which renders the component when called. This can be used when the render() method depends on some other data instead of just this. props and this.state, as changes to other data don't trigger the render method.

componentWillUpdate(nextProps, nextState)

The componentWillUpdate(nextProps, nextState) method is invoked immediately before rendering when new props or state are being received. This method is not called for the initial render.

Note that you cannot use this.setState inside this method.

componentDidUpdate(prevProps, prevState)

The componentDidUpdate(prevProps, prevState) method is invoked immediately after the component's updates are flushed to the real DOM. This method is not called for the initial render.

componentWillUnmount()

The componentWillUnmount() method is invoked immediately before a component is unmounted from the real DOM.

Mixins

There are times when multiple components share the same code; in such cases, we can use mixins instead of writing the same code again and again.

A **mixin** is an object that holds component methods that can be easily plugged in to any component.

Let's look at an example to demonstrate mixins. Here is the code to create a new container element. Place it in the body tag:

```
<div id="container8"></div>
```

Here is the code for our example. Place it in the script tag that will be compiled by Babel.

```
var Mixin1 = {
  componentWillMount: function(){
    console.log("Component will mount now");
  }
}

var Mixin2 = {
  componentDidMount: function(){
    console.log("Component did mount");
  }
}

var HeadingComponent = React.createClass({
  mixins: [Mixin1, Mixin2],
  render: function(){
    return <h1>React is Awesome</h1>
  }
});

ReactDOM.render(<HeadingComponent />,
document.getElementById("container8"));
```

This is the output of the code on the page:

React is Awesome

And this is the output on the console:

```
Component will mount now
Component did mount
```

Here, we've created two mixins and added them to `HeadingComponent`.
These mixins can be used in any number of methods. Mixins simply increase
code reusability.

Using Refs

Refs are used inside components to return references to real DOM elements
rendered by React. So, instead of assigning an `id` or `class` value to elements, we can
assign refs. It's easier to get references to real DOM elements using refs than `id` or
`class` attributes.

Let's look at a basic example of how to use refs by creating a form. First, create a
container element and place it inside the `body` tag. Here is the code:

```
<div id="container9"></div>
```

Here is the code for the form, which uses refs:

```
var FormComponent = React.createClass({
  clicked: function(){
    console.log(this.refs.myInput.value);
  },
  render: function(){
    return (
      <div>
        <input type="text" placeholder="Write Something"
        ref="myInput" />
        <input type="button" value="Click to Submit"
        onClick={this.clicked} />
      </div>

    )
  }
})

ReactDOM.render(<FormComponent />,
document.getElementById("container9"));
```

The output of this code on the webpage is as follows:

If we enter `Hello World` in the text field and click on the button, then the output of the console is this:

```
Hello World
```

In the previous code, we're assigning a `ref` attribute to the button element. To refer to the button in the methods of the component, we use `this.refs`.

ReactDOMServer.renderToStaticMarkup

Earlier in this chapter, we used React on the server side to generate HTML. The HTML generated by React on the server and client side contains `data-reactid` attributes, which are used by React internally. On the client side, it makes sense to have `data-reactid`, as it is used during reconciliation and other processes and features.

You must be wondering what the point of adding this attribute on the server side is. Actually, it is added so that if you call `ReactDOM.render()` on the client side on a node that already has React server-rendered markup, React will preserve it and only reconcile it.

If you don't want `data-reactid` attributes to be generated on the server side, you can use `renderToStaticMarkup` instead of `renderToString`.

Summary

In this chapter, we learned React up to an intermediate level by covering in depth its features and components, JSX, using it for server-side rendering, reconciliation, and so on. We also learned miscellaneous features such as mixins and refs. Now, you should have a basic understanding of how and when to integrate React into your websites.

In the next chapter, we will learn React in more depth by building an application that uses the Flux and SPA architectures.

11

Building an RSS Reader
Using React and Flux

React is not enough to build a complete application, as it's just the view layer. We
need an architecture for holding the application logic and data, and this is where
Flux comes in. Obviously, React can be used with any other architecture, but Flux
is what is mostly used with React, as Flux is based on unidirectional data flow, like
React. In this chapter, we will build a single-page RSS reader using React and Flux.

We will cover the following topics:

- Flux architecture in depth
- Routing using the React Router library
- Using Flux.js to create a dispatcher
- Using MicroEvent.js to emit events
- Integrating Flux and routing

Understanding Flux

Flux is an application architecture and not a framework. You can think of it as
an alternative to MVC. It was primarily developed to be used with React as both
of them are based on unidirectional data flow. The Flux architecture enforces
unidirectional data flow.

Here is a diagram that shows all the parts of the Flux architecture and how data flows in it:

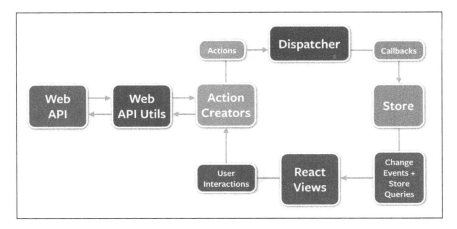

Here is how each part works:

- **Actions**: An action is an object that describes what we want to do and the data that we need to do it. In Flux, all events and data from all sources are converted to actions. Even UI events are converted to actions.

- **Dispatcher**: The dispatcher is a special type of event system. It is used to broadcast actions to registered callbacks. What the dispatcher does is not the same as a pub/sub system, as callbacks are not subscribed to particular events. Instead, every action is dispatched to every registered callback. An application should contain only one dispatcher.

- **Action creators**: Action creators are methods that dispatch actions to the dispatcher.

- **Stores**: Stores are objects that store the application data and logic. Stores react to actions. Callbacks ping the store to take appropriate action whenever an action that the store depends on is dispatched by the dispatcher.

- **React views**: React views are the React components that can retrieve data from stores and display as well as listen to events emitted from stores whenever there is a change in the data stored by them. Note that the events emitted by stores are not converted into actions.

So, in Flux, all the events and data from different sources are dispatched to the dispatcher as actions, then the stores update themselves whenever the dispatcher dispatches actions, and finally, views get updated whenever stores update.

Here is an another diagram, which provides a much higher-level abstraction of how Flux works:

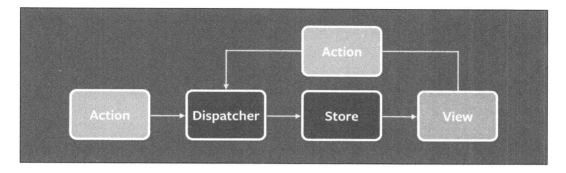

Here you can see that the data flows in a single direction, that is, data and events first go to the **Dispatcher**, then to the **Store**, and finally to the **View**. So, we can say that dispatcher, store, and view are the three major parts of the Flux architecture.

Just as there are many MVC frameworks, such as Angular, Ember, and Backbone, there are many Flux frameworks, such as Fluxible, Reflux, Alt, and Redux. But to keep things simple and easier to learn, we will not use any of these frameworks. Instead, we will use the Flux.js and MicroEvent.js libraries to implement the Flux architecture.

Using Flux.js

The **Flux.js** is a library created by the creators of Flux. It is used to build dispatchers. You can find the Flux.js source code at `https://github.com/facebook/flux` and the CDN version at `https://cdnjs.com/libraries/flux`.

A dispatcher is created using the `Dispatcher` constructor. It has five methods, as follows:

- `register(callback)`: This method lets us register a callback. It returns a string called the `callback` ID to uniquely identify a callback.
- `unregister(id)`: This is a method lets us unregister a registered callback. To unregister, we need to pass the ID of the callback that we want to unregister.
- `waitFor(array)`: This waits for the specified callbacks to be invoked before continuing with the execution of the current callback. This method should only be used by a callback in response to a dispatched action.

- `dispatch(action)`: This dispatches an action to registered callbacks.

- `isDispatching()`: This returns a Boolean indication of whether the dispatcher is currently dispatching.

We will go through example code while building the RSS feed reader.

Using MicroEvent.js

MicroEvent.js is an event emitter library, which provides the observer pattern to JavaScript objects. We need MicroEvent.js for triggering events from stores to update views.

You can get MicroEvent.js from `http://notes.jetienne.com/2011/03/22/microeventjs.html`.

To make an object or constructor be able to emit events and others to be able to subscribe to it, we need to integrate a `MicroEvent` interface into the object or constructor using the `MicroEvent.mixin` method.

Now, inside the object or constructor, we can trigger events using `this.trigger()`, and others can subscribe to events using the `bind()` method of the object. We can also unbind using the `unbind()` method.

We will look at example code while building the RSS feed reader.

Introduction to React Router

The RSS feed reader application we will create is going to be a single-page application. In single-page applications, routes are defined on the frontend instead of the backend. We need some sort of library that lets us define routes and assign components to them, that is, it can keep the UI in sync with the URL.

React Router is the most popular and recommended routing library for React. It provides a simple API with powerful features such as dynamic route matching and location transition handling built in.

You can find the source code of React Router at `https://github.com/reactjs/react-router` and the CDN version at `https://cdnjs.com/libraries/react-router`.

Here is a code sample of how to define routes using React Router and assign components to them:

```
var Router = ReactRouter.Router;
var Route = ReactRouter.Route;
var Link = ReactRouter.Link;
var BrowserHistory = ReactRouter.browserHistory;

var Routes = (
  <Router history={BrowserHistory}>
    <Route path="/" component={Home}></Route>
    <Route path="/profile/:username" component={Profile}></Route>
    <Route path="*" component={NotFound}/>
  </Router>
)

ReactDOM.render(Routes, document.body);
```

Here is how the preceding code works:

1. React Router lets us define routes and their components using React components themselves. This makes it easy to write routes.

2. A `Route` component is used to define individual routes. The paths of the routes are of the same pattern as the paths in Express.

3. All the `Route` components are wrapped with the `Router` component and the `Router` component is rendered on the page. The `Router` component finds the matching route for the current URL and renders the component assigned to the route.

4. We assigned the `history` property of the `Router` component to `ReactRouter.browserHistory`, which makes `Router` use the HTML5 History API.

5. The `Link` component should be used instead of the `<a>` tag as this component prevents full-page reloads and instead just changes the URL and renders the matching component.

Creating the RSS feed reader

The RSS feed reader we will create will let you add feed URLs, view a list of added URLs, and view the content of each feed URL. We will be storing the URLs in HTML5 local storage.

Setting up the project directories and files

In the exercise files of this chapter, you will find two directories: Initial and Final. Final contains the final source code of the application whereas Initial contains the files to help you quickly get started with building the application.

In the Initial directory, you will find app.js, package.json, and a public directory containing files to be served to the frontend. The app.js file will contain backend code. Currently, app.js and package.json contain no code.

We will put our HTML code in public/html/index.html, and in the public/js/ index.js file, we will place our frontend JavaScript code, that is, React code.

Let's first build the backend, after which we will build the frontend.

Building the backend

First, let's download the packages required for the backend. Place this code in the package.json file:

```
{
  "name": "rss-reader",
  "dependencies": {
    "express": "4.13.3",
    "request": "2.69.0",
    "xml2json": "0.9.0"
  }
}
```

Now, run npm install in the Initial directory to download the packages. Here, we require the express, request and xml2json npm packages.

Place the following code in the app.js file:

```
var express = require("express");
var app = express();
var request = require("request");
var parser = require("xml2json");


app.use(express.static(__dirname + "/public"));

app.get("/feed", function(httpRequest, httpResponse, next){
  request(httpRequest.query.url, function (error, response, body)
  {
    if (!error && response.statusCode == 200)
```

```
    {
      httpResponse.send(parser.toJson(body));
    }
  })
})

app.get("/*", function(httpRequest, httpResponse, next){
  httpResponse.sendFile(__dirname + "/public/html/index.html");
})

app.listen(8080);
```

This is how the preceding code works:

1. At first, we import the libraries.

2. Then, we add a middleware program to serve static files.

3. We then create a route that takes a URL as a query parameter, fetches the content of the URL, and sends it back as a response. We cannot fetch the feeds from the frontend because of CROS; therefore, we will fetch it through this route. It also converts the XML to JSON, because JSON is easier to work with.

4. Then, for all other paths, we return the index.html file.

5. Finally, we listen on port number 8080.

Building the frontend

In the public/js directory, you will find all the libraries that we will be using in the frontend. In the public/css directory, you will find Bootstrap 4, which we will use for designing.

Place this code in the index.html file to enqueue the JS and CSS files as well as creating a container for React components to render:

```
<!doctype html>
<html>
  <head>
    <title>RSS Feed Reader</title>

    <link rel="stylesheet" type="text/css"
    href="/css/bootstrap.min.css">
  </head>
  <body>
```

```
            <div id="appContainer"></div>

            <script src="/js/react.js"></script>
            <script src="/js/react-dom.js"></script>
            <script src="/js/ReactRouter.js"></script>
            <script src="/js/Flux.js"></script>
            <script src="/js/microevent.js"></script>
            <script src="/js/index.js"></script>
        </body>
    </html>
```

At first, we enqueued Bootstrap 4. Then, we enqueued the React, React Router, Flux, and MicroEvent libraries. Finally, we enqueued the index.js file, in which we will put our application code.

The appContainer element is the one inside which all of the UI will be displayed.

Defining routes

Here is the code to define routes for our application. Compile it using Babel and place it in the index.js file:

```
var Router = ReactRouter.Router;
var Route = ReactRouter.Route;
var Link = ReactRouter.Link;
var BrowserHistory = ReactRouter.browserHistory;

var Routes = (
  <Router history={BrowserHistory}>
    <Route path="/" component={FeedList}></Route>
    <Route path="/feed/:id" component={Feed}></Route>
    <Route path="submit" component={SubmitFeed}></Route>
    <Route path="*" component={NotFound}/>
  </Router>
)

ReactDOM.render(Routes,
document.getElementById("appContainer"));
```

We've defined four routes here, as follows:

1. The first route is for the home page. When a user visits the home page, we will display a list of feed URLs that the user has added.

2. The second route is for displaying the content of a feed.

3. The third route is for adding a new feed URL.

4. Finally, if nothing matches, then the fourth route displays a
   not found message.

Creating dispatcher, actions, and stores

Let's create the dispatcher, a store that lets us manage feed URLs, and the `FeedList`
component for displaying the feed URLs on the home page. To create all these,
compile and place the following code in the `index.js` file:

```
var AppDispatcher = new Flux.Dispatcher();

var FeedStore = {
  addFeed: function(url){
    var valid = /^(ftp|http|https):\/\/[^ "]+$/.test(url);

    if(valid)
    {
      var urls = localStorage.getItem("feed-urls");
      urls = JSON.parse(urls);

      if(urls == null)
      {
        urls = [url];
      }
      else
      {
        urls[urls.length] = url;
      }

      localStorage.setItem("feed-urls", JSON.stringify(urls));

      this.trigger("valid-url");
    }
    else
    {
      this.trigger("invalid-url");
    }
  },
  getFeeds: function(){
    var urls = localStorage.getItem("feed-urls");
    urls = JSON.parse(urls);
```

```
    if(urls == null)
    {
      return [];
    }
    else
    {
      return urls;
    }
  }
}

MicroEvent.mixin(FeedStore);

var Header = React.createClass({
  render: function(){
    return(
      <nav className="navbar navbar-light bg-faded">
        <ul className="nav navbar-nav">
          <li className="nav-item">
            <Link className="nav-link" to="/">Home</Link>
          </li>
          <li className="nav-item">
            <Link className="nav-link" to="submit">Add</Link>
          </li>
        </ul>
      </nav>
    )
  }
})

var FeedList = React.createClass({
  getInitialState: function(){
    return {
      urls: FeedStore.getFeeds()
    };
  },
  render: function(){
    var count = 0;
    return(
      <div>
        <Header />
        <div className="container">
          <br />
          <ul>
```

```
{
  this.state.urls.map(function(url)
  {
    count++;
    return <li> <Link to={"/feed/" +
    count}>{url}</Link></li>;
  })}
</ul>
</div>
</div>
)
}
})
```

This is how the code works:

1. First, we create a dispatcher for our app.

2. Then, we create a store named `FeedStore`, which provides us methods to add or retrieve a list of feed URLs. If we try to add an invalid URL, it sends out an `invalid-url` event; otherwise, it sends out a `valid-url` event so that we can display a message to the user indicating whether the URL was successfully added. This store stores and retrieves feed URLs from the HTML5 local storage.

3. Then, we call `MicroEvent.mixin` by passing `FeedStore` as an argument so that the store is able to trigger events and others can bind to those events.

4. Then, we create a `Header` component, which will be our application header. The `Header` component currently displays only two links: the root path and the path to add a new URL.

5. Finally, we create the `FeedList` component. The `getInitialState` method of the component retrieves the list of feed URLs from `FeedStore` and returns them to be displayed. Note that we are not using the `<a>` tag while displaying the list; instead, we are using the `Link` component. The ID of a feed is its position in the array stored in local storage.

Now, let's create the `SubmitFeed` component, which lets us add a new feed URL and then displays whether the URL has been added successfully. Here is the code for it. Compile and place it in the `index.js` file:

```
var SubmitFeed = React.createClass({
  add: function(){
    AppDispatcher.dispatch({
      actionType: "add-feed-url",
      feedURL: this.refs.feedURL.value
```

```
      });
    },
    componentDidMount: function()
    {
      FeedStore.bind("invalid-url", this.invalid_url);
      FeedStore.bind("valid-url", this.valid_url);
    },
    valid_url: function()
    {
      alert("Added successfully");
    },
    invalid_url: function()
    {
      alert("Please enter a valid URL");
    },
    componentWillUnmount: function()
    {
      FeedStore.unbind("invalid-url", this.invalid_url);
      FeedStore.unbind("valid-url", this.valid_url);
    },
    render: function(){
      return(
        <div>
          <Header />
          <div className="container">
            <br />
            <form>
              <fieldset className="form-group">
                <label for="formGroupURLInput">Enter URL</label>
                <input type="url" className="form-control"
                id="formGroupURLInput" ref="feedURL"
                placeholder="Enter RSS Feed URL" />
              </fieldset>
              <input type="button" value="Submit" className="btn"
              onClick={this.add} />
            </form>
          </div>
        </div>
      )
    }
  })
```

```
AppDispatcher.register(function(action){
  if(action.actionType == "add-feed-url")
  {
    FeedStore.addFeed(action.feedURL);
  }
})
```

Here is how this code works:

1. The `SubmitFeed` component displays a form with a text field and a button to submit it.

2. When a user clicks on the **Submit** button, the `add` handler is invoked. The `add` handler dispatches an action with the `add-feed-url` action type and the URL to be added as the data.

3. As soon as the component is mounted, we start listening to the `invalid-url` and `valid-url` events from `FeedStore`. If a URL is added successfully, we display a success message; otherwise, we get a failure message.

4. And, as soon as the component is unmounted, we stop listening to events from `FeedStore`. We should unbind, or we will end up with multiple listeners.

5. Finally, we register an action callback that checks for the `add-feed-url` action type and invokes the `addFeed` method of the `FeedStore` store.

Now, let's create the `Feed` component, which displays the content of an individual feed URL. Here's the code for it. Compile and place it in the `index.js` file:

```
var SingleFeedStore = {
  get: function(id){
    var urls = localStorage.getItem("feed-urls");
    urls = JSON.parse(urls);

    var request_url = urls[id - 1];

    var request;
    if(window.XMLHttpRequest)
    {
      request = new XMLHttpRequest();
    }
    else if(window.ActiveXObject)
    {
      try
      {
```

```
        request = new ActiveXObject("Msxml2.XMLHTTP");
      }
      catch (e)
      {
        try
        {
          request = new ActiveXObject("Microsoft.XMLHTTP");
        }
        catch (e)
        {}
      }
    }

    request.open("GET", "/feed?url=" +
    encodeURIComponent(request_url));

    var self = this;

    request.addEventListener("load", function(){
      self.trigger("feed-fetched", request.responseText);
    }, false);

    request.send(null);
  }
}

MicroEvent.mixin(SingleFeedStore);

var Feed = React.createClass({
  getInitialState: function(){
    return {
      data: []
    };
  },
  componentDidMount: function(){
    SingleFeedStore.get(this.props.params.id);
    SingleFeedStore.bind("feed-fetched", this.update);
  },
  update: function(data){
    var data = JSON.parse(data);
    this.setState({data: data.rss.channel.item});
  },
  componentWillUnmount: function(){
    SingleFeedStore.unbind("feed-fetched", this.update);
  },
  render: function(){
    return(
```

```
      <div>
        <Header />
        <div className="container">
          <br />
          <ul>
              {this.state.data.map(function(post) {
                  return <li><a href={post.link}>{post.title}</a></
li>;
              })}
          </ul>
        </div>
      </div>
    )
  }
})
```

Here's how it works:

1. At first, we create `SingleFeedStore`, which has a `get` method that returns the content of a feed URL. It uses our server route to fetch the content of the URL. Once the content has been fetched, it triggers the `feed-fetched` event with that content.

2. Then, we called `MicroEvent.mixin` by passing `SingleFeedStore` as an argument so that the store is able to trigger events and others can bind to those events.

3. Then, in the `getInitialState` method of the `Feed` component, we return an empty data array, and inside the `componentDidMount` method, we make a request to `SingleFeedStore` as the `get` method of `SingleFeedStore` gets the data asynchronously.

4. In `componentDidMount`, we bind an event handler for the `feed-fetched` event and update the view as soon as the event occurs.

5. As usual, we unbind the event handler as soon as the component is unmounted.

Finally, let's create the `NotFound` component. Here is the code for it. Compile and place it in the `index.js` file:

```
var NotFound = React.createClass({
  render: function(){
    return(
      <h1>Page Not Found</h1>
    )
  }
})
```

Testing the application

We are now done with building the application. To run the webserver, inside the `Initial` directory, run `node app.js`. Now, in a browser, open `localhost:8080`. You will only be able to see the header as we haven't added anything yet. Here is how it should look:

Now, click on the **Add** menu item. You would see a form like this:

Enter a valid feed URL, such as `http://qnimate.com/feed/`, and click on **Submit**. Now, go back to the home page, and you will see this output:

Now, click on the URL to see the content of the feed. The output will be something like this:

Home   Add

- Pointing Domain to AWS Elastic Load Balancing
- Find Recorded Audio File Location in Cordova
- ES6 Reflect API Tutorial
- Express.js Middleware Tutorial
- Storing Data Locally in a Intel XDK App
- Streaming File Uploads to Storage Server with Node.js
- Generate Unique Number in JavaScript
- JSON.parse() throws "unexpected token" error for valid JSON
- Best Photo Straightening Online Tool

Clicking on any of the titles will open the URL in the same tab.

Summary

In this chapter, we learned how to build a single page application using React and Flux. We also explored many libraries, such as `xml2json`, `Flux.js`, `MicroEvent.js`, and React Router. Afterwards, we built a fully operational RSS feed reader.

You can now go ahead and add new things to the app, such as real-time feed updates and notifications.

12
New Features of Angular 2

Angular 1 was based on the MVC architecture whereas Angular 2 is based on a components-and-services architecture. Angular 1 and Angular 2 are completely different in terms of architecture and APIs, so previous knowledge of Angular 1 is unlikely to help you much in learning Angular 2. In this chapter, we will learn Angular 2 without comparing it with Angular 1 as doing that will create confusion and is unnecessary. Even if you don't have knowledge about Angular 1, you can continue with this chapter.

We will cover the following topics:

- Web components
- The Angular 2 architecture
- Template language
- Component inputs and outputs
- The component life cycle
- Events
- Forms
- Services

And much more...

The Angular 2 architecture

Angular 2 is a framework for building the client side of web applications, based on a services-and-components architecture.

An Angular 2 application is composed of a view and various services. Services are simple JavaScript objects that hold application logic and state. Services should be reusable. Views consume services, and services can also interact with each other.

Views and services are loosely coupled so that an Angular 2 view can be used with any other architecture, such as Flux. Similarly, services can be used with any other view, such as React.

Angular 2 views are based on component-oriented architecture. In component-oriented architecture, the application UI is divided into reusable components. A component has a UI with code to update the UI and handle user actions on the UI. A custom tag is associated with a component, and whenever the custom tag appears, a new instance of the component is created and rendered. So, we can say that component-oriented architecture is architecture for the view of an application. Actually, the components consume the services.

> In the previous two chapters, we studied React, which is also based on component-oriented architecture, since with React, we build an application as a set of components.

Here is a diagram from the official Angular 2 website (`https://angular.io`) that shows the complete architecture of Angular 2:

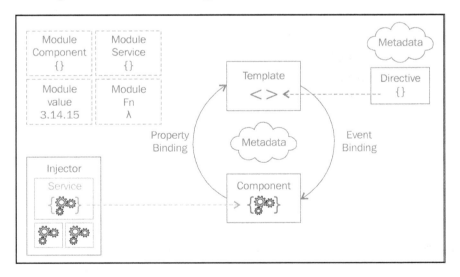

Here, you can see that the UI of a **Component** is defined using a **Template**. Templates are written using template HTML, that is, a combination of HTML and many other tokens. A component also holds the UI state and event handlers of the UI.

We shouldn't store application logic and state inside a component, as it will have an impact on code reusability and cause issues while developing large and complex apps. Application state and logic should be stored in services.

Angular 2 only implements one-way data binding. This makes large and complex apps easier to debug.

Services are injected into specific components that need them, and not all the components.

Introducing web components

Before we get into web components, you need to know why we are learning about them. Well, we are learning about web components because Angular 2 components utilize shadow DOM and templates, which are a part of web components.

In a nutshell, web components are a collection of four different browser specifications that enable the creation of reusable components in web pages. These four specifications are **HTML imports**, **shadow DOM**, **templates**, and **custom elements**. They can be used together or separately.

Web components provide native implementation of component-oriented architecture. A component created using web components is called a web component as well.

Before we learn about web components, let's consider a project for demonstration purposes. Create a directory named `web-components`, and then create a file named `index.html` in it. Web components have pretty poor browser support, so let's download `webcomponents.js polyfill`. Download the `webcomponents.js` file from `https://github.com/webcomponents/webcomponentsjs` and place it in the `web-components` directory.

Now, place this code in the `index.html` file:

```
<!doctype html>
<html>
  <head>
    <title>Web Components Demo</title>
    <script src="webcomponents.js"></script>
  </head>
  <body>
    <script>
      //place JavaScript code here
    </script>
  </body>
</html>
```

Let's now look at an overview of shadow DOM, templates, and custom elements by building a component to display a card that has an image, title, and description.

Templates

Templates are used to define reusable code. A template is defined using the `<template>` tag. Code for the template is placed inside this tag. We can place any tag, such as `<script>` and `<style>`.

The code inside the `<template>` tag is only parsed, not rendered.

Here is an example of how to create a template. Place this code in the body tag:

```
<template id="cardTemplate">
  <style type="text/css">
    .container
    {
      width: 250px;
      float: left;
      margin-right: 10px;
    }

    img
    {
      width: 100%;
    }
  </style>
  <div class="container">
    <img src="" />
    <div>
      <h3></h3>
      <p></p>
    </div>
  </div>
</template>
```

Here, the template holds the UI code for the card component. Now, if you open the `index.html` file in a browser, you won't see anything because the `<template>` tag is only parsed, not rendered.

Custom elements

Custom elements let us define new types of HTML elements (that is, new types of HTML tags). When we use a tag name that's not recognized by the browser, the browser simply treats it like a <span> tag. But when we register a custom tag, it gets recognized by the browser. It can inherit other elements, lets us perform different operations on different stages of the element lifecycle, and much more.

Let's create a custom element for our component. Wherever the tag appears, a new instance of the component will be displayed.

Here is the code to display the custom element. Place it in the <body> tag:

```
<custom-card data-img="http://placehold.it/250x250" data-
title="Title 1" data-description="Description 1" is="custom-
card"></custom-card>
<custom-card data-img="http://placehold.it/250x250" data-
title="Title 2" data-description="Description 2"></custom-
card>
```

We have to use the - character in the custom element name. This is compulsory because this restriction allows the parser to distinguish custom elements from regular elements and ensures forward compatibility when new tags are added to HTML. Here, we are passing properties of the component as data attributes.

Now, let's define <custom-card> as a custom element and place the template code inside the tag whenever a new instance of <custom-card> is created. To do that, place this code in the <script> tag:

```
var customCardProto = Object.create(HTMLElement.prototype);
customCardProto.createdCallback = function(){
  var template = document.querySelector("#cardTemplate");
  template.content.querySelector("img").src =
  this.getAttribute("data-img");
  template.content.querySelector("h3").innerHTML =
  this.getAttribute("data-title");
  template.content.querySelector("p").innerHTML =
  this.getAttribute("data-description");

  var clone = document.importNode(template.content, true);
  this.appendChild(clone)
}
var customCard = document.registerElement("custom-card", {
  prototype: customCardProto
});
```

Here is how the code works:

- By default, custom elements inherit methods and properties of `HTMLElement`.

- To register a custom element, we need to use the `document.registerElement` method. The first argument is the custom tag name and the second argument is an optional object. This optional object can take a property called **prototype**. The `prototype` property defines the HTML element it inherits, that is, the properties and methods of the HTML element it inherits. By default, it's assigned to `Object.create(HTMLElement.prototype)`.

- We can also add new properties and methods to our custom element by adding new properties and methods to the object assigned to the `prototype` property.

- Here, we've added a method called `createdCallback`, which is invoked whenever an instance of a custom element is created, that is, either an instance created using JavaScript or HTML.

- Inside `createdCallback`, we are retrieving our template and setting the image source, title, and description and then appending it to the custom element by creating a clone of it, as many custom elements will share the same template.

Now, if you open `index.html` in a browser, you will see this output:

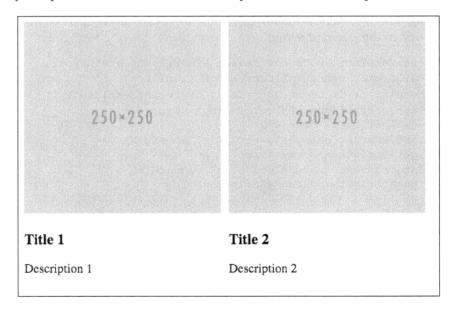

Shadow DOM

Shadow DOM allows HTML elements to get a new kind of node called a shadow root associated with them. An element that has a shadow root associated with it is called a shadow host. The content of a shadow host isn't rendered; the content of the shadow root is rendered instead. A shadow root can have another shadow root below it.

The benefit of shadow DOM is that CSS styles defined inside a shadow root won't affect its parent document, and CSS styles defined outside the shadow root will not affect the elements inside the shadow root. This is useful to define styles specific to the components. In short, we can say that shadow DOM provides style encapsulation.

Style encapsulation is not the only benefit of shadow DOM. The HTML inside the shadow root is protected from accidental modification from JavaScript. We can still inspect the shadow root in browser developer tools.

Many native element, such as `<video>` and `<audio>`, have a shadow root, but when you inspect it, you won't see the shadow root. Browsers by default hide the shadow roots of these elements. To see their shadow roots, you need to change browser-specific settings.

Let's modify the previous custom element code to render the template inside shadow DOM. Replace the previous `createdCallback` method with this one:

```
customCardProto.createdCallback = function(){
  var template = document.querySelector("#cardTemplate");
  template.content.querySelector("img").src =
  this.getAttribute("data-img");
  template.content.querySelector("h3").innerHTML =
  this.getAttribute("data-title");
  template.content.querySelector("p").innerHTML =
  this.getAttribute("data-description");

  var clone = document.importNode(template.content, true);

  var shadow = this.createShadowRoot();

  shadow.appendChild(clone);
}
```

Here, instead of appending the template code directly to the custom element, we created a shadow root using `createShadowRoot` and appended the template code to it.

Setting up an Angular 2 project

Angular 2 code can be written in JavaScript, TypeScript, or Dart. In case you are writing Angular 2 code in TypeScript or Dart, you will need to transpile the code to JavaScript before serving to the client. We will use JavaScript to write Angular 2 code.

Create a directory named angular2-demo. Then, inside the directory, create the app. js and package.json files. Then, create a directory named public, and inside the directory, create four more directories named html, js, componentTemplates, and componentStyles. Now, create a file named index.html and place it in the html directory.

Then, download angular2-polyfills.js, Rx.umd.js, and angular2-all.umd. js from https://cdnjs.com/libraries/angular.js/ and place them in the angular2-demo/js directory. These files are what they sound like. You can also enqueue the CDN links directly if you want to.

Inside the index.html file, place this starting code:

```html
<!doctype html>
<html>
  <head>
    <title>Angular 2 Demo</title>
  </head>
  <body>

    <script src="/js/angular2-polyfills.js"></script>
    <script src="/js/Rx.umd. js"></script>
    <script src="/js/angular2-all.umdn.js"></script>
    <script>
      //App code here
    </script>
  </body>
</html>
```

Inside the app.js file, place this code:

```js
var express = require("express");
var app = express();

app.use(express.static(__dirname + "/public"));

app.get("/", function(httpRequest, httpResponse, next){
  httpResponse.sendFile(__dirname + "/public/html/index.html");
})

app.listen(8080);
```

This is the server-side code. It's self-explanatory.

Now, in the `package.json` file, place this code and run `npm install` to download the `express` package:

```
{
  "name": "Angular2-Demo",
  "dependencies": {
    "express": "4.13.3"
  }
}
```

To start the server, run `node app.js`. Then, open the app using `localhost:8080` as the address in a browser.

Angular 2 fundamentals

An Angular 2 application is completely split into components. Technically, an Angular 2 component is a reusable `custom` tag that is mutable and encapsulated with an embedded state, that is, changes to the state or properties will mutate the UI.

 Remember that Angular 2 doesn't register the custom tag name as a custom element.

All the components of the application are arranged in a tree structure, with a component as the root node.

Here is an example of how to create a component. It creates a card component that displays an image, title, and description. Place this code in the `<script>` tag:

```
var Card = ng.core.Component({
  selector: "card",
  inputs: ["src", "title", "desc"],
  templateUrl: "templates/card-template.html",
  styleUrls: ["templateStyles/card-style.css"]
})
.Class({
  constructor: function(){
  }
})
```

Then, create a file named `card-template.html`, and place it in the `componentTemplates` directory. Place this code in the file:

```
<style>
  .container
  {
    width: 250px;
    float: left;
    margin-right: 10px;
  }

  img
  {
    width: 100%;
  }
</style>
<div class="container">
  <img src="{{src}}" />
  <div>
    <h3>{{title}}</h3>
    <p>{{desc}}</p>
  </div>
</div>
```

After that, create a file named `card-style.css` and place it in the `componentStyles` directory. Place this code in the file:

```
.container
{
  width: 250px;
  float: left;
  margin-right: 10px;
}

img
{
  width: 100%;
}
```

This is how these three code snippets work:

- A component needs to be created by chaining `Component` and `Class` methods that belong to an `ng.core` object.

- The `Component` method takes a configuration object with various properties, whereas the `Class` method takes an object with component lifecycle methods, constructors, and UI action handlers.

- Here, the configuration properties we've provided are `selector`, `inputs`, `templateUrl`, and `styleUrls`. The `selector` property is used to define the custom tag for the component. The `inputs` property is used to define the attributes that the custom tag takes. The `templateUrl` property is used to define the file containing the template of the component. You can also use `template` if you want to inline the template code. Finally, `styleUrls` is used to define the CSS files containing the style for the component. You can also use the `styles` property to inline CSS code, or you can define CSS using a `<style>` tag inside the template itself. CSS defined in any of these three ways won't affect other components, that is, it's encapsulated to the component itself.

- In the `Class` method, we will have to provide the `constructor` method even if it does nothing. It's invoked during the construction of a new instance of the component. By construction of the component, I mean the construction of the component in memory—not resolving attributes, resolving its children, rendering its view, and so on. The primary use of the `constructor` method is to inject services into the component. Services cannot be injected automatically as we may sometimes need to initialize services for every component, and Angular is unaware of how to do this. The `constructor` method has access to the state of the component but not its properties. Here, we shouldn't do any heavy work or something else that would slow down or cause the construction of the component to fail. `constructor` is not a component lifecycle method.

- Then, we have the component template code. In this template file, we are simply rendering the properties passed to the component. To render anything that's in the component state, we need to use the {{}} token.

Let's create another component called `Cards`, which displays a list of cards. It gets information about cards from a service.

Place this code in the `<script>` tag of the `index.html` file:

```
var CardsService = ng.core.Class({
  constructor: function() {
  },
  getCards: function() {
    return [{
      src: "http://placehold.it/350x150",
      title: "Title 1",
      desc: "Description 1"
    },
    {
      src: "http://placehold.it/350x150",
      title: "Title 2",
      desc: "Description 2"
    },
    {
      src: "http://placehold.it/350x150",
      title: "Title 3",
      desc: "Description 3"
    }]
  }
});

var Cards = ng.core.Component({
  selector: "cards",
  viewProviders: [CardsService],
  directives: [Card],
  templateUrl: "componentTemplates/cards-template.html"
}).Class({
  constructor: [CardsService, function(cardsService){
    this.getCards = cardsService.getCards;
  }],
  ngOnInit: function(){
    this.cards = this.getCards();
  }
})
```

```
var App = ng.core.Component({
  selector: "app",
  directives: [Cards],
  templateUrl: "componentTemplates/app-template.html"
}).Class({
  constructor: function(){

  }
})

ng.platform.browser.bootstrap(App);
```

Now, create a file named `cards-template.html` in the `componentTemplates` directory and place this code in it:

```
<card *ngFor="#card of cards" title="{{card.title}}"
src="{{card.src}}" desc="{{card.desc}}"></card>
```

Now, create a file named `app-template.html` in the `componentTemplates` directory and place this code in it:

```
<cards></cards>
```

Now, in the `<body>` tag of the `index.html` file, place this code:

```
<app></app>
```

Here is how these four code snippets work:

- To create a service, we need to use the `ng.core.Class` method. It takes an object with the `constructor` method and other methods or properties that the service exposes. While injecting the service into other services or components, a new instance of the service is created and injected. While creating a new instance of a service, the `constructor` method is called. We have to provide this method even if it doesn't do anything. The primary purpose of this method is to inject services that this service depends on. Here, our `CardsService` method is not dependent on any other service, so we have no code inside the `constructor` method. Then, we defined a `getCards` method, which returns data of three different cards to display.

- Then, we created a `Cards` component. It takes the data from `CardsService` and renders a `Card` component for each card data. While creating the `Cards` component, we provide `viewProviders` and `directives` properties to the configuration object. `viewProviders` is the list of services the component is dependent on, and `directives` is the list of other components this component renders. Here, you can see that instead of directly assigning a function to the `constructor` property, we are assigning an array with a list of services the component depends upon and the last array item as the actual function. This is the format of injecting services into components. Inside the `constructor` method, we store references to the methods or properties of the service that the component needs, that is, we can use services inside the `constructor` method. We will learn more about `viewProviders` later on. The `this` keyword in any of the methods passed to the `Class` method points to the state of the component. After a component instance has been created, whenever the component state changes, the template bindings are updated. We have another method here, called `ngOnInit`. It's a lifecycle method that's invoked after a new instance of the component has been created and its attributes resolved. Inside this, we call the `getCards` method and store the returned value inside the `cards` property of the state. Note that the attributes passed to a component tag are accessible using the `this` keyword after the component instance has been created.

- Inside the template of `CardsComponent`, we are using the `*ngFor` directive to display the cards. We will learn more about directives later.

- Then, we create an `App` component, which acts as the root of our component. Inside this component, we are displaying the `Cards` component.

- Finally, we initialize the application. An Angular 2 application is initialized explicitly. While initializing it, we need to provide a reference to the root component. This is done to ensure that applications are composed of nested components all the way down. The root component is the one that's added to the `<body>` tag. Adding tags of other components to the body tag will not do anything.

Now, if you refresh your `localhost:8080` page in your browser, you will see this output:

350×150	350×150	350×150
Title 1	**Title 2**	**Title 3**
Description 1	Description 2	Description 3

Styling components and shadow DOM

Earlier, we saw that there are three ways of defining styles specific to components (styles encapsulated in the component template scope). A component's CSS doesn't even affect the components it owns.

Angular 2 doesn't use shadow DOM by default; instead, it uses a different technique to achieve style encapsulation. This is due to the lack of browser support.

By default, Angular 2 modifies the CSS selector in such a way that it only targets the elements in the component, and it then places the CSS in the `<head>` tag of the page. If you inspect our current app using browser developer tools, you will see this:

```
···<!DOCTYPE html>
<html>
▶ #shadow-root (open)
▼ <head>
    <title>Angular 2 Demo</title>
  ▼ <style>
      .container[_ngcontent-wik-3]
      {
          width: 250px;
          float: left;
          margin-right: 10px;
      }

      img[_ngcontent-wik-3]
      {
          width: 100%;
      }
    </style>
  </head>
▼ <body>
  ▼ <app>
    ▼ <cards>
        <!--template bindings={}-->
      ▶ <card _nghost-wik-3>…</card>
      ▶ <card _nghost-wik-3>…</card>
      ▶ <card _nghost-wik-3>…</card>
      </cards>
    </app>
    <script src="/js/angular2-polyfills.min.js"></script>
    <script src="/js/Rx.umd.min.js"></script>
    <script src="/js/angular2-all.umd.min.js"></script>
  ▶ <script>…</script>
  </body>
</html>
```

Here, you can see that the CSS has been modified and inserted into the `<head>` tag.

To force Angular 2 to use shadow DOM, we need to assign the encapsulation property of the component configuration object to `ng.core.ViewEncapsulation.Native`. By default, it's assigned to `ng.core.ViewEncapsulation.Emulated`.

When you inspect the app after assigning the encapsulation property of the `Card` and `Cards` components to `ng.core.ViewEncapsulation.Native`, you will see something like this:

```
<!DOCTYPE html>
<html>
▶ #shadow-root (open)
▼ <head>
    <title>Angular 2 Demo</title>
  </head>
▼ <body>
  ▼ <app>
    ▼ <cards>
      ▼ #shadow-root (open)
          <!--template bindings={}-->
        ▼ <card>
          ▼ #shadow-root (open)
            ▼ <style>
                .container
                {
                    width: 250px;
                    float: left;
                    margin-right: 10px;
                }

                img
                {
                    width: 100%;
                }
              </style>
            ▶ <div class="container">…</div>
          </card>
        ▶ <card>…</card>
        ▶ <card>…</card>
      </cards>
    </app>
    <script src="/js/angular2-polyfills.min.js"></script>
    <script src="/js/Rx.umd.min.js"></script>
    <script src="/js/angular2-all.umd.min.js"></script>
  ▶ <script>…</script>
  </body>
</html>
```

Here, you can see that shadow DOM was used to achieve style encapsulation.

 In case you don't want style encapsulation for a component, you can assign the encapsulation property to `ng.core.ViewEncapsulation. None`. In this case, all of the CSS will be placed directly in the `<head>` tag.

Angular 2 change detection

Change detection is the process of detecting component state change. The state of a component is stored and manipulated using the `this` keyword. Therefore, there is no direct way for Angular 2 to detect when the state changes. So, Angular 2 uses complex algorithms and third-party libraries to detect state changes.

The first thing Angular 2 does for detecting state changes is that it pretends that all the changes happen asynchronously. Then, it uses the `zone.js` library to monitor browser events, timers, AJAX requests, WebSockets, and other asynchronous things that are supported by `zone.js`.

Now, whenever any of these asynchronous activities takes place, it checks everything that could change, including object properties and array elements of the `this` keyword of all the components from the root node; if any change is detected, then the template bindings of the component are updated. Angular 2 doesn't simply re-render the whole component. Instead, it checks for the bindings that have changed and selects and updates them specifically.

Some components can have a lot of state data, and checking the state for every asynchronous operation will unnecessarily impact app performance if their state has not changed. Therefore, Angular 2 provides an option to mark such kinds of components so that it does not check their states unless the component itself tells Angular 2 to check its state during the next detection cycle, that is, when the next asynchronous activity occurs. Let's look at an example to demonstrate this.

Place this code above the `App` component code in the `<script>` tag of the `index. html` file:

```
var SampleComponent1 = ng.core.Component({
    selector: "sampleone",
    template: "{{value}}",
    viewProviders: [ng.core.ChangeDetectorRef],
    changeDetection: ng.core.ChangeDetectionStrategy.Detached
}).Class({
```

```
  constructor: [ng.core.ChangeDetectorRef, function(cd){
    this.cd = cd;
  }],
  ngOnInit: function(){
    this.value = 1;
    setInterval(function(){
      this.value++;
      this.cd.markForCheck();
    }.bind(this), 2000)
  }
})
```

Then, add `SampleComponent1` to the `directives` array of the `App` component.
So now, the `App` component's code should be this:

```
var App = ng.core.Component({
  selector: "app",
  directives: [Cards, SampleComponent1],
  templateUrl: "componentTemplates/app-template.html"
}).Class({
  constructor: function(){
  }
})
```

Now, add this code to the end of the `app-template.html` file:

```
<br style="clear: both">
<sampleone></sampleone>
```

Here is how these three code snippets work:

1. In this example, we are displaying a value that gets incremented every 2 seconds and the template is re-rendered to display the updated value.

2. At first, we create a component called `SampleComponent1`. It simply displays `value`. We have set the `changeDetection` property to `ng.core.ChangeDetectionStrategy.Detached`, which tells Angular 2 to not check its state change. By default, the `changeDetection` property is assigned to `ng.core.ChangeDetectionStrategy.Default`, which tells Angular 2 to check its state change during every change-detection cycle. We then inject the `ng.core.ChangeDetectorRef` service into the component, which provides various APIs related to change detection. And then, in the `ngOnInit` method, we increment the value of `value` every 2 seconds, after which we call the `markForCheck` method of `ng.core.ChangeDetectorRef`, which tells Angular 2 to check for changes in the state of the component during the next change-detection cycle. `markForCheck` will make Angular 2 check for a change in state for the next detection cycle only, not for the ones after that.

3. Then, we simply display `SampleComponent1` in the `App` component.

If a component depends only on its inputs and/or UI events or if you want a component's state change, check only whether its inputs have changed or events have been fired; then, you can assign changeDetection to ng.core.ChangeDetectionStrategy.OnPush.

> If at any time you want to force a change-detection cycle instead of waiting for an asynchronous operation to happen, you can call the detectChanges method of the ng.core.ChangeDetectorRef service.

Understanding view children and content children

Elements present inside the tags of a component are called **content children**, and elements present inside the template of a component are called **view children**.

To display the content children of a component in the component's view, we need to use the `<ng-content>` tag. Let's look at an example of this.

Place this code above the App component's code:

```
var ListItem = ng.core.Component({
  selector: "item",
  inputs: ["title"],
  template: "<li>{{title}} | <ng-content></ng-content></li>",
}).Class({
  constructor: function(){}
})

var List = ng.core.Component({
  selector: "list",
  template: "<ul><ng-content select='item'></ng-content></ul>"
}).Class({
  constructor: function(){}
})
```

Now, change the App component's code to this:

```
var App = ng.core.Component({
  selector: "app",
  directives: [Cards, SampleComponent1, List, ListItem],
  templateUrl: "componentTemplates/app-template.html"
}).Class({
  constructor: function(){}
})
```

To the end of the `app-template.html` file, add this code:

```
<br>
<list>
  <item title="first">first</item>
  <item title="second">second</item>
</list>
```

The output of this code is as follows:

- first | first
- second | secon

This is how these three code snippets work:

1. In the App component's template file, we add a `<list>` tag, which displays a list. And inside its opening and closing tags, we define the individual list items that it should display.

2. We create `ListItem` and `List` components that are bound to `<list>` and `<item>` tags, respectively.

3. We add `List` component to the `directives` property of the App component, not List, because the `<list>` tag is present in the template of the App component, and the App component is responsible for creating its instances.

4. The App component looks for the `<ng-content>` tag in the template of the List component and renders the List component instances there.

5. `<ng-content>` takes an optional `select` attribute that's assigned to a CSS selector that indicates which elements of the content children we want to display. There can be multiple `<ng-content>` tags in a template. If the `select` attribute has not been provided, then all the content children will be rendered. Here, the `select` attribute is not required; we are using it just for demonstration.

Getting the reference of components of content children and view children

To get access to the reference of components of view children or content children, we can use the ng.core.ContentChildren, ng.coreViewChildren, ng.core. ContentChild, and ng.core.ViewChild constructors. The difference between ng.core.ContentChildren and ng.core.ContentChild is that the first one returns all the references of a given component whereas the second one returns the reference of the first occurrence. The same difference also stands for ng.core.ViewChild and ng.core.ViewChildren.

Here is an example to demonstrate ng.core.ContentChildren. Replace the code for the List component with this:

```
var List = ng.core.Component({
  selector: "list",
  template: "<ul><ng-content select='item'></ng-content></ul>",
  queries: {
    list_items: new ng.core.ContentChildren(ListItem)
  }
}).Class({
  constructor: function(){},
  ngAfterContentInit: function(){
    this.list_items._results.forEach(function(e){
      console.log(e.title);
    })
  }
})
```

The output of this code in the console is as follows:

first

second

Most of this code is self-explanatory. What's new is the `ngAfterContentInit` lifecycle method. It's triggered after the content children have been initialized. Similarly, if we want to access the view children, we need to use the `ngAfterViewInit` lifecycle method.

Note that we only have access to the state of the components—nothing else.

Local template variables

We can assign a local template variable to a content child or view child. Local template variables let us get the reference of any element of the content children or view children, that is, component references or HTML element references.

To assign a local template variable to an element of the view children or content children, we need to place #variable_name in the opening tag.

Here is an example to demonstrate how local template variables work. Place this code above the App component:

```
var SampleComponent2 = ng.core.Component({
  selector: "sampletwo",
  template: "<input type='text' #input />",
  queries: {
    input_element: new ng.core.ViewChild("input")
  }
}).Class({
  constructor: function(){},
  ngAfterViewInit: function(){
    this.input_element.nativeElement.value = "Hi";
  }
})
```

Change the App component's code to this:

```
var App = ng.core.Component({
  selector: "app",
  directives: [Cards, SampleComponent1, List, ListItem,
  SampleComponent2],
  templateUrl: "componentTemplates/app-template.html"
}).Class({
  constructor: function(){}
})
```

And then, add this code to the end of the app-template.html file:

```
<sampletwo></sampletwo>
```

The output of this code is as follows:

Here is how these three code snippets work:

1. We create a new component named `SampleComponent2`, which displays an HTML input text element. We assign the input element to a local template variable named `input`.

2. Then, we use the `ng.core.ViewChild` to get a reference to the element. If we pass a string to `ng.core.ViewChild`, `ng.core.ViewChildren`, `ng.core.ContentChild`, and `ng.core.ContentChildren`, then they will look for the elements with the same local variable name as the string, and if we pass a component, they will look for the component, like we saw before.

3. The reference of the components we get from the local template variable is of the same interface we got before. But for HTML element references, we can access the real DOM of the element by using the `nativeElement` property.

Component lifecycle methods

When a `component` tag appears, Angular 2 creates an instance of a component, renders it, checks for changes in attributes, checks for changes in state, and destroys it when it's no longer needed. These steps together form the lifecycle of a component.

Angular 2 lets us register methods that are called at various stages of the component lifecycle.

Here are the various lifecycle methods provided by Angular 2; lifecycle hooks are explained in the order they occur:

- `ngOnChanges`: This is invoked whenever the attributes of a component change. It's also invoked after the attributes of a component are resolved for the first time after the creation of a new instance of the component. It's invoked after the state has been changed due to the attributes but before the view is updated. This method receives the current and previous values of the attributes.

- `ngOnInit`: This is invoked after the first instance of `ngOnChanges`. It states that the component has been successfully created and attributes have been read.

- ngDoCheck: This is called during every change-detection cycle and right after ngOnInit. We can detect and act upon changes that Angular 2 can't or won't detect on its own. This is invoked after Angular 2 is done checking state changes for the component and has updated the state if there was any change in the attributes but before the component view is updated. After this call is over, the view is rendered, and while rendering it, ngAfterContentInit, ngAfterContentChecked, ngAfterViewInit, and ngAfterViewChecked are invoked.

- ngAfterContentInit: This is invoked after content children have been initialized but not yet rendered, that is, after the ngOnChanges, ngOnInit, ngDoCheck, ngAfterContentInit, and ngAfterContentChecked methods of the content children have been called.

- ngAfterContentChecked: This is invoked whenever the change-detection cycle checks whether the content children have changed as well as right after ngAfterContentInit. If there is a change, it's invoked before the views of the content children are updated. Before invoking it, the query results of ng.core.ViewChildren, ng.core.ContentChildren, and so on are updated, that is, it's invoked after ngAfterContentChecked of the content children has been invoked. After this call, the content children views are updated.

- ngAfterViewInit: This is invoked after view children have been initialized but not yet rendered, that is, after the ngOnChanges, ngOnInit, ngDoCheck, ngAfterContentInit, ngAfterContentChecked, ngAfterViewInit, and ngAfterViewChecked methods of the view children have been called.

- ngAfterViewChecked: This is invoked whenever the change-detection cycle checks whether the view children have changed as well as right after ngAfterViewInit. If there is a change, it's invoked before the views of the view children are updated but after the ngAfterViewChecked methods of the view children have been invoked.

- ngOnDestroy: This is invoked before a component is destroyed. The ngOnDestroy method of a component is invoked before the ngOnDestroy methods of its content children and view children.

Writing templates

We need to use template language to write component templates. Template language is composed of HTML along with the {}, [], (), [()], *, |, and # tokens. Let's see what each of these is used for and how to use them.

Rendering a value

To simply render a property of the `this` keyword, we need to use the {{}} token. Inside these braces, we can simply place the property name.

We can only place expressions inside braces. The expressions we place inside them look like JavaScript. But there are a few JavaScript expressions that we are not allowed to use inside these braces. Here they are:

- Assignments (=, +=, -=)
- The `new` operator
- Chaining expressions with ; or ,
- Increment and decrement operators (++ and --)
- The bitwise operators | and &

Pipes

We can also place `pipes` in braces. A pipe is a function that accepts an input value and returns a transformed value. A pipe is represented by the | operator. The final result of expressions inside braces can be transformed using pipes. There can be as many pipes in the braces as we want. A pipe can also take parameters.

Angular 2 provides some built-in pipes: `date`, `uppercase`, `lowercase`, `currency`, and `percent`. We can also create our own pipes.

Here is an example of using {{}}. Place this code above the `App` component:

```
var SampleComponent3 = ng.core.Component({
  selector: "samplethree",
  template: "{{info.firstname + info.lastname | uppercase}}"
}).Class({
  constructor: function(){
    this.info = {
      firstname: "firstname",
      lastname: " lastname"
    }
  }
})
```

Replace the App component code with this:

```
var App = ng.core.Component({
  selector: "app",
  directives: [Cards, SampleComponent1, List, ListItem,
  SampleComponent2, SampleComponent3],
  templateUrl: "componentTemplates/app-template.html"
}).Class({
  constructor: function(){}
})
```

And then, place this in the `app-template.html` file:

```
<br><br>
<samplethree></samplethree>
```

The output of the code is as follows:

FIRSTNAME LASTNAME

 Note that the final result of the expression inside the braces is converted into a string if the final value is not a string.

Handling events

To handle events of elements in a template, we need to use the () operator. Here is an example of how to handle events. Place this code above the App component code:

```
var SampleComponent4 = ng.core.Component({
  selector: "samplefour",
  template: "<input (click)='clicked($event)'
  (mouseover)='mouseover($event)' type='button'
 value='Click Me!!!' />"
}).Class({
  constructor: function(){
    this.clicked = function(e){
      alert("Hi from SampleComponent4");
    };

    this.mouseover = function(e){
      console.log("Mouse over event");
    }

  }
})
```

Replace the App component code with this:

```
var App = ng.core.Component({
  selector: "app",
  directives: [Cards, SampleComponent1, List, ListItem,
  SampleComponent2, SampleComponent3, SampleComponent4],
  templateUrl: "componentTemplates/app-template.html"
}).Class({
  constructor: function(){}
})
```

Place this code in app-template.html:

```
<br><br>
<samplefour></samplefour>
```

The preceding code is self-explanatory.

Binding state to element attributes

To bind the value of a property of the this keyword to the attribute of an element in a template, we can simply use {{}}, like this, for example:

```
<component title="{{title}}"></component>
```

But if you want to pass an object, this method will not work, as the expression inside the {{}} token is always converted to a string. Therefore, Angular 2 provides the [] operator, which enables a component to pass an object through attributes to a component in its template.

Here is an example to demonstrate this. Place this code above the App component code:

```
var SampleComponent5 = ng.core.Component({
  selector: "samplefive",
  inputs: ["info"],
  template: "{{info.name}}"
}).Class({
  constructor: function(){}
})

var SampleComponent6 = ng.core.Component({
  selector: "samplesix",
  directives: [SampleComponent5],
  template: "<samplefive [info]='myInfo'></samplefive>"
}).Class({
```

```
constructor: function(){
  this.myInfo = {
    name: "Name"
  }
}
})
```

Replace the App component's code with this:

```
var App = ng.core.Component({
  selector: "app",
  directives: [Cards, SampleComponent1, List, ListItem,
  SampleComponent2, SampleComponent3, SampleComponent4,
  SampleComponent6],
  templateUrl: "componentTemplates/app-template.html"
}).Class({
  constructor: function(){}
})
```

Place this code at the end of the app-template.html file:

```
<br><br>
<samplesix></samplesix>
```

The output of this code is as follows:

Name

 Note that while assigning attributes to an HTML tag, if we assign an attribute that's not native to the element, we need to prefix the attribute name using attr.. For example, to assign a value attribute to a <span> tag, we need to name the attribute attr.value, not simply value. Otherwise, Angular 2 will throw an error. This is because while interpreting a template and creating its DOM, Angular 2 sets the attributes by assigning the values to the properties of DOM elements. So when we use the attr. prefix, it signals Angular 2 to use setAttribute instead.

Two-way data binding

By default, Angular 2 doesn't use two-way data binding. It uses unidirectional binding but offers the `[()]` operator for two-way data binding, if needed.

Here is an example to demonstrate `[()]`. Place this code above the `App` component's code:

```
var SampleComponent7 = ng.core.Component({
  selector: "sampleseven",
  template: "<input [(ngModel)]='name' /><input
  (click)='clicked()' value='Click here' type='submit' />"
}).Class({
  constructor: function(){},
  clicked: function(){
    alert(this.name);
  }
})
```

Replace the `App` component code with this:

```
var App = ng.core.Component({
  selector: "app",
  directives: [Cards, SampleComponent1, List, ListItem,
  SampleComponent2, SampleComponent3, SampleComponent4,
  SampleComponent6, SampleComponent7],
  templateUrl: "componentTemplates/app-template.html"
}).Class({
  constructor: function(){}
})
```

Place this code in the `app-template.html` file:

```
<br><br>
<sampleseven></sampleseven>
```

The output of this code is as follows:

Here, enter something in the text field and click on the button. You will see an alert box with the text field's value.

To capture the value of HTML form elements, we need to place ngModel inside the [()] brackets. We can place an attribute name if we are setting up two-way data binding between inputs and outputs. We will learn more about outputs later.

Directives

Directives are used to change the DOM based on the state. There are two types of directives: attribute directives and structural directives. Let's look at each of them.

Attribute directives

An **attribute directive** changes the appearance or behavior of a DOM element based on a change in state. ngClass and ngStyle are the built-in attribute directives. We can also create our own attribute directives.

The ngClass directive is used to add or remove CSS classes from an element whereas the ngStyle directive is used to set inline styles.

Here is an example of how to use the ngClass and ngStyle directives. Place this code above the App component's code:

```
var SampleComponent8 = ng.core.Component({
  selector: "sampleeight",
  template: "<div [ngStyle]='styles' [ngClass]='classes'></div>"
}).Class({
  constructor: function(){
    this.styles = {
      "font-size": "20px",
      "font-weight": "bold"
    }

    this.classes = {
      a: true,
      b: true,
      c: false
    };
  }
})
```

Replace the `App` component's code with this:

```
var App = ng.core.Component({
  selector: "app",
  directives: [Cards, SampleComponent1, List, ListItem,
  SampleComponent2, SampleComponent3, SampleComponent4,
  SampleComponent6, SampleComponent7, SampleComponent8],
  templateUrl: "componentTemplates/app-template.html"
}).Class({
  constructor: function(){}
})
```

And then, place this code at the end of the `app-template.html` file:

```
<sampleeight></sampleeight>
```

Now, if you inspect the `<sampleeight>` tag in browser developer tools, you will see this:

```
▼<sampleeight>
    <div class="a b" style="font-size: 20px; font-weight: bold;"></div>
  </sampleeight>
```

Most of this code is self-explanatory. You can see that the same `[]` token is also used for attribute directives. When the `[]` token is used, Angular 2 first checks to see whether a built-in attribute directive or custom directive is present with that name, and if not, it treats it as an attribute.

Structural directives

A **structural directive** changes the DOM layout by adding or removing DOM elements. `ngIf`, `ngSwitch`, and `ngFor` are the three built-in structural directives. We can also create our own custom structural directives.

Here is an example to demonstrate `ngIf` and `ngSwitch`. We have already seen an example of `ngFor` previously. Place this code above the `App` component's code:

```
var SampleComponent9 = ng.core.Component({
  selector: "samplenine",
  templateUrl: "componentTemplates/samplecomponent9-template.html"
}).Class({
  constructor: function(){
```

```
        this.display1 = true;
        this.display2 = false;
        this.switchOption = 'A';
    }
})
```

Create a file named `samplecomponent9-template.html,` and place it in the `componentTemplates` directory. Place this code in that file:

```
<br><br>

<div *ngIf="display1">Hello</div>
<div *ngIf="display2">Hi</div>

<span [ngSwitch]="switchOption">
  <span *ngSwitchWhen="'A'">A</span>
  <span *ngSwitchWhen="'B'">B</span>
  <span *ngSwitchWhen="'C'">C</span>
  <span *ngSwitchWhen="'D'">D</span>
  <span *ngSwitchDefault>other</span>
</span>
```

Replace the `App` component's code with this:

```
var App = ng.core.Component({
  selector: "app",
  directives: [Cards, SampleComponent1, List, ListItem,
  SampleComponent2, SampleComponent3, SampleComponent4,
  SampleComponent6, SampleComponent7, SampleComponent8,
  SampleComponent9],
  templateUrl: "componentTemplates/app-template.html"
}).Class({
  constructor: function(){}
})
```

Finally, place this code in the `app-template.html` file:

```
<samplenine></samplenine>
```

The output of this code is as follows:

Most of this code is self-explanatory. You can see that we are using the * token for structural directives. The * token treats the element as a template, that is, it doesn't render the element but uses it as a template to create the DOM.

Actually, both attribute and structural directives are written using the [] token, but writing code using structural directives with the [] token makes the code longer. Therefore, Angular 2 introduced the * token, which makes it easy to write code using structural directives. Internally, Angular 2 translates the code that uses the * token to use the [] token. Learn more about it here:

```
https://angular.io/docs/ts/latest/guide/template-syntax.html#!#star-
template
```

Outputs

Outputs allow components to emit custom events. For example, if we have a component that displays a button and we want the parent component to be able to add an event handler for the click event of the child component, we can achieve this using outputs.

Here is an example of how to integrate outputs. Place this code above the App component's code:

```
var SampleComponent10 = ng.core.Component({
  selector: "sampleten",
  outputs: ["click"],
  template: ""
}).Class({
  constructor: function(){
    this.click = new ng.core.EventEmitter();
    setInterval(function(){
      this.click.next({});
    }.bind(this), 10000)
  }
})

var SampleComponent11 = ng.core.Component({
  selector: "sampleeleven",
  directives: [SampleComponent10],
  template: "<br><sampleten
  (click)='clicked($event)'></sampleten>{{value}}"
}).Class({
  constructor: function(){
    this.value = 1;
```

```
      this.clicked = function(e){
        this.value++;
      }
    }
  })
```

Replace the App component's code with this:

```
var App = ng.core.Component({
  selector: "app",
  directives: [Cards, SampleComponent1, List, ListItem,
  SampleComponent2, SampleComponent3, SampleComponent4,
  SampleComponent6, SampleComponent7, SampleComponent8,
  SampleComponent9, SampleComponent11],
  templateUrl: "componentTemplates/app-template.html"
}).Class({
  constructor: function(){}
})
```

Finally, place this code at the end of the app-template.html file:

```
<sampleeleven></sampleeleven>
```

Now, you will start seeing a counter appear on the page.

The outputs property is used to define the events the component emits. We need to create a property in this keyword with the same name as the output and assign it to a new instance of ng.core.EventEmitter so that it can emit events. ng.core. EventEmitter provides observer patterns to objects.

To capture events, we need to use the () token, just like we used it to capture native UI events.

 Note that we need to assign output to a new instance of ng.core. EventEmitter inside the constructor property, that is, during the creation of a new instance of the component.

Two-way data binding with inputs and outputs

You can implement two-way data binding between inputs and outputs. For example, if a parent component passes an attribute to a component of the view children and the child component notifies the parent component whenever the input value changes, then instead of using () and [] separately, we can use [()].

Here is an example to demonstrate this. Place this code above the `App` component's code:

```
var SampleComponent12 = ng.core.Component({
  selector: "sampletwelve",
  inputs: ["count"],
  outputs: ["countChange"],
  template: ""
}).Class({
  constructor: function(){
    this.countChange = new ng.core.EventEmitter();
    setInterval(function(){
      this.count++;
      this.countChange.next(this.count);
    }.bind(this), 10000);
  }
})

var SampleComponent13 = ng.core.Component({
  selector: "samplethirteen",
  directives: [SampleComponent12],
  template: "<br><sampletwelve
  [(count)]='count'></sampletwelve>{{count}}"
}).Class({
  constructor: function(){
    this.count = 1;
  }
})
```

Replace the `App` component's code with this:

```
var App = ng.core.Component({
  selector: "app",
  directives: [Cards, SampleComponent1, List, ListItem,
  SampleComponent2, SampleComponent3, SampleComponent4,
  SampleComponent6, SampleComponent7, SampleComponent8,
  SampleComponent9, SampleComponent11, SampleComponent13],
  templateUrl: "componentTemplates/app-template.html"
}).Class({
  constructor: function(){}
})
```

Finally, add this code to the end of the `app-template.html` file:

```
<samplethirteen></samplethirteen>
```

Here, the output is same as the previous example. Most of the things are self-explanatory. The only thing you need to know is that both these code snippets do the same thing:

```
<sampletwelve [(count)]='count'></sampletwelve>
<sampletwelve [count]='count' (countChange)=
'count=$event'></sampletwelve>
```

Understanding providers

A **provider** tells Angular 2 how to create an instance of a service while injecting it. A provider is set using the `providers` or `viewProviders` properties of a component.

Let's look at an example of how to create providers. Place this code above the `App` component's code:

```
var Service1 = ng.core.Class({
  constructor: function() {
  },
  getValue: function() {
    return "xyz"
  }
});

var Service2 = ng.core.Class({
  constructor: function() {
  },
  getValue: function() {
    return "def"
  }
});

var Service3 = ng.core.Class({
  constructor: function() {
  },
  getValue: function() {
    return "mno"
  }
});
```

```
var Service4 = ng.core.Class({
  constructor: [Service2, Service3, function(s2, s3) {
    console.log(s2);
    console.log(s3);
  }],
  getValue: function() {
    return "abc"
  }
});

var ServiceTest1 = ng.core.Component({
  selector: "st1",
  viewProviders: [
    ng.core.provide(Service1, {useClass: Service4}),
    ng.core.provide(Service2, {useValue: "def"}),
    ng.core.provide(Service3, {useFactory: function(){
      return "mno";
    }})
  ],
  template: ""
}).Class({
  constructor: [Service1, function(s1){
    console.log(s1.getValue());
  }]
})
```

Replace the App component's code with this:

```
var App = ng.core.Component({
  selector: "app",
  directives: [Cards, SampleComponent1, List, ListItem,
  SampleComponent2, SampleComponent3, SampleComponent4,
  SampleComponent6, SampleComponent7, SampleComponent8,
  SampleComponent9, SampleComponent11, SampleComponent13,
  ServiceTest1],
  templateUrl: "componentTemplates/app-template.html"
}).Class({
  constructor: function(){}
})
```

Finally, add this to the end of the app-template.html file:

```
<st1></st1>
```

This is the console output of the code:

```
def
mno
abc
```

This is how it works:

- First, we create four services: `Service1`, `Service2`, `Service3`, and `Service4`. They all have a `getValue` method, which returns a string. `Service4` is dependent on `Service2` and `Service3`.

- Then, we create a component called `ServiceTest1`. It's dependent on `Service1`. In the `viewProviders` property, we passed an array of providers. A provider is created using the `ng.core.provide` method. It takes two arguments; the first one is the service name, and the second one is the configuration object, which states how to create an instance of this service. The `useClass` property tells Angular 2 to create a instance of this service when an instance of the service in the first argument is requested. So here, when an instance of `Service1` is required, an instance of `Service4` is what is actually created. Similarly, `useValue` is used to provide a value, and `useFactory` is used to pass control to a function to decide what to return when a new instance is requested. So here, when an instance of `Service2` is requested, we get the `def` string, and when `Service3` is requested, we get the `mno` string.

Earlier in this chapter, we were simply assigning `viewProviders` to the services themselves. A service also implements the interface of a provider such that it creates the instance of the service itself.

If there are multiple providers matching a service, then the latest one overrides the previous one.

The difference between providers and the viewProviders property

The `viewProviders` property allows us to make providers available to the component's view only, whereas the `providers` property makes a provider available to its content children and view children.

The `providers` property creates a service instance only once and provides the same to whichever component asks for it. We have already seen how `viewProviders` works. Let's look at an example of how `providers` works. Place this code above the App component's code:

```
var counter = 1;

var Service5 = ng.core.Class({
  constructor: function(){}
})

var ServiceTest2 = ng.core.Component({
  selector: "st2",
  template: ""
}).Class({
  constructor: [Service5, function(s5){
    console.log(s5);
  }]
})

var ServiceTest3 = ng.core.Component({
  selector: "st3",
  providers: [ng.core.provide(Service5, {useFactory: function(){
    counter++;
    return counter;
  }})],
  directives: [ServiceTest2],
  template: "<st2></st2>"
}).Class({
  constructor: [Service5, function(s5){
    console.log(s5);
  }]
})
```

Replace the App component's code with this:

```
var App = ng.core.Component({
  selector: "app",
  directives: [Cards, SampleComponent1, List, ListItem,
  SampleComponent2, SampleComponent3, SampleComponent4,
  SampleComponent6, SampleComponent7, SampleComponent8,
  SampleComponent9, SampleComponent11, SampleComponent13,
  ServiceTest1, ServiceTest3],
  templateUrl: "componentTemplates/app-template.html"
}).Class({
  constructor: function(){}
})
```

Finally, at the end of the `app-template.html` file, place this code:

```
<st3></st3>
```

The console output of this code is as follows:

2

2

Most of the things in this code are self-explanatory. We are using `providers` instead of `viewProviders`. The `ServiceTest2` component is dependent on `Service5`, but it doesn't have a provider for `Service5`, so Angular 2 uses the provider provided by `ServiceTest3`, as `ServiceTest3` is its parent. If `ServiceTest3` hadn't had a provider for `Service5`, Angular 2 would have gone further above and looked for the provider in the `App` component.

> The `ng.platform.browser.bootstrap` method also takes a second argument, which is a list of providers that is available to all the components. So, instead of passing providers in the `App` component, we can pass them through the `ng.platform.browser.bootstrap` method.

Summary

In this chapter, we learned about Angular 2. We saw what components are, how to write templates, how to create services, and so on. We also learned about web components and how Angular 2 takes advantage of them. You should now be comfortable with building Angular 2 applications.

In the next chapter, we will learn how to build an SPA using Angular 2 by building a complete app.

13
Building a Search Engine Template Using AngularJS 2

To build **single page applications (SPAs)** using Angular 2, we need to learn how to implement routing in Angular 2. Angular 2 comes with built-in routing APIs, which are very powerful, feature rich, and easy to use. In this chapter, we will build a basic search engine template to demonstrate routing in Angular 2. We won't be building a complete search engine because that's out of the scope of this book. We will use Bootstrap 4 to design the search engine template. At the end of this chapter, you will be comfortable with building SPAs using Angular 2.

In this chapter, we will cover the following topics:

- Routing in Angular 2
- The built-in HTTP client provided by Angular 2
- Generating random textual data using the Chance.js library

Setting up the project

Follow these steps to set up your project:

1. In the exercise files of this chapter, you will find two directories, initial and final. The final directory contains the final search engine template whereas the initial directory contains the files to quickly get started with building the search engine template.

2. In the `initial` directory, you will find `app.js` and `package.json`. In the `package.json` file, place this code:

```
{
  "name": "SearchEngine-Template",
  "dependencies": {
    "express": "4.13.3",
    "chance": "1.0.3"
  }
}
```

Here, we are listing `Express.js` and `Chance.js` as dependencies. Express will be used to build the web server whereas `Chance.js` will be used to generate random textual data to populate the template's search results.

3. Now, run `npm install` inside the `initial` directory to download the packages.

Inside the `initial` directory, you will find a directory named `public`, inside which all the static assets will be placed. Inside the `public` directory, you will find the `componentTemplates`, `css`, `html`, and `js` directories.

Inside the `css` directory, you will find `bootstrap.min.css`; `index.html` inside the `html` directory; and finally, `index.js`, `angular2-all.umd.js`, `angular2-polyfills.js`, and `Rx.umd.js` inside the `js` directory.

4. In `index.html`, place this starting code to load Angular, Bootstrap, and the `index.js` file:

```
<!doctype html>
<html>
  <head>
    <title>Search Engine Template</title>
    <link rel="stylesheet" type="text/css"
    href="/css/bootstrap.min.css">
  </head>
  <body>

    <script src="/js/angular2-polyfills.js"></script>
    <script src="/js/Rx.umd.js"></script>
    <script src="/js/angular2-all.umd.js"></script>
    <script src="/js/index.js"></script>
  </body>
</html>
```

This code is self-explanatory.

5. Now, in the `app.js` file, place this code:

```
var express = require("express");
var app = express();

app.use(express.static(__dirname + "/public"));

app.get("/*", function(httpRequest, httpResponse, next){
  httpResponse.sendFile(__dirname +
  "/public/html/index.html");
})

app.listen(8080);
```

Here as well, most of the code is self-explanatory. We are simply serving `index.html` regardless of what the HTTP request path is.

Configuring routes and bootstrapping the app

In SPA, the routes for our app are defined in the frontend. In Angular 2, we need to define the paths and a component associated with the path that will be rendered for that path.

We provide the routes to the root component, and the root component displays the component bound to the route.

Let's create the root component and routes for our search engine template:

1. Place this code in the `index.js` file to to create the root components and routes:

```
var AppComponent = ng.core.Component({
  selector: "app",
  directives: [ng.router.ROUTER_DIRECTIVES],
  templateUrl: "componentTemplates/app.html"
}).Class({
  constructor: function(){}
})

AppComponent = ng.router.RouteConfig([
    { path: "/", component: HomeComponent, name: "Home" },
    { path: "/search-result", component:
    SearchResultComponent, name: "SearchResult" },
```

```
    { path: "/*path", component: NotFoundComponent, name:
"NotFound" }
]) (AppComponent);

ng.platform.browser.bootstrap(AppComponent, [
  ng.router.ROUTER_PROVIDERS,
  ng.core.provide(ng.router.APP_BASE_HREF, {useValue : "/" })
]);
```

2. Now, create a file named `app.html` in the `componentTemplates` directory and place this code in it:

```
<nav class="navbar navbar-light bg-faded">
    <ul class="nav navbar-nav">
        <li class="nav-item">
            <a class="nav-link"
            [routerLink]="['Home']">Home</a>
        </li>
    </ul>
</nav>
<router-outlet></router-outlet>
```

Here is how this code works:

1. At first, we create the root component, called `AppComponent`. While creating the root component, we add the `ng.router.ROUTER_DIRECTIVES` directive to it, which lets us use the `routerLink` directive.

2. Then, we use `ng.router.RouteConfig` to configure the routes for our application. We are providing an array of routes as an argument to the `ng.router.RouteConfig` method. A route consists of a path, component, and the name of the route. The paths can be static, parameterized, or wildcard, just like Express route paths. Here, the first route is for the home page, second for displaying the search result, and finally, the third for handling invalid URLs, that is, URLs for which routes are not defined. The `ng.router.RouteConfig` method returns a function that takes the root component and attaches the routes to it.

3. We then initialize the application. While initializing the app, we're passing the `ng.router.ROUTER_PROVIDERS` provider, which will be used to create instances of various services related to routing. Also, we are providing a custom provider, which returns the / character when an instance of the `ng.router.APP_BASE_HREF` service is requested. `ng.router.APP_BASE_HREF` is used to find the base URL of the app.

4. In the `AppComponent` template, we are displaying a navigation bar. The navigation bar has an `anchor` tag that doesn't have an `href` attribute; instead, we are using the `routerLink` directive to assign the redirect link so that when clicked on, instead of a complete page reload, it only changes the URL and component. And finally, `<router-outlet>` is what displays the component based on the current URL.

Generating random search results

To populate our template, we need to generate some random search result data. For this, we can use the `Chance.js` library. We will generate random data on the server side, not on client side, so that we can later demonstrate how to make an HTTP request using Angular 2.

`Chance.js` is available for both client-side and server-side JavaScript. We earlier downloaded the `Chance.js` package to use with `Node.js`. Here is the code to generate random data. Place it in the `app.js` file above the `/*` route so that `/*` doesn't override the random data route:

```
var Chance = require("chance"),
chance = new Chance();
app.get("/getData", function(httpRequest, httpResponse, next){

  var result = [];

  for(var i = 0; i < 10; i++)
  {
    result[result.length] = {
      title: chance.sentence(),
      desc: chance.paragraph()
    }
  }

  httpResponse.send(result);
})
```

Here, we first create a route for the `/getData` path, which sends an array of search results as a response. The route callback uses `chance.sentence()` to generate random titles for the search result and `chance.paragraph()` to generate a description.

Creating route components

Let's create `HomeComponent`, `SearchResultComponent`, and `NotFoundComponent`. Before that, let's create a component to display the search form. The search form will have a textbox and a search button. Follow these steps:

1. Place this code in the `index.js` file, above the `AppComponent` code:

```
var FormComponent = ng.core.Component({
  selector: "search-form",
  directives: [ng.router.ROUTER_DIRECTIVES],
  templateUrl: "componentTemplates/search-form.html",
}).Class({
  constructor: function(){},
  ngOnInit: function(){
    this.searchParams = {
      query: ""
    };

    this.keyup = function(e){
      this.searchParams = {
        query: e.srcElement.value
      };
    };
  }
})
```

2. Now, create a file named `search-form.html` in the `componentTemplates` directory, and place this code in it:

```
<div class="m-a-2 text-xs-center">
  <h1>Search for Anything</h1>
  <form class="form-inline m-t-1">
      <input (keyup)="keyup($event)" class="form-control"
      type="text" placeholder="Search">
      <a [routerLink]="['SearchResult', searchParams]">
          <button class="btn btn-success-outline"
          type="submit">Search</button>
      </a>
  </form>
</div>
```

This is how the code works:

1. At first, we create a component called `FormComponent`. It uses the `ng.router.ROUTER_DIRECTIVES` directive.

2. In the template of the component, we display an HTML form. The form has a textbox and button.

3. We handle the `keyup` event of the text input box and store the value in the `searchParams.query` property.

4. The button redirects to the `SearchResult` component. Note that here we are passing `searchParams` object to `routerLink`, which becomes the query parameter when redirecting.

Now, let's create the `HomeComponent` component. This component is displayed on the home page. It displays the search form.

Here is how to create `HomeComponent`:

1. Place this code in the `index.js` file, above the `AppComponent` code:

```
var HomeComponent = ng.core.Component({
  selector: "home",
  directives: [FormComponent],
  templateUrl: "componentTemplates/home.html",
}).Class({
  constructor: function(){}
})
```

2. Now, create a file named `search-form.html`, and place it in the `componentTemplates` directory:

```
<search-form></search-form>
```

Here, the `HomeComponent` code is self-explanatory.

3. Now, let's create the `SearchResultComponent` component. This component should display the search form and the search result below it. It should fetch the result by making an HTTP request to the server. Here is the code for the `SearchResultComponent`. Place it in the `index.js` file, above the `AppComponent` code:

```
var SearchResultComponent = ng.core.Component({
  selector: "search-result",
  directives: [FormComponent],
  viewProviders: [ng.http.HTTP_PROVIDERS],
  templateUrl: "componentTemplates/searchResult.html"
}).Class({
```

```
constructor: [ng.router.RouteParams, ng.http.Http,
function(params, http) {
    this.params = params;
  this.http = http;
  this.response = [];
}],
ngOnInit: function(){
  var q = this.params.get("query");
  this.http.get("getData").subscribe(function(res){
    this.response = JSON.parse(res._body);
  }.bind(this));
}
})
```

4. Now, create a file named `searchResult.html` and place it in `componentTemplates`. Place this code in the file:

```html
<style>
  ul
  {
      list-style-type: none;
  }
</style>

<div class="container">
  <search-form></search-form>
  <div class="m-a-2 text-xs-center">
      <ul>
        <li *ngFor="#item of response" class="m-t-2">
          <h4>{{item.title}}</h4>
          <p>{{item.desc}}</p>
        </li>
      </ul>
  </div>
</div>
```

This is how the code works:

1. Here, we are providing the `ng,http.HTTP_PROVIDERS` provider, which is used when using the HTTP client service provided by Angular 2. Using the HTTP client service, we can make HTTP requests.

2. In the constructor property, we are injecting the HTTP service along with the `ng.router.RouteParams` service, which is used to obtain the query parameters of the current URL.

3. In the `ngOnInit` method, you can see how to make a GET request using the HTTP service and also how to get the query parameters using the `ng.router.RouteParams` service.

4. In the template of the component, we are displaying the fetched search result using the `ngFor` directive.

> You can learn about the HTTP service provided by Angular 2 at `https://angular.io/docs/ts/latest/guide/server-communication.html`.

Now, let's create `NotFoundComponent`. Here is the code for that:

1. Place this code in the `index.js` file, above the `AppComponent` code:

```
var NotFoundComponent = ng.core.Component({
  selector: "name-search",
  templateUrl: "componentTemplates/notFound.html"
}).Class({
  constructor: function(){}
})
```

2. Now, create a file named `notFound.html` and place it in the `componentTemplates` directory. Place this code inside the file:

```
<div class="container">
  <div class="m-a-2 text-xs-center">
    <h1>The page your are looking for is not found</h1>
  </div>
</div>
```

The code is self-explanatory.

Testing the template

To test the template, we will follow these steps:

1. Inside the `initial` directory, run the `node app.js` command.

2. Now, in a browser, open the `http://localhost:8080/` URL. You should see this output:

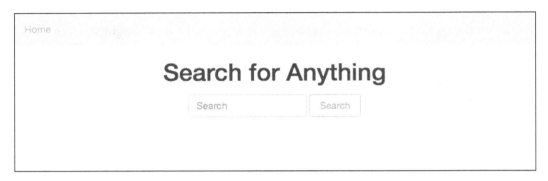

3. Now, type something in the search box and click on the **Search** button. You should then see this output:

4. Now, enter an invalid path in the address bar. You should be able to see this output:

> Home
>
> # The page your are looking for is not found

Routing life cycle methods

When a path matches a component, Angular 2 activates the component, and when the path changes, Angular 2 deactivates it. When we say that a component has been activated, it means that Angular 2 has created an instance of the component, that is, called the constructor method of the component, whereas when we say a component has been deactivated, it means the component has been removed from the DOM and instance is deleted.

The methods of a component that are called while activating or deactivating it are called routing lifecycle methods.

Here is the list of routing lifecycle methods:

- `CanActivate`: This hook is invoked before activating the component. It should return a boolean value or a promise indicating whether to activate the component.

- `routerOnActivate`: This method is invoked after the component has been activated.

- `routerCanReuse`: This method is invoked to find out whether to reuse the previous instance of the component when the next URL change is the same URL again. It should return a boolean value or a promise indicating whether to reuse. It's invoked only if an instance had been created earlier.

- `routerOnReuse`: This method is invoked if the component is being reused. It's called after `routerCanReuse`.

- `routerCanDeactivate`: This method is invoked before deactivating the component. It should return a boolean value or a promise indicating whether to deactivate the component.

- `routerOnDeactivate`: This method is invoked after the component has been deactivated.

Let's look at a code example of the routing lifecycle methods. Replace the HomeComponent code with this:

```
var HomeComponent = ng.core.Component({
  selector: "home",
  directives: [FormComponent],
  templateUrl: "componentTemplates/home.html",
}).Class({
  constructor: function(){},
  routerOnActivate: function(){
    console.log("Component has been activated");
  },
  routerCanReuse: function(){
    console.log("Component can be reused");
    return true;
  },
  routerOnReuse: function(){
    console.log("Component is being reused");
  },
  routerCanDeactivate: function(){
    console.log("Component can be deactivated");
    return true;
  },
  routerOnDeactivate: function(){
    console.log("Component has been deactivated");
  }
})

HomeComponent = ng.router.CanActivate(function(){
  console.log("Component can be activated");
  return true;
})(HomeComponent);
```

Now, visit the home page. There, click on the home button again. Now, type something in the search box and click on the **Search** button. This is the console output you will see:

```
Component can be activated
Component has been activated
Component can be reused
Component is being reused
Component can be deactivated
Component has been deactivated
```

Production mode versus development mode

Until now, we have been running Angular 2 in development mode. The difference between development and production mode is that in development mode, Angular 2 starts change detection immediately after the first run and logs a **value has changed after it was checked** error if anything changes between the first and second run. This helps locate bugs.

To enable production mode, place this code above the `ng.platform.browser.bootstrap()` method call:

```
ng.core.enableProdMode();
```

Summary

In this chapter, we learned routing in Angular 2 by building a basic search engine template. Along with learning routing in depth, we also learned about the Angular 2 HTTP client service as well as how to switch to production mode in Angular 2.

You should now be comfortable with building the frontend of any kind of web application using Angular 2.

14

Securing and Scaling Node.js Applications

It's very important to scale and secure your applications. Scaling and securing are not one-time tasks. You need to keep making changes to your code as you add new features to increase application security, and as your application traffic and data increases, you need to scale your servers. In this chapter, you will learn how to make Node.js applications more secure and how to scale Node.js applications. I will be assuming that your are using Express for creating your web server as it is the most common.

In this chapter, we will cover:

- Application vulnerabilities
- Non-vulnerability attacks
- Various third-party services to protect your application
- Checking security issues in third-party packages
- Techniques of distributing traffic

Common vulnerabilities in applications

According to Wikipedia, a **vulnerability** is a weakness in the application that allows an attacker to reduce a system's information assurance. Applications expose different types of vulnerability.

Let's look at some important vulnerabilities and how to prevent them.

Helmet

Helmet is a Node.js library that helps you prevent various attacks by setting various security-related HTTP headers.

Here are the various headers added by Helmet:

- `Strict-Transport-Policy`: This header is used to enforce secure (HTTP over SSL/TLS) connections to the server. HTTPS prevents man-in-the-middle attacks. In a man-in-the-middle attack, an attacker secretly alters the communication between the client and server. This is done to steal data, add ads to web pages, and so on.

- `X-Frame-Options`: This header provides clickjacking protection. **Clickjacking** is a technique by which an attacker uses multiple transparent or opaque layers to trick a user into clicking on a button or link on another page when they intended to click on the top-level page. Thus, the attacker is "hijacking" clicks meant for their page and routing them to some other page, most likely owned by another application, domain, or both. This header prevents the application from being viewed inside an iFrame, therefore providing clickjacking protection.

- `X-XSS-Protection`: This header prevents reflective XSS attacks. Reflective XSS attacks are a type of XSS attack. **Cross-Site Scripting** (**XSS**) attacks are a type of injection in which malicious scripts are injected into otherwise benign and trusted web sites. XSS attacks occur when an attacker uses a web application to send malicious code, generally in the form of a browser-side script, to a different end user. Reflected XSS is the most frequent type of XSS attack. They are also known as non-persistent XSS attacks since the attack payload is delivered and executed via a single request and response. Reflected XSS occurs when the attacker injects executable JavaScript code into the HTML response by injecting the code into the URL.

- `X-Content-Type-Options`: Browsers can override response `Content-Type` headers to guess and process data using an implicit content type. While this can be convenient in some scenarios, it can also lead to some kinds of attack, such as a MIME confusion attack, authorized hotlinking, and so on. Returning `X-Content-Type-Options` will cause browsers to use the provided `Content-Type` header and not interpret the content as a different content type.

- `Content-Security-Policy`: This header lets us provide a list of trusted sources to the browser, from which content such as JavaScript, CSS, HTML frames, fonts, images, and embeddable objects (Java applets, ActiveX, audio, and video) can be loaded onto a page. This helps us prevent XSS attacks.

To learn more about Helmet, visit `https://www.npmjs.com/package/helmet`

Cross-site request forgery

Cross-site request forgery (**CSRF**) is a type of attack in which requests from a user are sent to servers without the user knowing about it.

For example, if an attacker is able to find a reproducible link that executes a specific action on the target page while the victim is logged in to it, he is able to embed such a link on a page he controls and trick the victim into opening it. The attack-carrying link may be placed in a location that the victim is likely to visit while logged in to the target site sent in a HTML e-mail body or attachment.

There are various ways to prevent CSRF attacks. Most CSRF prevention techniques work by embedding additional authentication data into requests, which allows the web application to detect requests from unauthorized locations.

There is a library named `csrf` (`https://www.npmjs.com/package/csrf`) for Node. js that lets you prevent CSRF attacks. It provides you middleware to protect Express web servers from CSRF attacks.

Cross-site scripting

We saw earlier what the XSS vulnerability is. We basically saw what a reflected XSS attack is. There is another type of XSS attack called **stored XSS**.

Stored XSS occurs when the application stores user input that is not correctly filtered. For example, while chatting, if a message is not sanitized, then both users can run scripts on each other's browsers by sending JS code within `<script>` tags as messages.

To prevent both types of XSS attack, we should always filter/sanitize user input.

Session fixation

Session fixation is an attack that permits an attacker to hijack a valid user session. Here are several techniques to prevent session fixation:

*   Set session timeouts
*   Regenerate session tokens frequently
*   When logged out, expire the session token
*   Store the user agent and IP address of the user when creating a session and check whether the value matches during the following HTTP requests.

Non-vulnerability based attacks

There are various kinds of attack that can be made on any kind of application, as they depend on loopholes in the application. Still, applications can do a lot to prevent these attacks.

Let's see a few of the most common non-vulnerability-based attacks and how to prevent them.

Denial-of-service attacks

A **denial-of-service (DoS)** attack is an attempt to make a server machine unavailable to its intended users temporarily. An attacker uses one or many machines to make continuous requests to the server to take it down.

The best way to prevent DoS is to use an external service such as CloudFlare, which uses a lot of different techniques and data from various sources to block malicious requests on your server. It's always better to avoid handling DoS on your server and leave it to a service created by DoS experts.

Brute force attacks

A **brute force attack** aims at being the simplest kind of method to gain access to a site: trying usernames and passwords, over and over, until it gets in.

Here are several ways to prevent brute force attacks:

- We can embed CAPTCHA in forms that can completely prevent bots from making brute force attacks and slow down brute force attacks made by humans.
- There is a middleware program for Express servers called **express-brute** that limits the rate of incoming requests based on several factors. You can find out more about **express-brute** at `https://www.npmjs.com/package/express-brute`.

Using secure packages

The npm packages you use may contain critical security vulnerabilities that could also affect your application. It's not possible to go through every package's code or test each of them separately.

There is a database called `Node Security Project` that has a list of the most important vulnerable packages. You can use command-line tools such as nsp (https://www.npmjs.com/package/nsp) and requireSafe (https://requiresafe.com/) to check the vulnerable dependencies of your application.

You should always keep an eye on the new version releases of the packages that your application is dependent on and update it, as a new release often fixes issues related to security.

Scaling Node.js servers

If your application has lots of users accessing the system simultaneously, then obviously a single server cannot handle all the traffic. It will slow down and crash. Therefore, we need to deploy the application on multiple servers and then distribute the traffic equally between them.

To distribute traffic between servers, we need to use something called a **load balancer**. A load balancer is a server that sits in front of the application servers. The client communicates with the load balancer instead of the application servers, and instead of handling the request, the load balancer forwards it to an application server; when the application servers sends the response, it sends the same response to the client.

As a load balancer doesn't actually process the request, it can handle many more requests than an application server. Obviously, a load balancer cannot handle unlimited requests, so we can use multiple load balancers. When we use multiple load balancers, the traffic between them is distributed by using the round-robin DNS technique. In round-robin DNS, the IP address of the domain pointing to the load balancer changes according to an appropriate statistical model.

Amazon Web Services (**AWS**) provides a load balancer called Amazon ELB, which can be used to distribute traffic between Amazon EC2 servers, that is, application servers. Obviously, it difficult to predict the total number of EC2 instances you would need to scale your application; therefore, AWS also provides something called **auto scaling**, which can add/remove EC2 instances as needed. Therefore, to host a large-scale application, Amazon is the best choice. It also provides lots of other cloud services to scale and deploy your application.

In case you don't want to worry about scaling, deploying, and managing your servers, then you can use cloud services such as Heroku, which makes it much easier to achieve all this, and you just need to worry about the application code—that's it.

Summary

In this chapter, we saw a lot of services and libraries to scale and secure Node.js applications. We saw various vulnerabilities and how to prevent them. Make sure you take regular backups of your data so that even if your app is hacked, you will still have a chance to get the application running again as the data is not lost. Obviously, there is a lot more to learn about scaling and securing Node.js applications as this is an unending topic and new things come up regularly.

Index

A

Angular 2
  architecture 243-245
  change detection 259-261
  fundamentals 251-256
  shadow DOM 257, 258
  styling components 257, 258
  URL 244
angular2-all.umd.js
  URL 250
angular2-polyfills.js
  URL 250
Angular 2 project
  setting up 250
API key
  URL 67
architecture 26, 27
attribute directive 272, 273
auto scaling 301

B

Babel
  URL, for installing 209
Babel compiler
  reference link 209
backend, live score website
  admin panel, protecting 119, 120
  HTML, serving to administrator 119, 120
  HTML, serving to users 119
  message, broadcasting
     to namespace 121, 122
  socket.io cookie, authentication 121, 122
  socket.io server, integrating with
     Express server 118

  static files, serving to users 119
Bacon.js
  about 136
  errors 147, 148
Bacon.js APIs
  about 138
  EventStream, creating 138, 139
  EventStream, filtering 142
  EventStream, merging 142
  EventStream, transforming 143-145
  properties, creating 139-141
  properties, filtering 142
  properties, merging 142
  properties, transforming 143-145
Bacon.js library
  URL 136
Bacon.retry function
  delay 149
  isRetryable 149
  retries 149
  source 149
basic plugin 15
Bootstrap 4
  21:9 aspect ratio class 195
  about 173
  browser support 174
  card component 183-188
  CSS units, em 174, 175
  CSS units, rem 174, 175
  customizing 195
  device support 174
  downloading 173, 174
  Flexbox support 194
  glyphicons, removing 196
  grid system 175-179
  heading, displaying 181

G

GitHub repository, WebRTC
  reference 76
glyphicons 196

H

headers, Helmet
  about 298
  Content-Security-Policy 298
  Strict-Transport-Policy 298
  X-Content-Type-Options 298
  X-Frame-Options 298
  X-XSS-Protection 298
Helmet
  URL 298
HTML imports 245
HTTP
  relationship, with WebSocket 100, 101
HTTP service, Angular 2
  URL 291

I

image upload server
  creating 36-38
Interactive Connectivity
      Establishment (ICE) 65
Isomorphic development 207-209

J

JavaScript syntax extension. *See* JSX
jQuery
  URL, for download 136
JSX
  about 209
  compiling 209, 210
JSX syntax 210-213

L

lazy evaluation
  about 155, 156
  implementing 155
Less version
  URL 193

live score website
  about 117
  backend, building 117, 118
  frontend, building 123, 124
  testing 125

M

media consumer 56
media source 56
MediaStream
  transferring 65, 66
MediaStream API 58
MediaStream constructor
  URL 59
MediaStreamTrack interface
  URL 58
mem-store plugin 15
merging 142
MicroEvent.js
  about 228
  reference link 228
  using 228
microservices
  implementing, Seneca used 11, 12, 16
microservices architecture
  about 5-7
  data management 10
  demerits 9
  merits 7
  services, scaling 7, 8
  using 9, 10
mixin 222
monolithic architecture
  about 2
  demerits 2
  issues 5
  scaling 2-4
monolithic core
  creating 38-49
monolithic server side applications
  writing 4

N

namespaces 110-112
navigator.getUserMedia 60-63

www.ingramcontent.com/pod-product-compliance
Lightning Source LLC
Chambersburg PA
CBHW062103050326
40690CB00016B/3181